Corpse Magic

MICHAEL TAUSSIG

Corpse Magic

ECHOES ACTIVE IN THE SLAYER-SLAIN NEXUS

THE UNIVERSITY OF CHICAGO PRESS | CHICAGO AND LONDON

The University of Chicago Press, Chicago 60637

The University of Chicago Press, Ltd., London

© 2025 by The University of Chicago

Published 2025

Printed in the United States of America

34 33 32 31 30 29 28 27 26 25   1 2 3 4 5

ISBN-13: 978-0-226-83739-0   (cloth)

ISBN-13: 978-0-226-83741-3   (paper)

ISBN-13: 978-0-226-83740-6   (e-book)

DOI: https://doi.org/10.7208/chicago/9780226837406.001.0001

Library of Congress Cataloging-in-Publication Data

Names: Taussig, Michael T., author.

Title: Corpse magic : echoes active in the slayer-slain nexus / Michael Taussig.

Description: Chicago : The University of Chicago Press, 2025. | Includes bibliographical references and index.

Identifiers: LCCN 2024038374 | ISBN 9780226837390 (cloth) | ISBN 9780226837413 (paperback) | ISBN 9780226837406 (ebook)

Subjects: LCSH: Homicide. | Violent deaths. | Violence—Colombia. | Violence—United States. | Violence—Psychological aspects. | Violence—Social aspects.

Classification: LCC HV6535.C7 T38 2025 | DDC 364.15201/9—dc23/eng/20241021

LC record available at https://lccn.loc.gov/2024038374

♾ This paper meets the requirements of ANSI/NISO Z39.48-1992 (Permanence of Paper).

In memory of Gabriel Izquierdo, SJ

Asked if they believed in ghosts during their debate, the three Democratic Party candidates for the governorship of New York responded: Suozzi said he believes in "spirits," Williams said he believes in the afterlife, and [acting governor] Hochul said she speaks to her deceased mother.

WNYC radio news, June 8, 2022

CONTENTS

ILLUSTRATIONS

METHOD IN THE MADNESS
AND VICE VERSA

Killing unites as much as it severs.

In some cases, it is said, the victim inhabits the slayer after being killed.

It can happen automatically or as the result of maneuvers I call "corpse magic," which I shall presently relate.

What to think, then, today, of the killing by US police of three people per day, disproportionately Native American, Black, and Hispanic, in that order? What to think of massacre after massacre at schools, shopping malls, sports events, Memorial Day parades, discos, and music festivals, and of gang shootings in that fair land where, in 2021, 54 people a day were shot dead over the first five months, and more than 180 over the July 4th holiday weekend.[1]

Does the bond by which the slain inhabits the slayer exist in those situations?

Impossible, you say. After all is not the USA bound to Rule of Law?

But here's the question: Which is more fearsome, corpse magic or its absence? Which is stranger?

And what of phone videos of the killings? Are they not streaming corpse magic?

* * *

In the pages that follow, I join distinct realities that share one feature, assassination. One name for this method is *montage*, a word I take from film and photography. Montage highlights the power of images and image manipulation as something other than what we usually mean by explanation, as if what can be shown cannot be said. This is not comparison so much as nervy reaction to what is generated by difference, unstable and venturing.

At first, I thought this book had two parts, spliced together in a Jesuit seminar room in Bogotá. There was the magic part, focused on corpse magic from biblical times in the Holy Land to present-day plantation towns in western Colombia. And there was the cell phone part focused on the auto-mobilized death-space, meaning videos of US police killing African Americans at traffic stops.

But as the text evolved, so did metaphors for the relation of the two parts. Alongside *montage*, I was drawn to the idea of *mosaic* and close on its heels the idea of *constellations* as deployed by Walter Benjamin with reference to his concept of history wherein montaged images he called "dialectical images," combining something past with something present with nothing in between, unexpectedly surface in states of emergency.

In the case of corpse magic, my approach has been not so much historical as "colonial," centering on connections between the US-instigated War on Drugs and its impact in the Global South, particularly but not only in Colombia.

Benjamin's concepts of montage and constellation owed much to a curious mix of Marxism and magic (which at one point he called "theology"). The maverick art historian Aby Warburg, whom Benjamin admired and wished to befriend, also showed much interest in magic, as visitors to his immense library in Woburn Square, London, can verify.

Rooted in image, magic can nevertheless be emphatically bodily, as the stories herein attest. Such is the case whether the bodies be alive or *dead-come-alive* in the cause of justice and vengeance, like this book itself.

As regards the image basis of montage, I have spent a good deal of time in the past decade thinking about the role of drawings in ethnographic fieldwork notebooks. But only toward the end of writing this book on corpse magic did its resemblance to those notebooks occur to me, interspersing words with drawings, thoughts in one key careening off another like cell phone videos of police assassination.

* * *

Realities: Multiple, Magical, and Invisible. In Colombia there exists a steady drum beat of inner-city, small town, and hamlet homicides that is so common it has come to seem natural, like rainfall or traffic accidents. Hence it is invisible, or should I say, it is accepted and forgotten because it is an everyday occurrence. The gangs kill each other, and merchants, police, and paramilitary types surreptitiously and sometimes quite openly carry out murderous *limpiezas*, or "cleansings" of gangs. What is more, they do so with at least the tacit support of the populace whenever some arbitrary level of gang violence is reached. It seems to me like genocide.

As vengeance hums along the slayer-slain nexus, there is an undertow of rumor and strife mystifying social life more than magical realism ever could. What's more, gangs not only kill each other. They can be paid by obscure forces to kill other sorts of people, for instance those who stand for human rights, or those who try to take over sections of large landholdings so as to grow food, as is happening to the vast sugar plantations abutting the western slopes of the Cordillera Central, not far from the plantation town on which I focus a good deal of this book.

Since the peace treaty in 2016 with the FARC guerrilla (the largest guerrilla army in Latin America by far), violence has gotten more unpredictable and in some ways greater as paramilitaries, FARC dissidents, and other groups swarm into the power vacuum. As regards gangs, however, it is worth noting that the current vice president, a Black woman, Francia Márquez, from a town close to the one that lies at the center of this book, has recently initiated a well-funded program in several towns in western Colombia offering alternatives to kids and young adults in gangs.

This is not only a Colombian story. It is a Global South story and, to a critical extent, one of the US as well. These distinct realities are juxtaposed, separated, then brought together newly born, nowhere more so than with regards to the body of Christ and the corpse magic I describe, funneled through sorcery into vengeance.

It is thus a sorcery story in the sense that it regards not just tales of sorcery but sorcery itself as both fictitious and real yet, unlike much of magical realism, highlights deception and terror; more *El señor presidente* or *Chronicle of a Death Foretold* than *One Hundred Years of Solitude* except for the latter's account of a banana freight train in 1928 carrying not bananas through the darkness of night, but three thousand corpses of striking banana workers and their families shot by the Colombian army. But nobody knows. Nobody remembers.

As for the magic in my title and in the pages that follow, I leave it to the reader to decide what that might be.

The Living and the Dead

Let us beware of saying death is opposed to life. The living is
a merely a type of what is dead, and a very rare type.

Nietzsche, *The Gay Science*

1 *Thickening*

On New Year's Eve 2014, intruders broke into the cemetery in the western Colombia agribusiness town I think of as my second home. The freshly buried body of a young gang member was exhumed and hacked to pieces. How the assailants got to it is a mystery, as the priest had recently had a concrete-brick wall thirty feet high built around the cemetery, which occupies an entire block in a town with one of the nation's highest homicide rates.[1] Two weeks later, a cemetery in Guachené, a smaller town five miles away, was also broken into, and the same thing happened. Rumor had it that in both cases the exhumation and mutilation was done to stop a magically prepared corpse from killing its killer.

The French anthropologist Robert Hertz, who died young in the trenches of World War I, opined in 1907 that no amount of ritual could appease the souls of the slain. More than a century later I am asking, is that why they're ripe for sorcerers to practice vengeance or, in the case of Jesus, lead us unto the Promised Land?

Almost half a century after Hertz wrote his essay on the corpse, Rogerio Velásquez, born in the jungle-clad, gold-rich, ex-slave province of Colombia known as the Chocó, just south of Panamá, where the rain rarely stops, wrote that vagrant souls of the dead may manifest as strange bodies that shine with blinding light or move with incredible speed.[2] Velásquez does not specify what these strange bodies are. *Cuerpos*, he says, perhaps cadavers presenting as shooting stars. But they could be anything. What he says next is even stranger, beautiful and a little frightening. An assassin cannot move, he says; thanks to the machinations of a sorcerer, the shadow of the person killed is now covered in a baffling dazzlement.[3]

On this reckoning, killing not only unites as much as it severs but does so with aesthetic zest and cosmic charge. Like sacrifice, it creates anew from what it destroys.

Out of the blue, Luz Marina told me of a neighbor taken from his home at night to a village three miles away. "Piece by piece," she said, "his body was cut up with a power saw. People heard the screams throughout the night until there came silence. After the family buried the body, they found a piece of it, so they dug up the body and reburied it along with the missing piece." This happened more than once, she said.

She spoke in a nonchalant way. The neighbor was caught up, she explained, in *la vida fácil*, the easy life, meaning drug trafficking. Years later, when I reminded her of this story, she could not remember it. It was part of the "everyday uncommon," if there is such a thing. But a few blocks away, also caught up in *la vida fácil* and the everyday uncommon, lay young Miguel, unable to move, a bullet in his spine, withering away, just eyes it seemed, dark pools reflecting the light as his body disappeared into the empty space that was that room without furniture, not even a cardboard box. Just mildewed walls and those burning coals of eyes. I tried to talk with him, encouraged by his mother, Carmen. He told me to fuck off.

I think of stories like these as rites of passage that get stuck in transmission, leaving you hanging. Like the time long ago when a heavyset potato farmer high in the Andes—just below the tundra with its drizzle, bogs, and stranger than strange vegetation like the spiky-headed *frailejón*—cacti that grow in tall clusters like ghosts in the mist—asked me, "Do you know how people smuggle cocaine up from the lowlands?" He answered his own question: "The abdominal cavity of an infant is packed with cocaine paste. Holding the infant to the breast, a woman gets through no matter what checkpoint." He chuckled.

I didn't believe him, but my middle-class friends in Bogotá certainly did, and the symbolism was more than true, the work of poetry. The story propels you into a body, and what's more the body is dead, the body of a baby at breast.

And the intestines? What did they do with the intestines?

Mutilation is not lost on Vladimir either, an ex-paramilitary in El Sur de Bolívar, where oil palm plantations use paramilitary killers to force peasant colonists off the land. (Like most Latin American peasants they do not have land titles.) He spares no detail as he chats with me and my fellow passengers, bone-thin peasant colonists and a chubby woman schoolteacher suffering from fainting spells, in our small launch threading its way amid flowers floating like a carpet on a small tributary of the Río Magdalena.

Vladimir tells us of cutting open the body of a guerrilla fighter, stuffing it with cocaine, then driving it to Medellín in a hearse. Another time he was working on a dairy farm in Antioquia, he says, and had to walk somewhere early in the morning with the mist still on the ground. He saw the headlights of three pickup trucks in a stream and then he saw two bodies, one being cut to pieces, with a belt around his mouth to stop him screaming. The other man was dead, and his body was being packed with what was most likely cocaine or a derivative. Vladimir crept past. Walking up the hill, he heard the sound of a motorbike of *alto cilindraje* coming down the hill, *muy suave*. The driver stopped. "Have you seen anything down at the stream?" "Oh, no." "Are you sure?" "Of course, I'm sure."

When I tried to draw this, I drew on my imagination, as stimulated by the story. And that's my point, or rather two points:

First, drawing makes you look harder, which in this case means repeating the story in your mind, sharpening some things, ignoring others, adding others, until the brittle essence and imagined reality of another world emerges.

So, the "brittle essence": those ghastly eyes, staring like the end of the world; the belt tightened across the mouth; arms bound bowerlike above the head (a detail I added); the gaping wound in the abdomen, like that in late medieval and early Renaissance paintings showing the stigmata of the crucified Christ; the river; headlights beaming in the dark, illuminating all as in a theater.

Second, stories of horror like these *narcorelatos* work on your imagination. Consider, for instance, the frequently told stories of smugglers swallowing cocaine-filled condoms, only to have them explode in midair on flights north. Imagine those last moments at thirty thousand feet, trapped in your body, realizing it's all over, heart pounding, sweat pouring,

eyes wide. My young friend Davison—named after the Harley Davidson motorbike, I think—told me without flourish or drama that his uncle died like that.

All of which raises a question: Why is so much attention focused on dark inner worlds in relation to cocaine, worlds of intestines and hollowed-out abdominal cavities?

In his book on crowds and power, Elias Canetti makes much of secrecy—of the secret as a living entity with a mind of its own. In Canetti's account, the secret passes through the mouth into the intestines, which are the dark unknown and something more. That something more is the flip-flop between exposure and concealment. Canetti's figure for that, cliched as it may be, is the tiger, lying in wait, hidden, then leaping into the open, seizing and swallowing its prey—the victim then disappearing into the darkness of the invisible interior. But eventually, as if following a natural law, the secret shall burst like a cocaine-filled condom and issue forth as *narcorelato*.

You have to wonder about Canetti's idea of the secret. Does he make too much of it? Is it alive, as he says, bound to self-destruction as well as the destruction of everything associated with it? And why is it so corporeal, so intestinal, dark, and dangerous?

It seems to me unlikely that secrets are as hermetically sealed as he postulates, especially when it comes to cocaine. What exists is the public secret, known to many but resistant to speech other than through the *narcorelato* emerging like magma from decidedly Other realities.

On March 16, 2007, the Colombian magazine *Semana* (roughly equivalent to *Time* in the USA) published a lengthy extract from, it claimed, the 2005 diary of an important paramilitary chieftain with the nom de guerre "Don Mario."[4]

In 2004 Don Mario had been part of the Bloque Centauro, said to comprise five thousand killers on the eastern plains of Colombia, led by Miguel Arroyave, known as the Archangel and also as the Chemist, on account of his skill at synthesizing cocaine.

Don Mario's diary provides a picture of overflowing affluence, an update of the medieval peasant's land of Cockaigne, awash in money, luxury goods, whores, magic, killing, cocaine, fleets of all-terrain vehicles, and thousands of combatants and corpses—as well as much by way of Colombian government assistance. (Yes, Colombian government assistance!) Even if the diary is made up or wildly exaggerated, the imagination displayed is revealing. But stunning anthropological fieldwork by Johanna Pérez Gómez confirms at least one of its key features to be terribly real, namely that of using magic to protect oneself from bullets.[5]

War had erupted between the paramilitaries. Before the first confrontation, according to Don Mario's diary, the twenty-nine hundred combatants aligned with Arroyave sought, without his knowledge, the help of a local woman famous for her magical powers, said to make men bulletproof. She prayed and sprinkled holy water over the fighters and gave each what she said was earth from a cemetery to keep on their person during combat.

With their confidence thus fortified, Arroyave's troops met the enemy head-on. The casualties were colossal, and the woman of magic, it is insinuated, was murdered as the cause of the debacle.

Arroyave, who arrived a few days later, called on the Colombian air force to attack his enemies with rockets. With victory achieved, he proclaimed a celebration but was told his men could find no more than fifty prostitutes and would have to raffle them. Six outstanding commandants got special prizes: Voluntario got a Hilux Toyota pickup; Belisario, an apartment in Bogotá; Polvora, a farm in Urabá; and the rest did pretty well too.

* * *

Don Mario's diary continues: As the fiesta was finishing, I asked Belisario to show me the twenty-five prisoners of the Buitrago group who had surrendered rather than face certain death. Belisario wanted to kill them but was waiting my permission.

I asked the prisoners, "Which of you wants to work with us?" Some fifteen said yes, but two preferred to be killed, one of whom attracted my attention. He was very badly wounded, but what was strange was that there was no blood emerging from his bullet wounds.

I called for a doctor but the kid said, "Señor, let me die. Believe me Señor, I am not crazy nor a coward, but I implore you to let me die."

"Let me explain," he continued. "Since quite a while I made a pact with that Other Being asking for protection. I prayed with the cross following the instructions of the person making the pact so that bullets would not kill me. But I had to follow the rules that the spirits of the dead demanded. Today they informed me that the hour had come: "You have to ask to be killed!"

I AM ROTTING THRU & THRU

SOME WENT RIGHT THRU HIS BODY

IT WOULD BE BETTER TO KILL HIM

LET ME DIE

He raised his shirt and said, "Look at these wounds, through and through."

I looked. The wounds were profound. Some went right through his body. It is a miracle he is still alive, I said to Belisario, who replied it would be best to kill him.

I gave the order to two of the toughest men we had. The wounded man was put on the back of a pickup truck to be killed.

Half an hour later the two men reported that it was practically impossible to kill him, that they had emptied their magazines into him but could not kill him and so they cut him to pieces.

***

Let me break into the narrative to note that, according to Johanna Pérez Gómez, a specific person, meaning a specific spirit of a dead person, has control over the body and soul of the bulletproof man.[6] An ex-paramilitary told her that he was thus "closed" by a Guahibo indigenous woman healer/sorcerer of the eastern plains of Colombia. She wrote out a spell; he was to memorize it, burn it, and then drink the ashes.[7] The paper had been dipped in the blood of a dead person, and he was told to summon the spirit of that person by name every time he went into battle.[8]

Note that the rite was administered by a Guahibo indigenous woman and that it is claimed Guahibos were massacred throughout the twentieth century by large landowners with military and paramilitary assistance.[9] These massacres, including the killing of children, suggest to me not simply that the indigenous people are regarded as less than human, as is often said. Rather, they are regarded as both infrahuman and superhuman, below and above the human. Such doubleness implicates mystical powers, making the person or group thus designated as much liable to be slaughtered as to be sought after for magical purposes . . . like being made bulletproof.[10]

A SUPERSTITIOUS LOT

As we have just seen, paramilitaries tend to be a superstitious lot. In stories told to my young anthropologist friend Elizabeth Gallón Droste when she was a kid, what scared the paramilitaries occupying a town outside of Bogotá she often visited as a child were women witches:

That very night, the paisa's kids told me that the witches frighten the paramilitaries at night-time.

They were the only people that actually scared them.[11]

Every night the witches flew to frighten the paramilitaries, causing them eventually to leave. At sunrise, kids taking stones from the river for construction would see the witches flying back to their homes like flocks of birds. What scared the paramilitaries was that they could neither identify nor trap nor kill these women. Apart from targeting the paramilitaries, my young friend heard that the witches were motivated by envy of pregnant women, beautiful girls, and the girl with green eyes.

Paramilitaries are callous killers who make a big deal of their nastiness—wildly operatic, you could say—yet underneath all that it seems they may be shit-scared of the spirits of the people they have killed and of other sorts of spirits as well. After all, if the dead can give you the power to resist bullets, what else might they be able to do? They can, for instance, turn on the person with whom they have a compact and afflict their family with years of misfortune.[12] It's an old story, not limited to the tale of Dr. Faustus. Pacts with supernatural forces must eventually be paid for. The gift demands reciprocity.

And if my bodyguard, who served seventeen years in the Colombian Special Forces and then five in the French Foreign Legion, is any guide, the regular army is no less superstitious. He anointed his revolver, bullets included, with holy oil blessed by a priest, to which he added the juice from a special plant, which gave the bullets a green hue. Preferring magic spells in Latin to Spanish, he nevertheless attached great importance to lighting a candle each morning and praying to the *ánimas*, the souls of the dead locked in purgatory, whom I will discuss later. You help them escape, and they reciprocate.

The prayer goes like this, he said:

Que la Santa Cruz sea mi luz
Que no sea el dragón [el diablo]
Mi Señor, vete atrás Satanás

No me tientes con cosas malas

Es malo lo que das de probar

Bebe tu propio veneno

This is strange. It registers a world in which one is continually tempted by evil in the form of a devil who, with your saint's assistance, is obliged to turn on himself, drinking his own poison. It seems a frenzy of unabated reciprocation of evil with evil. Every morning the freshly lit candle illumines a world whose default position is evil, a world in which killing is bad but to which, this soldier maintains, you become accustomed.

Until you die, he solemnly adds. Then it catches up with you. Big time.

Meanwhile, concealed under his shirt, he has a bunch of talismans hung around his neck. When he extracts them, they spill forth like tropical fruit. He gave me one, a miniature San Benito, his patron saint, that I keep with my mobile phone. After all, his job was to protect me—along with the leaders of the indigenous school who had invited me to visit.

But I think his real religion, if I can put it that way, was the flattering power trip that came from the sense of being in the know, privy to the "inside story." Everywhere and everything was, to his way of thinking, saturated by double-talk. The world was masked, but experts like him, blessed with the magic of knowing what not to know, could unmask it. That is what being a bodyguard entails, the conceit and self-assurance that one is possessed of a sixth sense, like a mastiff with claws and teeth to match.

This came across in his stories of the French Foreign Legion, with which he fought, he says, mainly in Iraq and North Africa—doing what the French army preferred not to do, much as the paramilitaries do for the Colombian regular army. When the Légion étrangère went into Brazil to rescue kidnapped French citizens, the Brazilian government cut its radar so the French helicopters could enter unrecorded from French Guiana. The mission was similar to the famous night helicopter incursion into Ecuador when he was in the Colombian Special Forces, to capture or kill the FARC leader Raúl Reyes, with a wink and a nod to sovereignty and international law. As things turned out, the soldiers killed Reyes. All around us, my bodyguard assured me, lurked the FARC—under every bed, under every bush, despite the 2016 peace treaty it signed with the government.

It now seems his paranoia was warranted; toward the end of 2023 FARC dissidents seem every day more formidable. The government has only itself to blame for not abiding by the treaty.

Buttressed now by movies and stories of magic and terror on social media, as well as continual exchanges via cell phone with military intelligence, I think that this magico-paranoic atmosphere provides the ground for sorcery as much as the need for daily intercourse with San Benito.

As I read the testimonies of family members of the six thousand Unidad Popular Party members assassinated directly or indirectly by the army over a mere decade starting in the late 1980s, I cannot but be sorely puzzled by this charming bodyguard with his amulets, his prayers, his generosity, and his gift for storytelling.

So, yes! they are a superstitious lot. Wouldn't you be?

THE BELLS

Today is All Soul's Day. From dawn till dusk the bells toll in the remote ex-slave gold-mining village of Santa María on the banks of the Timbiqui River on the Pacific coast of Colombia. Until 2010 the mining consisted of women washing river sand and gravel for gold, or men and women excavating fifteen-foot-deep holes with pick and shovel, then making horizontal galleries. Others tried their luck going back into the horizontal tunnels excavated under the virtual slavery created by a British and French mining company in the late 1920s, which lasted about twenty years.

But after 2010 came mafia gold mining (called *entables*) with heavy equipment. Backhoes clambered upriver; there are no roads, but such machines are amazingly agile as well as destructive. The *entables* got locals with land to give them a free hand excavating enormous craters in return for giving the owners, the FARC, and the village junta each about 10 percent of the gold they mined. Boom times arrived way upriver, deep in the forest. Prostitutes arrived from the interior of the country, brought by a charmingly naive illiterate middle-aged man from Huila who also bought three cement billiard tables and crates of beer, all of which he housed in a sprawling brothel made of neon green plastic at the edge of the village. Indeed, such neon green plastic soon supplanted the forest as people from all over Colombia came and built makeshift housing with it. The billiard tables had belonged to a suddenly rich local who owed his fortune to cocaine and gold and built a towering white multistory "hotel" on the forested riverbank downstream. Then just as suddenly, he disappeared like a whiff of smoke.

But now the gold fever has subsided. The prostitutes have gone. Army helicopters sporadically attack the mining equipment, but the mining, deemed "illegal" by the government, continues, albeit at a reduced rate.

1 GRANO = $2.000,⁰⁰

Most of the locals depend on picking at the tailings left in the wake of the backhoes.

Today, All Souls' Day, is the day of the *ánimas*, although it is not easy to define an *ánima* (or a soul). From dawn to dusk, kids climb the hill to the church to pull the bell ropes. It is a faltering sound that keeps you in suspense, concussive yet continuous, each peal of the bells a little different from the one before.

Or so it seems. You lose track. Hours pass. The bells never stop. The sun burns. Clouds gather. The afternoon rains pelt down. But today is different. The bells remembering the dead are what dominate. It's a comfort to think of the young'uns climbing the hill all day, bridging the generations, bringing us close to the dead like that. Up and down they go, up and down, some giving the bells a special cadence, others, it seems, ringing randomly.

They say that children too young to talk are ever-sensitive to the presence of the dead, who are around us all the time and not just on the day of the *ánimas*. If they do see the dead, they are in danger. The body convulses and goes into shock. *Espanto*—spooked out—it's called.

Some old people are like that too. They can see the dead walking past on their way to the river. Lightning rods they be, the prevocal young and the very old, taking the charge. Why does the acquisition of speech cancel

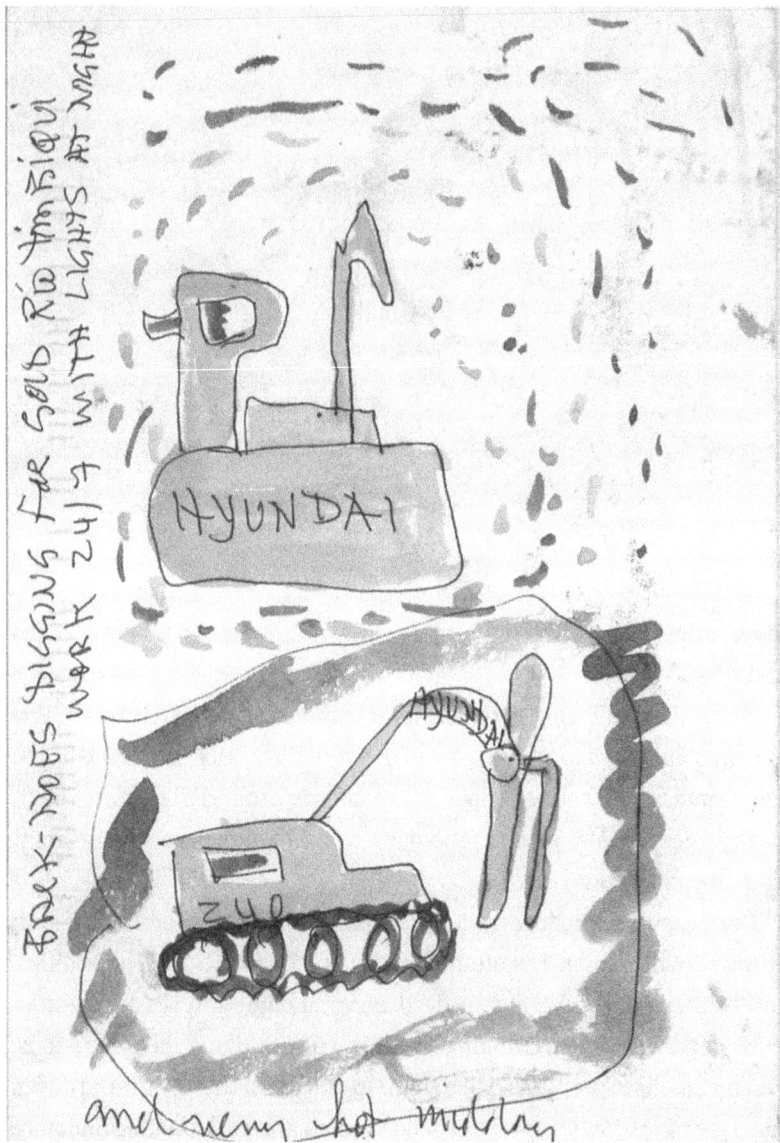

this sensitivity, and why does it sometimes return? It's as if the very young and the very old are threshold people, skirting the border between life and death, the infant half-emergent into life, the aged half-departing. Is that what's happening with me now, both infant in my visitor status and physically old, convulsing in that *espanto* state known as writing?

Historians of death in the West tell us there used to be a lot of contact between the living and the dead. A pesky lot they were, the dead, to be held at arm's length, or even lamed to prevent their walking. E. Louis Backman tells us of needles being inserted into corpses' feet, of feet being nailed to coffins. Or the legs or big toes being bound together, as was practiced as late as 1926 in Lincolnshire, England.[13] That's not so long ago. We were modern then.

In a remote mountain village in Colombia studied in the mid-twentieth century by two anthropologists, old people were miserable. Poorly fed and grumbling, they would warn, in effect, "Just wait till I die, then you'll see who's in charge."[14] A disturbing threat, and how it contests what I take to be mainstream attitudes in the Global North today. Yet despite being modern, do we not still evince fear when we avoid the word *dead* or *death* and instead say someone has "passed," as if they were not really dead but headed to some unnamed, unknowable place, like the mariners who set forth from Old Europe?

Today the words *death* and *dead* weigh heavy on the tongue. They are tabooed words in search of euphemisms, making death all the more unreal. The headline of a *New York Times* op-ed made timely by COVID caught my eye: "Where Do the Dead Go in Our Imaginations?"[15] The question seems to capture the psychic internalization and privatization of what in other times and other places has been a common belief in the continuous existence of the dead as ancestral spirits. But by and large in the Global North, spirits of the dead do not exist except "in our imaginations"—and during the strange moment in 2022 (the source of this book's epigraph) when gubernatorial candidates in New York, caught by a surprise question, admitted fidelity to the dead.

Could it be that such internalization in our imaginations accentuates the power the dead possess, especially since Black Lives Matter, and COVID, when the dead came forth in droves? Photos of COVID deaths were taboo in the Global North, but death and dying have made another, surprising appearance in the USA in these past decades with cell phone videos of police killings, an appearance that drives home in totally new ways the existence of police assassination.

As for the strange, almost physiological power of the dead even without visual imagery, think back to my description of that day of pealing bells in the village in the forest by the river. The sound those bells make is bigger than mind, if such be possible, more encompassing, more penetrating, unstoppable. You can close your eyes, you can stop thinking, but you can't close your ears. It's a sound that covers everything, smothers everything, and is in everything: in your food, in your thoughts, when you eat, when you shit, and when you write—yes, right here—the reverberation creeping along your skin onto the page.

Now that I am far away from the bells, dare I write that sound? Can I do so without breaking the spell between the living and the dead, when your body is no longer your body, your mind no longer your mind; that state when it is possible to imagine the use of the slain body to slay the slayer and you wonder if killers feel no remorse, while each day makes that question more urgent and more naïve—like what happens when you confront the statistics on police killing in the USA?

There, where the police kill three people a day, a rare thing recently happened: a policeman was found guilty of murder. He forced an African American man named George Floyd from his car—his *auto-mobile*—handcuffed him, and forced him to lie on the pavement face-down. He then knelt on his neck for nine minutes while increasingly agitated witnesses, mostly African American, recorded video on their cell phones.

One video in particular, taken by a Black teenager on her way to the store, spread across the world and was decisive in the verdict of guilt. Viewers were mesmerized. Like early Dada cinema, the phone video exploded into our collective consciousness as a meteorological disturbance, like a lightning strike or eclipse of the sun.

Later I will discuss in some detail an instance of this convergence between the metaphysical and the physical as it relates to killing. I call this convergence the "Nuer-Effect," by which the spirit of the victim enters into the body of the killer and can spread further, as we shall learn, to enmesh humans, animals, and things. Such force extends like the plague of which, via COVID and mass shootings, we have recent, first-hand knowledge.

BASE MATERIALISM: TEXT AS SWURL

The thirty-foot-high wall the priest built around the cemetery was accompanied by a massive shift in the burial of the dead. Rarely are they now buried in the soil. Instead, they are slotted into niches in concrete walls.

What then of my old friend Regina Carabalí's fascination with the worms in the corpse? They don't enter it from the outside, she insisted. They emerge from within. Once you're dead, that is, suggesting that death is, in one way or another, a lively, squirming, eminently internal state of affairs. Similarly, the French historian Philippe Ariès, in his 1973 lectures on the Western history of attitudes toward death, describes a fifteenth- and sixteenth-century obsession with the macabre: with visions of the corpse as corrupted, worm-ridden, consumed in its "natural liquors." And Leopold Bloom, our modern Ulysses, on his way to the cemetery in Dublin, opines that "they must breed a devil of a lot of maggots. Soil must be simply swirling with them. Your head it simply swurls."[16]

Bloom's turn of phrase is close to Regina Carabalí's down-to-earth understanding of the corpse, which strikes me as what Georges Bataille in his early surrealist phase called "base materialism." With this he attempted to find ways of diverting the point of view which holds that opposites attract and implicate one another such that materialism is a form of idealism, and vice versa, thus churning the wheels of philosophy, very much including Hegel and therewith Marx. By contrast, "base materialism" would be a poetic, imaginative, and unexpected escape from the grip of dialectics, that seductive attraction of opposites. Base materialism would "swurl" with its own brand of sanctity, like this text you are reading.

As for Regina Carabalí's preference for burial in earth and her sense of the corpse's decay—is it too far off the mark to understand her image of auto-pustulence as "sacred," à la Bataille, here in the cemetery with the involuted innerness of the insides irrigated by foaming sewage water and who knows what else by way of them corpse-worms in holy congress with the earth? After all, Bataille's major concept was *dépense*, meaning waste, profitless spending for the hell of it, as with popular imagery of gangs trafficking little packets the size of love letters with cocaine derivatives while strutting in their quixotic pursuits of sex, extortion and, of course, revenge.

As for the niches gobbling up cemetery space, they are called *bóvedas*, a strange word, strange like so many of the terms used for containers of the corpse, like *sepulcher, catafalque,* or *sarcophagus,* from the Greek for flesh-eating.

Why are these names so strange, these containers of the corpse permeated by the strangeness of that which they would contain. How foreign, these names, bound not to another country but to a foreign state of being. As with mummification, these out-of-joint names that bristle with taboos are wrapped around the corpse on the first leg of its journey, ensuring its physical separation from the living. Not *coffin* but *casket*, notes Jessica Mitford in her 1950s best-seller *The American Way of Death*, as funeral homes burnish the terminology.

I read that *bóveda* comes from the Latin *volūta*, a form of the verb "to turn" that also names a spiral, curl, or roll, which makes me think of resurrection, the return of the dead or at least their transformation. *Volūta* shares its root with the English word *vault,* and I note in passing that the files making up Walter Benjamin's unfinished *Arcades Project*, published after his death, are called *convolutes,* one of which is devoted to the catacombs upon which Paris rests, as if the cadaverous infrastructure of that miraculous city is one vast cemetery and the buildings at street level are its tombstones—many of them, I was recently reminded, built with profits from the slave trade, a fact unmentioned in Benjamin's copious notes on Paris. But "Not even the dead shall be safe," he later wrote, en route to his own death, and you can only wonder how and why Haiti became famous for its voodoo and zombies.

What would it take to awaken the dead during states of emergency? This is the question posed by Haiti, no less than by Benjamin's Angel of History as he fled Paris ahead of the Gestapo in 1940. Pared down, this is the same question underlying corpse magic: How do sorcerers in a state of emergency awaken the dead—meaning, awaken them for revenge? After all, that famous last text of Benjamin's on the philosophy of history is overwhelmingly a text of vengeance in the name of justice with the return of the Messiah.

DIONYSUS AND THE CRUCIFIED ONE

Later I shall develop this idea of vengeance, magical and nonmagical, but here I wish to provide a striking example of vengeance magic described by Todd Ochoa in his 1990s account of Palo, an Afro-Cuban religious practice involving the dead.[17] When I say dead here, I mean both the spirits of the dead and their bodily remains, stolen from Havana cemeteries.

Ochoa's description of Palo peaks with his three final chapters, concerned with the use of parts of a corpse to kill one's enemies. This is done on Good Friday, after midnight, when the Christian god is said to lie powerless, nailed to the cross. Not just any corpse is used, but that of a Jew stolen from a Jewish cemetery or, better still, a Chinese corpse from the *cementerio chino*. Stronger still—*let me underline this*—is the corpse of a murderer who has been executed.

I cite this example not because I think the use of the corpse in western Colombia to kill its killer involves Palo in any direct way. No! Rather, Palo provides me with a striking instance of what corpse magic can be, an outer limit, if you will, of the *spiritual materiality* of what I see as the key aspect of Christianity, namely the Crucifixion.

Both Palo and the use of the corpse that I describe in western Colombia suggest how radical is Christianity's own understanding of corpse magic, using the corpse of Christ not to kill one's enemies but to love them and despair at one's sin-drenched Self.

Of all that happened in Western history, this must be the most decisive event, switching metaphysical and even physiological gears from vengeance to love and self-loathing (such a weird combination). That is certainly Friedrich Nietzsche's orientation, the Christian love in question being understood by him as an underhanded, coercive, controlling form striving for submission. Be it noted that at the beginning of his mental illness, Nietzsche signed his letters as both *Dionysus* and *The Crucified One*, as if his vision of Christ was not the suffering figure on the Cross but the inebriated dancing pagan Dionysus, who not only could imitate anything but could not *not* imitate, thereby existing in a state of continuous Becoming.[18] Could Christ as Dionysus be the sorcery-awoken corpses of the graveyard?

Thus, the corpse magic that I describe as the cause of the cemetery break-in can be thought of as a replay of Christ's resurrection, but set at right angles, so to speak. Through corpse magic, the dead body of the slain comes alive or the soul is animated such that it proceeds to its appointed task, not the path of Christian salvation but revenge. Nevertheless, the basic model is the same: aroused from its death-sleep a corpse is sent on a holy mission of vengeance, through humility and love, as with Christ, or with smoldering hate, as with an assassinated gangster.

PALESTINE AND MINNESOTA

In the USA killing by police is likely to involve an automobile, the sacred site where the police enter the human body. While kings were painted astride powerful horses and equestrian statues of important men were planted in city parks and at crossroads, today it is the automobile as death-space of inner-city America that commands attention. Or rather, it should, except we take automobiles so much for granted that we don't see them. They are the moving landscape. Until the Police Stop.

"History decays into images, not into stories," wrote Benjamin in the compendium of notes published as *The Arcades Project*.[19] It is perhaps an unexpected claim from the author of "The Storyteller," in which the focus is obviously on talk and words. But when it came to images, Benjamin held a historical, albeit nonchronological, theory: "wherein what has been comes together in a flash with the now to form a constellation. In other words, image is dialectics at a standstill." The "now" he had in mind was a mystical moment that, cutting through chronology, suspends time, providing "a revolutionary chance in the fight for the oppressed past."[20] Put another way, there are situations in which images are montaged, as in film, containing a salient element of the past within themselves, not so much as history but as history challenged.

This is what we see, or rather, feel, in the cell phone video streamed by Diamond Reynolds on July 6, 2016, as her companion, Philando Castile, was being shot dead through the driver's window by a policeman who had stopped his automobile for an alleged taillight problem.

She is live-streaming the video through Facebook. Castile is bleeding profusely from a chest wound. He is dying or already dead. She is talking all the time, describing what has just happened and pleading with the policeman or with whoever is listening or watching, "Please don't tell me he's dead!" Over and over, as her four-year-old daughter, in the back seat, cries.

Police videos show other officers approaching the car, crouching like hobbled animals, bent over in contorted postures with weapons drawn. It could be Vietnam, 1970. Yale Law professor and ex–public defender James Forman Jr. has described in detail the sleight of hand used by police to stop dark-skinned motorists for alleged violations such as faulty taillights as part of that war without end, that War on Drugs, most of the drugs in question having come from the jungles and mountainsides of Colombia.[21]

Henry Taylor made a painting of Reynolds's video that was exhibited in the 2017 Whitney Biennale. It's all angles accentuated by flat sheets of color. In the painting, the policeman is just a hand with a gun that looks more like a toy poking through the frame of the window, itself set at an angle as in a cartoon. Blood spreads across Castile's white T-shirt. He is laid back in his seat.

Like the video, the painting is in motion, albeit frozen with an explosive force as if predicting the day-after-day protests across the USA four years later following the phone video recording of police killing George Floyd, also in Minneapolis.

Splayed out under the dark canopy of the car's roof, Philando Castile can seem like a replay of the Crucifixion catapulted from the thin dry air of Jerusalem two thousand years ago to the bloody seat of an auto-mobile in inner-city Minnesota, USA, July 6, 2016. For the present to be touched by the past there should be nothing between, says Benjamin, evoking the practice of montage.[22]

2 *Hollowing*

The *narcorelatos* presented so far entail bodies thickened by violence, and do so in a way that thickens my body too, caught in a reality-effect at once hallucinatory and material, so material it becomes spiritual.

The first three stories deal matter-of-factly with fantastical events, their lack of astonishment heightening the horror. This lack of astonishment indicates where the middle classes today tend to differ from lumpen-rural people like Vladimir. With a wink and a nod, he winds us up. "Oh, no," he replies. "Are you sure?" "Of course, I'm sure."

As we meander upriver along the Sucursal de Papayal, a tributary of the Río Magdalena, he is inside and outside his tale. It is comic and bloody at once. It is hard to imagine anything even remotely like it being included in the well-meaning volumes documenting massacres put out by the preeminent Colombian Grupo de Memoria Histórica or countless other human rights groups.[1] Stories told the way Vladimir tells his would be censored, cut from the record by another act of violence.

His stories both diminish and accentuate the terror. He takes you into the morning mist rising by the river where the corpses are strung up. (Why always the river?) You echo in yourself Vladimir's changes of pace, and are held in suspense as we skid in our launch across the carpet of flowers, one strange reality layered over another.

He comes across as a person returned from the dead, this rambunctious Old Nick, our Vladimir. He has seen it all, this spirit of the wilderness of the soul. He relishes the traumas of which he speaks and of which to some degree, as a paramilitary by his own admission, he is the cause. But then he got sick of oatmeal. Challenging piety with absurdity, transforming cruelty into cartoons, he robs brutality of its capacity to scare us witless. He takes us to those forbidden places, raises an eyebrow, and whisks us away. This is similar to the laughter in the work of Rabelais, the fifteenth-century physician and Greek scholar whose bawdiness and scenes of dismemberment engaged the Russian critic Mikhail Bakhtin. Writing in the 1930s, in exile under Stalin, Bakhtin saw Rabelais as part of a millennia-old tradition of the carnivalesque in Western literature, including the early Socratic dialogues.[2] Corpse-humor coexisting with terror is but one form that this takes.

The epic poetry of the peasant Tomás Zapata provides another instance of this mix of terror and humor, violence and the comic. I first met him in 1970 in the town at the center of my corpse-magic chronicle. A Black man in his eighties and blind when we met, he was a giant, soft of speech and gentle, taking in the morning sun.

He had taught himself to read and write with the help of a trader in the marketplace and had composed many poems, which he knew by heart, such as the one about the classic *Violencia* that ripped through Colombia from 1948 to 1956 (although these dates can be extended forward and backward) leaving an estimated eighty-five thousand people dead (other serious estimates claim two hundred thousand) in a population of around ten million. There were terrifying mutilations, as with "the necktie cut," in which the tongue protrudes through a hole in the throat, and the *bocachica*, named for a commonly eaten freshwater fish prepared by cutting

slits along its side for frying, a practice which, applied to humans, caused slow exsanguination till death occurred. Pregnant women were murdered so as to extract and destroy the fetus.

La *Violencia* was a fratricidal conflict between the two major political parties, with the Conservatives in control of the army and the police. Peasant-based and elite-led, it is the subject of many studies by Colombian writers, some of whom provide a surfeit of grotesque photographs of mutilated bodies together with cold-blooded clinical descriptions.[3] This is what you could call a middle-class professional optic.

But in his epic poem concerning the impact of the *Violencia* on his own town, Zapata takes another direction. As with Vladimir talking about paramilitaries forty years later, his tone and rhythm are jocular. The fact that his lines rhyme (*aabb*) in itself lends a measure of lightheartedness to his blow-by-blow depiction of the violence exercised by the military mayor, Marco Polo Zambrano, and his *chulavita* police.[4]

Zapata begins thus:

Por Dios bendito, ¿qué hacemos con el gobierno de Zambrano?
Estamos como dos bestias, matándose los hermanos
Desde que llegó Zambrano, el pueblo comenzó a temblar
Y nos quitaron hasta las agujas para podernos matar

Dear God, what can we do with the government of Zambrano?
We are like two beasts, brother killing brother
Since Zambrano came, the town quakes with fear,
Even our sewing needles were taken so they could kill us all the easier

And it concludes (in my abbreviated translation):

Surely they will kill me, because I speak the truth
But my pen insists on writing
Just as a tiger is known by its stripes
People are known by the power of their pen
Here end my verses written by my hand [*mano*]
In this form was the government of Marco Polo Zambrano

There is no shortage of film comedy centered on the cadaver. Take *Milou en mai* (May Fools), a hilarious film by Louis Malle, focused on the serene cadaver of a matriarch lying in state in bed, staring at the ceiling with a smile on her face while around her swirl the rivalries of her descendants, echoing the turbulence of May '68 in nearby Paris. Or take *Belle de Jour*, directed by Luis Buñuel, starring Catherine Deneuve as a respectable wife *and* high-class prostitute, who acts as a beautiful corpse laid to rest in a raised coffin while the wealthy fantasist whose idea this is masturbates underneath with vigor sufficient to shake the coffin. For one solitary moment she breaks out of her act, eyelids fluttering open as she tries to figure out the cause of the motion. Then closed again. Or consider Alfred Hitchcock's film *The Trouble with Harry*. Harry's trouble is he's dead and nobody knows what to do with his corpse.

"His corpse." Isn't it strange that we speak here of a dead person as if he were not only alive but the owner of his corpse? As if the corpse were now a separate item, a piece of property possessed by the deceased, another example of the tricks death plays on language.

Now dead, now alive, now me, now an alien piece of real estate, part fetish, part trickster, the corpse is unfathomably prone to comedy, though if you tilt the frame ever so slightly nothing could seem more blasphemous.

Hitchcock had, by the time he directed *The Trouble with Harry* (1955), made many films for television involving corpses. In Cuba, Tomás Gutiérrez Alea made two hilarious corpse films poking fun at the bureaucratization of the revolution, *La muerte de un burócrata* (Death of a Bureaucrat; 1966) and *Guantanamera* (1995), a road movie with a difference, depicting the adventures that befall people in a hearse transporting a corpse from the east of Cuba to Havana. It's as if making a film about a corpse, especially a funny film about a corpse, improbably lets him off the hook of revolutionary censorship.

But why funny? Is it because breaking a taboo nearly always involves humor as well as shock (something Bataille never ceased to wonder at)? Indeed, is not humor the underbelly of shock?

Halloween in the USA is an especially good example of mixing death with the comic. On the stoops in Brooklyn, I see not only skeletons and ghosts but bloody body parts such as amputated hands and cracked-open skulls. Disney movies made for kids at Halloween show dancing skeletons identical with what five hundred years earlier was painted on church walls in France as the *danse macabre*.

One online list of dark comedies involving corpses stops arbitrarily at a hundred but presumably could include many more. Notable is *The Loved One* (1965), set in Los Angeles, directed by Tony Richardson, with a script adapted by those great talents, Terry Southern and Christopher Isherwood, from the very funny 1948 novel of the same name by Evelyn Waugh. Jessica Mitford's classic exposé, *The American Way of Death* (1968), is likewise a hilarious description of the US funeral industry.

But, again, why is the corpse funny? You really have to ask yourself. Look again at *The Loved One*, with its extended scenes of the embalmer cuddling the head of a corpse, purring with pride and pleasure at her handiwork. The corpse is not off-screen. Far from it. The corpse is the star of the film, occupying center stage, smiling at you in its deadness with a wink of recognition. If this is not corpse magic, what is?

Sex is a constant in this film, a corpse-tableau in which the world of corpse beautification and resurrection lends itself to sidesplitting humor. The nubile female attendants take their embalming seriously. It is an art as well as a science, an attitude that serves to increase the erotic innuendo. Marble statues of naked women abound, and at one point, when US Air Force brass come for a visit, the director of the funeral salon has half a dozen luxury coffins open by themselves, as if by magic, to display not corpses but scantily clothed young women, who then pull the officers in with them, ripping off their uniforms and proceeding to sex. Bataille could not have done better, only this is squeaky clean the Californian way and a lot funnier than Bataille's lugubrious prose, sluggish as treacle.

Alongside the elaborate descriptions of the beautification of the corpse as a veritable art-object is a vocabulary of euphemisms pussyfooting around the realities of death and the changes in color, appearance, and rigidity of the corpse, which is reconstructed as alive and comely.

The euphemistic richness surrounding death provides another instance of its linguistic acrobatics. Mitford tells us that it was the detailed chapter on embalming that at first caused mainstream US publishers to reject her book, yet this chapter proved the most popular with readers (again demonstrating the attraction and repulsion of the corpse). But pity the corpse beautician. Too lively a corpse can be more repulsive than a hunky-dory, dead-as-nails one.

Embalming got going in the USA only after the Civil War, when soldiers' bodies were prepared to be transported home. What was meant to be mere preservative became beautification, as if aimed at bringing the corpse back to life. The dead body that would previously have been prepared by the family or women in the community (as still happens in the sugar plantation town from which I write in western Colombia) and laid out in the front parlor of the home, was now taken to the new professionals, the undertakers with their "funeral parlor" or "funeral home," terms that linguistically preserved the husk of the original practice. And how strange and obfuscatory the term "undertaker."

The "denial of death" we hear so much about as a sign of modernity turns out to be more than an attitude. It would seem to start with the "home" no longer the home, the "parlor" no longer a parlor but a business. The humor in Waugh and Mitford depends on this commodification, the transaction in which a basic bodily function, namely death, is kidnapped, not so much by subterfuge as by performance art engaging the fearsome taboos concerning the corpse. It seems part of a modernization story, that of professional men supplanting the activity of community-bound women, similar to what happened with midwives and women herbalists throughout the world and identical to the story I will relate later regarding the disappearance of the death watch or wake.

At the same time that the home parlor was being commodified, Karl Marx was contemplating the dead in his world-changing book *Capital*, in which he analyzed economic value in capitalism as a result of a process where, in effect, people become like things and things become like people.[5] This was as much the lived experience of people as it was, in Marx's eyes, the paradigm underlying the leading economic theories of the day, put forward by David Ricardo, John Stuart Mill, and Adam Smith. This is markedly the case a century later in Waugh's novel, set in a vast cemetery in Los Angeles, city of Hollywood fantasy, and populated with corpses that can seem more alive than life itself. The oscillation between life and death is also the centerpiece of *Belle de Jour*, in which Deneuve, feigning death, opens her eyes in her coffin for one brief, forbidden second, as her rich client, fetishizing with zeal, jerks off below. Marx was not quite so daring.

Does not the humor of the corpse that fills the pages of Mitford and Waugh stem from the shameless commodification of death that they display? We laugh at the characters' double-talk and mock solemnity, the staff's wringing of hands and ever-lengthening faces of grief, while behind the scenes we can hear the money being counted.

Tracing the seriocomic or carnivalesque in Western literature from ancient Greece to the present, Bakhtin draws our attention to a short story written by Dostoevsky late in life, in 1873, and set in a timeless present, called "Bobok—From Somebody's Library" (*bobok*, a type of bean in Russian, means, idiomatically, "nonsense"). The narrator happens upon a funeral in a cemetery, a scene of much merrymaking and dissimulation. While sitting on a tomb, he overhears corpses arguing underground: "You made money, I suppose? You fleeced people?" says the corpse of a woman of high rank. "Fleece you, indeed?" replies the corpse of a shopkeeper. "We haven't seen the colour of your money since January. There's a little bill of yours at the shop." "Don't try to recover debts here," the corpse of the woman counters. "We all know things are different here," says the shopkeeper's corpse. "Different, how?" "We are dead, so to speak, your Excellency."[6]

"So to speak." At long last the corpses are free to talk truth to power, yet they preserve the decorum deemed necessary for dialogue no less than for the barbed tongue of aboveground repartee.

Thanks to transgression (in this case meaning satire), a moral topography is at work, one that seems as old as humankind, involving an oscillation between subterranean depths and the plane of social life. It is the confluence, thanks to the cemetery, of the underworld with the sanctimonious surface layers of society that provides the humor of the uncensored. The dreadful materiality of the dead body rubs up against the celestial heights of beauty and reason, reinforcing but also confounding schemes like those of Dante's *Divina Commedia*. It is as if life anywhere anytime is a roller-coaster pitching between levels whose conflicts and contradictions, absurdities, and mysteries are as likely to seem as funny as they are terrible, as one state of being passes into the other.

The intimacy of death with comedy struck Georges Bataille in numerous ways, as with his reference to James Joyce's *Finnegans Wake*. But he would have done better, I think, to cite *Ulysses*. "You must laugh sometimes so better do it that way," muses Leopold Bloom on his way to the cemetery, following the corpse of a friend. "Gravediggers in *Hamlet*," he continues. "Shows the profound knowledge of the human heart. Daren't joke about the dead for two years at least."[7]

So, Shakespeare shows profound knowledge of the human heart in having the gravediggers joke about the dead, but then "you daren't . . . for two years at least."

Had two years passed in the story James (not James Joyce) told me of the euthanasia of a noted anthropologist in his hometown who decided to hold a farewell party as he died? The whisky flowed. The nurse injected the host with the fatal chemical. The whisky flowed some more. The about-to-be dead man closed his eyes and passed away. But after an hour he woke up. "Am I dead?" he asked. The nurse applied another shot. This time, James assured me, he died.

You daren't joke. But we do. And the stories flow as freely as the whisky. Even the aspirant corpse joins in. We are all Shakespeare's gravediggers. Could this be why bodily violence and humor hang together in cartoon skirmishes between Bugs Bunny and Elmer Fudd, Wile E. Coyote and Road Runner, Tom and Jerry—about which Wikipedia writes:

> The cartoons are known for some of the most violent cartoon gags ever devised in theatrical animation: Tom may use axes, hammers, firearms, firecrackers, explosives, traps and poison to kill Jerry. Jerry's methods of retaliation are far more violent, with frequent success, including slicing Tom in half, decapitating him, shutting his head or fingers in a window or a door, stuffing Tom's tail in a waffle iron or a mangle, kicking him into a refrigerator, getting him electrocuted, pounding him with a mace, club or mallet, letting a tree or electric

pole drive him into the ground, sticking matches into his feet and lighting them, tying him to a firework and setting it off, and so on. While *Tom and Jerry* has often been criticized as excessively violent, there is no blood or gore in any scene.[8]

UN CHIEN DÉLICIEUX

Enough of cats. What about dogs, and specifically eating them, as in a surrealist spoof of surrealism, Ken Feingold's 1991 video *Un chien délicieux*. Implicitly referencing *Un chien andalou*, the classic 1929 surrealist film by Luis Buñuel and Salvador Dalí, Feingold's video shows, in its first half, an older man with a riveting Mohawk hairstyle and a parrot balancing awkwardly on his shoulder. Now and again, as it is about to fall, the parrot flaps its wings while the man speaks slowly and deliberately in dubbed English with a charming French accent. The camera never moves. There's just this man looking straight at you with a parrot scrambling for a claw-hold on his shoulder.

He has a tale to tell, and surreal it is: how foreigners blundered into his highland Thai village, were enchanted, and invited him to Paris to visit André Breton, the pope of surrealism. After a few months in Paris, however, his exoticism wears thin. The surrealists arrange a farewell dinner. "What would you like to eat?" they ask. "A dog," he replies. His hosts are shocked. "Impossible!" they reply. He has outshocked the surrealists.

"But now that you are here," he tells the camera, "I will show you how we eat dog."

Everything changes.

Before the screen held one image—a man with a strange haircut, a soft purring voice, and a parrot. Now it's all action, and the filming is composed, at first, of spooky long shots. Human figures sway in the background like two-dimensional puppets. They move jerkily. The wide-angle shot distorts everything into flat sheets, images blurring into one another like those of the bent-over police swarming toward Philando Castile's automobile.

Yet a little later not a detail is missed as we witness the killing of the dog. We zoom in on the blood pumping from the cut throat, see the extraction of the intestines—which are promptly eaten by other dogs—and then the burning of the dog's body hair prior to the quartering of its corpse, again in close-up.

You are witnessing killing like you have never seen or imagined, and you ask yourself, which is the more surreal? Which is the more avant-garde? The first half of the film, with the talking head in southeast Asia recounting a visit to surrealist HQ in Paris, or the second, with these intercut long shots and close-ups showing, step by step, the methodical act of killing and disemboweling a dog?

Then it dawns on you with even more of a shock that you have been duped, that the film, or at least its first half, is fake, a setup; there were no Europeans stumbling over the hill into a faraway village, and there was no trip to Paris to visit the pope.

But the killing. That is different. It seems so awfully real that it out-realizes both reality and surreality to the extent that, like the parrot, we scramble for a claw-hold.

What gives with these surreal animals, their pain, their slaughter, and their abundance? Tom and Jerry seem merely part of an endless genealogy of cruelty to animals as entertainment—and allegory.

FAMILY APPETITE

In Antioquia, the heartland of Colombia, famous for its entrepreneurship, textile industry, Pablo Escobar, and violence, it is common to have a party, killing a pig and eating it, at Christmas or New Year's celebrations. The fiesta is called *La Matada del Marrano*, the Killing of the Pig.

As for pigs and their importance in psychic life and ecological history, an anthropologist friend from Medellín tells me she was given the typical *paisa* gift, a sow, when she turned thirteen, a rite-of-passage gift whose significance would not be lost on Benjamin Franklin, who wrote centuries earlier of the parallel between a breeding sow and capital breeding more of itself. The idea of a "piggy bank" comes to mind. It should also be noted how strategic the pig was in the famous Antioqueño colonization of the interior of Colombia, the cutting down of the forest and its indigenous inhabitants as well.[9]

The scream of a pig being killed is hideous, prolonged, and unforgettable. It is easy, if not automatic, to hear it as human screaming, only it seems more human than human. It seems like a person struggling in the hold of people cutting its throat.

This sound briefly fills the screen midway through Medellín-born Clemencia Echeverri's seven-minute video *Apetitos de Familia*, made in 1998, a time when Colombia and especially the countryside around Medellín was undergoing extreme paramilitary and military predation. The screen flickers between shadowy depictions of people hugging and dancing in the dimmed lights of festive gaiety, while the pig screams and images of hands hauling out the viscera take the place of the dancers.

Before that, for the first minute and a half, the screen slowly fills from the bottom up with a purplish liquid, presumably the blood of the slain pig. Quietly, the sound of a beating heart continues.

BLOOD FILLS
THE
SCREEN

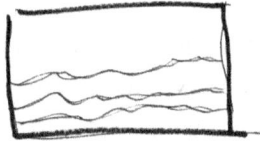

SOUND OF
HEART BEATING

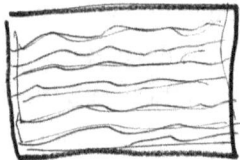

PIG
SCREAMING

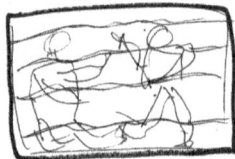

PEOPLE
DANCING

Killing, so long part of Colombian history, finds an echo in rites involving family and friends, where violence proceeds more or less thoughtlessly, at least without any overt sense of cruelty, as background noise.

HOME SWEET HOME

Taking *Apetitos de Familia* alongside other works by Echeverri, such as *Casa Intima* (14 minutes, 1996), which shows a middle-class family home being demolished, I feel I get a better understanding of what witnessing means, in a spiritual as well as a legal sense, *witnessing* being that which defines what writers and anthropologists do as well.

Yet is it not curious that my sense of witnessing—what it means to witness—is intensified and clarified by *destruction*—by "killing" the house and the dense family history its rooms contain, together with the artist's extravagant deployment of montage, here splitting the screen into quadrants?

Moreover, the sound keeps changing, setting up yet another channel of juxtaposition, sounds against sounds and sounds against visual imagery. At times the sound is a cacophony of hammer blows felling masonry and battering rams collapsing walls. A shovel pierces a wall like butter. Other times you zero into the optical unconscious and watch a chisel slowly prize apart a window with the precision of a surgeon.

Sometimes all four quadrants of the screen hold moving images, each of a different reality, say, the manual destruction of walls, the careful lowering from the second story of doors with colored glass panels, old family photos, and footage of the home's Black maid's strong arms spattered with white soap suds as she does laundry. Imagine, if you can, the screen split into four, each with its own story.

Occasionally there is a glimpse of that great fact of nature, the mountains of the *cordillera* rising steeply behind the ongoing wreck of what was a family home. But then there is that other "fact of nature," counterbalancing the mountain, namely the maid who holds the home together. Again and again, the film returns to her working arms. The sound of her scrubbing clothes on the laundry stone is the same as the sound of the demolition. Yes! This is flagrant montage, deliriously multiplex. But it has a center, so to speak, in those arms without which there could be neither middle class nor family home.

Most of the time, only one or two quadrants are occupied, leaving the others blank with their own eloquence.

Overall, an unnerving kaleidoscope is set in motion. Behind what we viewers directly experience with these images lies the worldwide process of gentrification and rapacious real estate raking in profits for the few and immiseration for the rest.

As I ponder the fourfold montage that brings this to light, I wonder about this book I am writing. For is this not also a montaged work whose whole and consuming point is to pit two realities against each other such that connections thicken and luminesce, each informing and illuminating the other while expanding frames of reference? On the one side is corpse magic involving killings in a western Colombian town, on the other, killings by police in the USA, killings that appear bereft of metaphysical or magical consequence yet which, recorded in cell phone videos, become spectral.

CHANGING CONTENT HERE IS LIKE THE
QUEEN IN CHESS

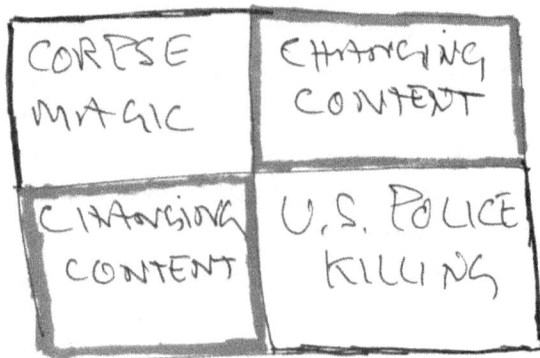

| CORPSE MAGIC | CHANGING CONTENT |
| CHANGING CONTENT | U.S. POLICE KILLING |

SHE CAN MOVE ANY WHERE

Fourfold split screen with corpse magic in one quadrant, US police in another, and the remaining two empty but radiant with possibility.

EVISCERATION

"Thickening" of the body involves hollowing out the corpse so as to pack in cocaine. We saw this with the disemboweled infant, and we saw it with the corpse and the half-alive body described by Vladimir as we headed up the river of flowers.

Evisceration of the corpse so as to embody cocaine achieves its mystical counterpart in the account of the young paramilitary's bulletproof body rent by bullets. Although cavernous, the wounds do not bleed. He is in a state of living death. "I am rotting through and through," he says, pleading with his captors for death. They riddle his body with more bullets, but to no avail.

The magic, the young paramilitary explains, makes him invulnerable to bullets, implying, I suppose, that only something other than a gun can kill him. Which seems absurdly literal, but there it is. So, his captors resort to cold steel, hacking his body to pieces with machetes on the back of a truck.

Killing with machetes differs from killing using guns by virtue of its intimate bodily engagement. Hacking a living body to death may involve, I imagine, a delirium, even a hysteria. Each thrust meets with physical resistance and heightens the sense of transgressing the taboo on killing until, perhaps, a sort of trance mixed with fury takes over and the killer becomes a machine, like a gun. It's not just killing but transforming, reducing a whole person to fragments. "Sausage meat" is the term Johanna Pérez Gómez found used in the *llanos* of Colombia when assailants were faced with the problem of eliminating a bulletproof person and had to cut the body into small pieces.[10] This furious bodily engagement with what is essentially already a corpse will emerge in more detail when I discuss the cemetery break-in I have already mentioned and distinctions between killing with a spear and killing with a firearm among the Nuer of southern Sudan.

Apparently loath to show someone being hacked to death, Hollywood directors commonly try to make guns equivalent. They explode in technicolor across the screen, but it's rarely more than background noise. Quentin Tarantino, however, had few such qualms in his 2019 film *Once Upon a*

Time in Hollywood, which certainly raises the hair on the back of your neck as he makes a movie version of eight-months-pregnant Sharon Tate and four friends being hacked to death by the Manson family on Cielo Drive in 1969. (*Cielo* is Spanish for sky or heaven.) It was as if killing by guns had exhausted itself as entertainment, and neoprimitivism was called for.

Is it not the case that in our high-tech killing culture today, it is hands-on, low-tech killing with a machete that is likely to be most scary and most effective as a strategy in paramilitary warfare aimed at terrorizing populations. (In June 2021 federal judge Roger Benitez in San Diego, California, tried the opposite tack. He defended the use of assault weapons such as the AR-15 by equating them with a Swiss Army penknife. This is a true story.[11])

I recall a conversation in the 1990s with an anthropologist born and educated in London's East End who had done fieldwork in highland New Guinea. I expressed amazement concerning the spread of guns among British youth. "Why do you want a gun?" I asked a twelve-year old boy from the north of England. "I want to be hard," he said, rolling his r's. At which point my anthropologist friend told me that when he went to school in the East End in the 1940s most boys carried a hammer as a weapon concealed under their trousers. A hammer! The question implied in his response was which is worse, a gun or a hammer? And the answer seemed to be the hammer.

Hacking a person to death with a machete unites the body of the killer with the body of the victim, thanks to the repeated arc of movement and resistance of flesh that firing a gun cannot equal. This corporeal intimacy seems crucial to what I call the Nuer-Effect, whereby killing with a spear provokes the blood (let's say "spirit") of the slain to enter into the body of the slayer.[12]

But does not the use of the power saw in stories of Colombian paramilitaries confronting unarmed civilians blend low and high tech? The power saw combines the savagery of the machete with the magic of the modern, snarling and screaming as you squeeze the trigger.

In the 1970s in downtown Bogotá, I would walk past a lurid poster advertising the film *The Texas Chainsaw Massacre* and wonder, in my then innocence, how anybody could enjoy watching something like that. It was called a "slasher film" and in the USA would become an industry. Eventually there were eight chainsaw massacre films, along with comic books and video games. That poster in downtown Bogotá still sticks in my mind now fifty years later.

In the 1980s in the small town of Mocoa in the cloud-forest foothills of the Andes that run into the Amazon basin, I saw eye-catching advertising for Stihl power saws. The poster showed a curvy young blonde woman seated with her legs apart. Between them was a power saw, teeth bared. Without underestimating the creative genius of the death squads that emerged in the 1980s in Colombia, empowered by US Cold War ideology and dollars, I can't help wondering how much iconography like that and the slasher films influenced the use of the chainsaw as a weapon to cut down people as well as forests.

ARE *NARCORELATOS* THEMSELVES CORPSE MAGIC?

Do drug stories tap into the bodily unconscious? Do the images evoked in *narcorelatos* such as those I've presented merge the body of the listener or reader with the actions depicted? Is the tale a flow like watching a film in which you are streamed, body and mind, into the film itself?[13] If so, this would parallel phone videos of police killing in the US, such as those showing the killings of Philando Castile and George Floyd.

In his 1907 book on wit and its relation to the unconscious, Sigmund Freud presents the concept of "ideational mimetics," the subtle body movements that accompany our reception of an idea such that cognition becomes corporeal empathy.[14] In accentuated form it is likely to occur when we follow the movements of Charlie Chaplin or Buster Keaton. We follow with our own bodies in synch. Sergei Eisenstein goes further when he explores, in his book on Disney, how fire functions in relation to animation: fire, he writes, "is capable of most conveying the dream of a flowing diversity of forms."[15]

As for fire, so for the *narcorelato*: it is the horror as much as the "slapstick" of disfigured bodies that triggers mimicry on the part of the viewer or listener. Of course, it is a disjointed mimicry, as befits attraction *and* repulsion, coming in close only to jerk away, then back in close . . . ad infinitum.

Am I alone in feeling my body parts hacked off? In feeling myself hung from a tree, dead or almost dead, as my abdomen fills with cocaine paste or powder? No! I don't think I'm the only one. My body has become your body no less than the body of the world.

With his notion of sympathetic magic, James Frazer in *The Golden Bough* famously set up a poetics of magical charms and spells as consisting of image magic, on the one hand, and physical contagion, on the other (later parsed as metaphor and metonymy by the linguist Roman Jakobson). Frazer noticed that the two were usually mixed in the charms he studied.

Then consider Proust's *mémoire involontaire* sparked by taste, smell, or sound, which works like one of these magical charms and can be exceedingly visceral. Indeed, in the first account Proust provides, the bodily reaction is orgasmic and the flood of memories triggered expands as if to encompass the world—not that different from what we shall see when I discuss the "Nuer-Effect" transposed to northeast Australia. This is a term I have coined based on a description provided in 1996 by the anthropologist Sharon Hutchinson for what occurred or was likely to occur when a Nuer man in the south of Sudan killed another Nuer man with a spear. She describes a mysterious blood bond forged at the moment of death when "some of the blood of the victim passed at death into the body of the slayer, being driven forth, as it were, by a mission of vengeance."[16]

IMAGE AS CONTAGION

With regard to images as understood in the West, the contagious aspect of an image impacting the viewer seems dubious at best. The gap between subjects and objects has at all costs to be preserved and corporeal empathy cut short to the extent possible. Me here, safely ensconced in my epistemological fortress; the image over there, basking in its ontology hanging on a wall or its equivalent; and never the twain shall meet. But is that the end of the story?

With the *narcorelato*, what happens, I submit, is that you the listener or you the reader actually travel or even transform for the briefest metaphysical moment into the drama of what is being depicted, but then you "snap out of it." Think of watching a violent movie, the moment before a shudder of fear or distaste distances you, a shudder that may actually exacerbate the mimesis between the image and what the image is an image of. The shudder comes in waves. It is physical, like nausea or heart-pumping shortness of breath.

Love can do this too. In *One-Way Street*, Walter Benjamin writes:

> If the theory is correct that feeling is not located in the head, that we sentiently experience a window, a cloud, a tree not in our brains but in the place where we see it, then we are, in looking at our beloved, too, outside ourselves. But in a torment of tension and ravishment.[17]

It is this engagement, be it momentary, illusory, a fairytale, or realer than real, that is the object of my attention in these pages. It fascinates. It holds me in thrall. For apart from its intrinsic interest and the ethical a priori of putting yourself in the shoes of the Other, *could this be the same as what is involved in corpse magic itself,* that magic that brings the slain corpse to life or activates something in it so as to slay the slayer?

This is where I come face to face with accounts in anthropology concerning the curious illness caused by homicide in so-called primitive societies, stories that describe a dangerous, life-threatening, mystical tie created by the act of killing a human being that may well extend beyond the killer to the killer's family, kin group, and environment. In ancient Greek accounts, it could take down an entire city.[18] Could this have any relevance in the USA today? Could the US police killing three people a day be susceptible, our cities as well? Does the magical bond between slayer and slain prevail in some way, if only as a potential?

And if not, what does that imply for the ethical basis of the modern world?

3 *Some Anthropology of Slaying*

My first inkling of the mystical impact on the killer of killing someone came many years ago while reading the Swiss missionary Henri Junod's famous two-volume, turn-of-the-century ethnographic account, drawn from his three decades in what is today called Mozambique. For a long time it was for me a strange fact isolated in the far reaches of my flagging memory.

Then I ran into Georges Bataille's suggestion that the drawings of animals in the Lascaux caves in the south of France could be considered testimony to the powers unleashed by transgressing the taboo on killing. For decades it had been Bataille's assumption that transgression is what makes humans human. Now, with the Lascaux drawings before him, he suggested that in killing a wild animal, art was born. Far-fetched, for sure, but suggestive, especially if we consider—as I shall, a little later—that animals are not only in some sense human but superhuman.

As for transgression, we might recall that the Old Testament begins with transgression, with Eve plucking forbidden fruit. But in Bataille's rendition vis-à-vis Lascaux, it is killing, not stealing, that is at issue, and instead of having to live thereafter in the wilderness with one's genitalia concealed, fearful of the wrath of God, you paint images on cave walls of what you have killed. The Hebrew Bible has its origin stories. Bataille has his.

While the god decrees that thou shalt not kill (humans) nor make graven images, in Lascaux cave culture, per Bataille, you must make graven images of (at least some of) what you are wont to kill. The image registers the transgression, meets it halfway, so to speak, and in doing so acquires power.

LASCAUX CAVE IMAGES

Aware that Lascaux is the graveyard of experts' attempts at interpretation, I nevertheless wish to suggest that the animals depicted are in some sense supernatural beings—if not gods, then rendered such in being slain, their killing amounting to a sacrifice of the god.

In a later commentary in *The Tears of Eros* (1961), focused on one particular image in a site in the caves known as "the pit" or "the well," Bataille offers a stark, more down-to-earth version of his idea of the hunter's relation to a slain bison: "The subject of this famous painting, which has called forth numerous contradictory and unsatisfactory explanations, would therefore be *murder and expiation*."[1]

As defined in the Merriam-Webster dictionary, *expiation* is "the act of extinguishing the guilt incurred by something." The entry quotes the example of the Christian Mass, "a ceremony that celebrates the sacrifice of Christ for the *expiation* of the original sin of Adam and Eve."

The image Bataille has in mind is of a fatally wounded bison with its guts spilling forth and a spear through its side. A human, drawn very crudely compared with the animal, is lying in front of the bison. The human has a phallic erection. Its head is not human. It is that of a bird.

This curious tableau seems tailor-made for Bataille's feverish attempts to relate the birth of art to death and eroticism, more specifically to finding a sacred nexus between sex as play, on the one hand, and its connection not just to death but to violent death, on the other. (More horrific illustrations accompany this image from "the pit" in Bataille's *The Tears of Eros*, which was censored by the French government for its violence.)

The bird's head was described by some Lascaux experts as a disguise and is of a piece with other man-animal hybrid figures on the walls of the caves, such as the startling "horned god," reproduced as a drawing by the pioneer explorer of Lascaux, the Abbé Breuil. This deity is a deerlike creature on two human legs with a deer's tail, a prominent phallus, huge antlers, and a quizzical humanlike face.

As described in ethnographies I discuss later, such hybrid creatures bring to mind the disguises hunters may use when pursuing game. (And let us not overlook hunting as a metaphor for what police do.) But the most riveting suggestion I would like to offer is that the figures on the cave walls are not animals as modern Westerners regard them but *animal-humans*, and hence divine.

Another way of expressing this is to suggest that the animals depicted in Lascaux are more human than humans and the paintings are thus of humans in their animal form. In painting the animal or bird, the painter resurrects the energy of the slain (read "corpse magic") in the slayer-slain nexus, reveling in its divinity.

To my mind, one of the puzzling features of the Lascaux paintings is that they are all or almost all of animals, not humans, and that there is a marked discrepancy between the fabulous images depicting the animal as a vibrant being and the tawdry lifeless representations of men, in the case of the Abbé Breuil's stick figure with a bird's head and a lot of phallus. (In other parts of the world such as Zimbabwe, humans in ancient cave paintings, beautiful, elegant, and manifold, are manifest and even predominant, as in the illustrated essay by Leo Frobenius in 1930 in *Documents*, the magazine edited by Bataille.[2])

THE SLAIN ANIMAL IS HUMAN BUT MORE GODLIKE

Let me suggest the following as an aid to exposition: that the pictured animals on those dark cave walls are the equivalent of Christian paintings of saints in churches. Let us go further. Imagine walking into a Catholic church and confronting, instead of Stations of the Cross lining the nave, a beaver, a bear, a reindeer, and a moose along one side, and a raven, an eagle, an earthworm, and a pussy cat on the other—each with a halo, a product of their "crucifixion."

These off-the-wall speculations lead me to the next Station of the Cross and to the following question: What if the hunted—and not only the hunter—could paint? After all, these hunted beings are supernatural and surely know a trick or two. What would their artwork consist of?

At the end of this book, I respond to this question by discussing cell phone videos made by people of color filming US police killing other people of color. But here, with the Abbé Breuil's hybrid image in mind, I wish to think more about the mimetic relationship between hunter and prey and about the emotional bonds therein.

According to some accounts of the painting in the "pit," the sticklike human figure may not be a corpse with an erect phallus (a strange idea, at best) but a shaman in trance (just as strange). But then, why the erect phallus? Is hunting per se erotic as well as ecstatic because of killing the god, meaning killing the animal as human and as god?

Regarding the latter, Bataille quotes at some length from *Les rites de chasse chez les peoples sibériens* by the anthropologist Éveline Lot-Falk, invoking her description of the Yukaghir people to support his notion that the slain animal is human—"only more godlike."[3]

"Human—only more godlike." A strange phrasing.

In a 2007 account of his fieldwork among the Yukaghir, the anthropologist Rane Willerslev describes hunters' disguises in terms of what he calls mimesis between the hunter and the animal.[4] This suggests "becoming Other."[5]

A MAN HUNTING ELK IS ALSO AN ELK

Willerslev describes, for example, a man hunting elk, among the biggest creatures in the forest. (In North America a male elk can weigh more than a thousand pounds.) The hunter wears an elk coat with the hair outward. He has big ears like an elk. The undersides of his skis are covered with the smooth skin of an elk's legs such that when he moves on the snow he *sounds like an elk.* What's more, when the hunter, thus "elked," moves his body, *he walks like an elk.* In the sauna the day before the hunt, he whips himself with birch leaves, losing his human smell and acquiring the odor of the leaves, which elk are fond of. It seems the elk are fooled. Or that they are curious and want to play. Perhaps it's all a game for the hunter, too, a game in which the animal obligingly plays its part?

I much appreciate the way the undersides of the skis, in this account, are covered in hide from the legs of an elk, and the assertion that this makes the Yukaghir hunter's movements sound like an elk walking. Supercharged mimesis, you might exclaim, mimesis of mimesis, albeit, perhaps, more in the mind of the hunter than of the hunted.

But does it matter whether the game is more in the mind of the hunter or of the hunted? Does it get any better, mimetically, than this? The skin of the legs of the elk become the skin of the "legs" of the hunter, whose walking, or waddling, then sounds like an elk's.

Well, yes, it does get mimetically better! Consider this fragment of text from the late nineteenth century, recording an indigenous person in Pine Ridge, South Dakota, USA, reporting that those who dream of elk must therefore

> wear sticks like elk horns with hide branches and rawhide ears. They must paint yellow. They must paint their hands and feet black and have black paint on their breast and back. They must have a circle made of eagle feathers on the right side. They must have a mask made of rawhide. They have poison in the circle. They can vomit poison in the hand. They can shoot poison. They can throw vomit poison from a wooden ring.[6]

I cannot resist relating the hunter's mimetic bond with the elk to Nietzsche's remark in *Genealogy of Morals* that police are like criminals, only worse, since they act like criminals but in the name of justice.[7] In contrast to the elk-legged hunter, US police don't walk much. Weighed down with guns, handcuffs, notebooks, tasers, and walkie-talkies, their natural habitat is the automobile with which they hunt other automobiles as game on roadways.

Might there be a sexual element in both sorts of hunting, a power stemming from sexual attraction? In fantastically mimetic terms, Joseph Ypes Brown describes such a power as conceived by the Oglala Sioux of South Dakota, in connection with the whirlwind, the spider, the dragonfly, and the cocoon.[8] Not only is mimesis utilized by the hunter of elk, but—a point not hinted at in the Siberian sources I cite—the elk itself is so profoundly mimetic that it is a source of mimetic power more generally, at least among the Oglala Sioux. We might suggest, further, that the animal's godlike character is tied up with that capability, which is also eminently sexual, being the power of attraction between the male and the female, and contingent, if not dependent, on the strange cry of the male, known as "bugling."

If this is a lot to take in, let me condense and abstract my train of thought, thus: I am suggesting (1) that police in the USA, if not elsewhere, can be thought of as hunters and thus hunting lore can be applied to them, including that of traditional, non-European hunters; (2) that hunting skills include mimesis not only as imitation of prey but more generally as spying, disguise, intimidation, and trickery of all sorts; and (3) that this accords with Nietzsche's observation that police act like criminals, only worse, because they do so in the name of justice.

RITUAL FOR THE SLAIN ANIMAL

We get insight, from another angle, into the meaning of the *expiation* Bataille has in mind when we come across a hunter dancing, singing, meditating, and smoking tobacco for up to an hour by the corpse of a freshly killed animal. This description comes from the anthropologist Frank Speck, whose fieldwork was undertaken between 1909 and the 1920s with the Naskapi-Montagnais people of Newfoundland.[9]

For sure this is not like the killing of animals for meat in slaughterhouses in the wastelands of rural America today. But while the anthropologist's conceit here is that the ritual serves to maintain the meat supply, material elsewhere in his account suggests a different notion: that the meat supply is dependent upon one's participation in the sacrifice of a fellow human being in animal guise.

Put another way, the act of killing converts an animal into first a human and then a god. Killing establishes not only a bond between the slayer and the slain but a morally generative bond pumping sacred energy into the universe.

My suggestion may seem vastly exaggerated to most readers, romanticized balderdash associated with the myth of the "noble savage," but the ethnography claims just that. Part of the problem for modern-day readers is that Naskapi religion, unlike Western monotheism with its one, overbearing, transcendent god, was a "religion of everyday life," not institutionally demarcated from other activities—a seamless part, I glean from Speck, of the whole of Naskapi life. Naskapi religion is immanent in life.[10] There are many "gods," or what Westerners call "spirits," but no dwelling set aside as a church, no one day of the week demarcated as sacred. If anything, the animal was the church and killing an animal intensified its status as sacred Other.

With his marvelous descriptions of the sacred character of animals, Speck provides more than sufficient material for such an interpretation.

Religion permeates everything and does so particularly through the hunt, through the killing relationship with animals, which, in Bataille's optic, will always be tied to transgression, to the rupture of Being that killing entails. This is tied in with the fact that *animals are humans in another form* and the hunt is the outcome of a dream in which the soul-spirit of the hunter connects with the soul-spirit of the animal. In Speck's words, the animals become "comparable to supernatural beings."[11]

Consider what Speck says about the beaver, toward whom the Naskapi "bear witness with all the fidelity of worshippers to its miraculous powers of magic and its sage intellect." The beaver can transform into other animal forms; geese and other birds are mentioned. The beaver can disappear by penetrating the ground, by rising into the air, or by diving into the depths of a lake or stream and remaining as long as desired.[12]

Is there anything more beautiful than this, I ask myself? Has not this beaver eclipsed Dante's *Divine Comedy* and enriched the two millennia of the carnivalesque described by Bakhtin?

The Naskapi, writes Speck, are "blessed with a feeling that they owe a debt to the animal world for its sacrifice of life in their behalf." Indeed, sacrifice captures what is here at stake. With his aphorism "sacrifice consecrates that which it destroys," Bataille focuses our attention on the bond between killing and the creation of sacredness, only he doesn't have the ethnographic material to do justice to his own insight.[13] He would have had a wonderful time, I suspect, reading Speck on the beaver, the bear, and the caribou.

In his analysis of Nuer sacrifice in Africa in the early 1930s, E. E. Evans-Pritchard comes close to Bataille's idea of sacrifice, though they remain miles apart in other ways. Scorning the idea that sacrifice is based on providing the gods with a gift—a mere token of meat or fat—Evans-Pritchard nevertheless concludes that through sacrifice the gods receive "the gift of life."[14] To say the least, this is puzzling. It encourages us to translate "gift of life" into what Derrida calls the "gift of death."[15]

This switches the tracks on which the contradictions run, reinforcing what I have been at pains to point out; that killing establishes a generative liaison between slayer and slain, something I need now to explore further in relation to homicide.

But before proceeding I need to point out that the cases I present are restricted to so-called warriors in battle, not, for instance, men killing women or defenseless people. We also have to be sensitive to the fact that "primitive warfare" may be largely or wholly a ritualized affair, war *games* with few casualties.[16] Such can by no means be equated with wars fought by Euro–North American armies against each other or in their colonies in the New World, Asia, or Africa against indigenous people, on occasion with the assistance of indigenous people. What's more, I hazard that what I describe below as the spiritual and physical consequences of warriors killing each other is neither inevitable nor always present, and could be largely fictitious, horror stories or war stories related for entertainment. The *Iliad*, with its skull-crushing, chest-piercing violence, comes to mind as exalted poetry, as do the *narcorelatos* I have related. How many people have actually suffered the fates described? For now, let the stories speak for themselves.

SOUTHERN AFRICA: THONGA (EARLY TWENTIETH CENTURY)

In his two-volume book *The Life of a South African Tribe*, based on thirty-two years among the Thonga of present-day Mozambique in the late nineteenth and early twentieth centuries, the Swiss missionary Henri Junod describes the danger that befalls a warrior who kills in battle.

The killer is "hot" or "toxic," and specific depolluting rites are necessary before he can reenter society. During his quarantine period, he wears old clothes. He eats with a special spoon because his hands are "hot." He is forbidden to drink water. Sex is prohibited. He is considered "black," and the black must be removed through medicines and inhalations administered by a specialist.[17] Junod explains that killing exposes the warrior to "the mysterious and deadly influence of nuru."

And what is *nuru*?

Nuru is the spirit of the slain which tries to take revenge on the slayer. It haunts him and may drive him into insanity: his eyes swell, protrude, and become inflamed. He will go out of his mind

and be attacked by giddiness and the thirst for blood may lead him
to fall upon members of his own family and to stab them with his
asagay [spear].[18]

The flesh of the enemy slain in battle is considered the most efficacious of
all charms. Made into a medicine, it is smeared on plants to foster growth.
The blacksmith who fails to use this medicine obtains not iron but slag.
The hunter inoculates himself with a powder obtained from tendons and
bones, smeared into incisions on his wrists and elbows.[19]

SUDAN: NUER (1980S)

That was in southern Africa. In Sudan, in the north of Africa, Sharon
Hutchinson describes the confusion she found in 1980–1983, and again
in 1990, concerning changes in vengeance magic among the Nuer as the
introduction of firearms and civil war distorted the traditional idea of spiritual pollution generated by killing a man with a spear.

In killing with a spear, what Hutchinson calls a mysterious blood bond
is forged when, at the moment of death, "some of the blood of the victim
passed at death into the body of the slayer, being driven forth, as it were, by
a mission of vengeance."[20] If the killer were to eat or drink before being ritually cleansed by a Leopard Skin Chief, he would die of a "highly dangerous
and contagious pollution" affecting both his kin and the kin of the victim.

How much of this mysterious blood bond exists when death is caused
by bullets is unclear. My understanding of Hutchinson's text is that guns
diminish the likelihood of contagious pollution, though this diminution
could be due to other factors, like the creation of state and quasi-state entities in this newly oil-rich nation, the state's appropriation of community
forms of justice, the spread of Christianity, and unending and terrible war,
with the Muslim state to the north as well as neighbors such as the Dinka.

MANA (TIMELESS)

Let us also consider another breach in everyday life, that of shock. Toward the end of his book on magic (1902), originally compiled with Henri

Hubert, Marcel Mauss wrote about the impact of shock on society as a whole, regarding it as a suspended but galvanizing force propitious to the eruption of magical force. Walter Benjamin held to a similar idea about the convulsive stasis accompanying the state of emergency in his last writing, "Theses on the Philosophy of History," where he posited a rhythm in history and social life in which flow is suspended by moments of stillness as necessary prelude to spiritual upheaval. Unlike Benjamin, Mauss and Hubert were thinking of "premodern" societies and, as for the type of shock, their attention was drawn to sudden changes in weather, war, the economy, and even the passing of a meteor in the night sky—events that turn the abnormal into what they call *mana*, the effluvium through which magic becomes manifest.[21] The question for me today is, how much is this the case with police assassination in the USA, when such killing occurs with impunity and there is now a good chance that video of assassination will be recorded on a cell phone such that it, too, might become a meteor in the night sky?

NORTHEAST AUSTRALIA: MURNGIN (1927)

The contagious and visceral force created by one man killing another man is unforgettably described in the monograph *A Black Civilization* by the anthropologist W. Lloyd Warner, based on his 1927–1929 fieldwork with the people then named Murngin in remote northeast Australia.[22]

"Another belief centered around killing as a cause for war," writes Warner, "is that the spirit of the dead man enters the body of the killer and gives him double strength and actually increases his body size."

The description continues for almost four pages. You sense the indigenous storyteller and then the ethnographer crafting the tale, lingering on the sound made by the spear that killed the man clanking against stones as the dead man walks with the spear in his body. He is walking toward the killer so as to enter his body through his foot. The killer can hear the sounds coming from the dead man's wound.

When the killer sleeps, he dreams that the soul of the dead man tells him where there is game, like a kangaroo or a turtle. The killer goes there, calls out the name of the dead man, hurls his spear, and kills the animal.

He finds that, like the body of the killer, it too has enlarged. In fact, it has grown huge, too heavy to lift, and is extremely tasty on account of so much fat. No woman can eat this. Sometimes a bird or a bee circles the killer. That too is the dead man's spirit.

The account by the anthropologist is slow-paced and bewildering, as if the story is an initiation into a mystery, not revealed so much as prodded and tested from a variety of angles that seem to have neither beginning nor end.

The killing exudes contagion. It spreads out from the slayer and the slain to affect animals. The wound makes noises. It seems as if the soul of the slain man enters not only the killer's body, via his foot, but also what we might call the soul of the world. You could say that killing puts the world on edge and, along with that, Being is magnified. Could it be that homicide thus enlarges the sense of life, and does so to a degree at least equal to what are sometimes referred to by anthropologists as "increase ceremonies" and "fertility rites"? In any event, personal guilt does not seem to be the issue here so much as the perturbation of the order of things.

The anthropologist tells us that warfare was endemic at the time of his study and sufficiently frequent to ensure unequal male-female ratios, allowing for polygyny. "Warfare is one of the most important social activities of the Murngin," he avers. "Without it, Murngin society as it is now constituted could not exist."[23] The principal causes were fighting over women and revenge.

Studies like this, based on 1927 fieldwork, tend to be silenced by modern-day anthropologists of aboriginal Australia who censor violence through omission. But to neglect what Warner provides regarding the slayer-slain nexus, and hence the spiritual impact of murder—of which there is plenty, and worse, in contemporary Aboriginal society—seems woefully miguided.[24]

MACBETH (1606)

With respect to the "collateral damage" of homicide, hearken to the day after the slaying of king Duncan by Macbeth, when an old man says he has seen strange things in his long life "but this sore night hath trifled former knowledge." With fear and wonder he tells us that a proud falcon, serene in power and flight, was taken down by a mere mouse-hunting owl. The horses of the slain king have become wild and broken out of their stables. They have "turned wild in nature." They "would make war with mankind. 'Tis said they eat each other."

Toward the end of Joel Coen's recent film version of *Macbeth*, the screen itself enlarges and Macbeth seems to be getting bigger, like the Murngin killer. Macbeth cannot sleep. He has "murdered sleep." "Blood will have blood," he says. "Stones have been known to move and trees to speak."[25] Admittedly this is not any old murder but the murder of a king. But does not that very fact make it easier for us to see that homicide upsets the natural order?

AMAZON: ARAWETE (1980)

Eduardo Viveiros de Castro called his major ethnographic work, published in 1986, *From the Enemy's Point of View*. But he could just as well have called it *From the Killer's Point of View*.[26] We find in his book, concerning the Tupi-Guaraní people called Arawete, the same phenomenon I've described above but with more elaboration on the identification—the mimesis—between the slain and the slayer.

Arawete say they kill for vengeance or "for the simple desire to kill enemies." Someone who is already a killer has this desire "inside his flesh."[27]

Upon killing a man, it seems that the killer himself dies. He lays in his house as if unconscious. His stomach is filled with the blood of the slain, and he vomits continuously. He does not eat. He is in a state of death. He mimics death. He becomes death. He hears bumblebees and the wings of vultures flapping. He is rotting. His bones soften. He drinks the tea used by women for menstruation and childbirth. He must have shamanic cleansing.

His weapons must be taken from him because the slain man's spirit is now within him exhorting him to revenge, to kill his own people. The spirit of the dead man cannot kill his killer as that would be to kill himself. The killer cannot have sex with his wife. The spirit of the slain is within him, and it is the slain man who would be having sex with her.

The spirit of the slain goes searching for songs, which he imparts to the killer through the latter's dreams. They become friends; the dead man exhorts him to dance, to "rise up," and this "rising" is also a metaphor for a renewed life-force that the killed person provides, for he is "behind" the killer as a mimetic double in his dancing and singing and much else that involves not just the killer but the killer's community.

The killer has in effect become the person he killed, "for the spirit of the enemy shall never leave him." Killers are therefore and thereafter "considered temperamental people prone to come to blows when irritated."[28]

You can see now the relevance of the mirror-image epigraph to Viveiros de Castro's book, taken from Heraclitus:

Mortal immortals, immortal mortals
living each other's death,
dying each other's life

We might ask what it means to cite a text such as this, more than twenty-five hundred years old? Of course, its venerable age and alluring pre-Socratic vibe make it a fine epigraph. But what of the anachronism, smuggling pre-Socratic Greece into mid-twentieth-century Amazonian Indian life and then into ours? What of my serving up these distinct realities, thus conjoined, in the text you are reading now, a text inquiring into killing in Colombia and killing by police in the USA?[29]

Crazy? Maybe? But don't we do this sort of thing all the time? Don't we make comparisons as an elemental activity of mind, to understand things better or just for fun? This is why we read anthropology. This is why we read history. This is why we read! The friction of same-but-different twitches thinking. Hence Heraclitus's phrase "living each other's death" not only adorns but strikes a chord with a book-length study of a group of Amazonian Indian men with a penchant for killing. This is made all the more auratic by the epigraph's being Greek, ancient Greek, symbolically foundational of Western culture.

The lines cross. Ancient Greece, contemporary Amazonia, and a motley crew of contemporary intellectual and social science types like me, many interested in the works of Gilles Deleuze and in Viveiros de Castro's indigenous teachers with their upside-down accounts of evolution spinning us in circles of enlightened confusion concerning animals who were once human and actually, really, still are. (Recall here the Naskapi.) Obviously, this is not to evoke linear history. Rather it is to question time and to question narrative, releasing the energy of montage, juxtaposing dissimilars in that pause where flow stops and the Messiah is at the threshold of your hybrid Self, teaching you new dance steps.

ANCIENT GREECE

What about ancient Greek views of corpse magic? To use Heraclitus as the heraldic leitmotif in an account of Amazonian views on killing raises questions about the way we unthinkingly think, assuming a phantasmatic liaison between what are taken to be the roots of Western culture and the exotic examples I offer concerning killing.

With this one stroke, with Heraclitus providing for Amazonian murder, the exotic starts to include us Westerners too, or at least our titular forefathers.

For it seems that in ancient Greece something similar to the effects of homicide in Arawete-land occurred. Madness along with terror and fear took hold of a killer. Plague, sterility, and famine could waste entire cities, such was the anger and power of the violently slain.[30]

This could be the work of the dead themselves or before the ninth century BC of the Furies acting on their behalf. The Furies were female underworld deities, one of whom in particular was charged with vengeance. And Greek ideas seem heavily influenced by earlier Mesopotamian beliefs concerning magic and the dead. The aggrieved slain in Mesopotamia could make their victim sleepless, nauseated, crazed, short of breath, anorexic, afflict them with cold sweats, hot flashes, frenzy, or pain in any part of the body and bring on miscarriages or neonatal illness.[31]

Hesiod, who lived around the same time as Homer, has it that the Furies descended from drops of blood that fell in the ocean when Cronus castrated his father, Uranus, god of the sky. The story seems awfully appropriate to the mystery of corpse magic in which the slain slays the slayer.

As for the psychic, or should we say spiritual, bond between the slain and the slayer, Sarah Johnston cites Plato, who says in *The Laws* that the slain person's soul lingers in the earth and "joins forces with the very memory of the murderer to bring all possible distraction upon him and all his works."[32] She cites as well Xenophon, who has Cyrus saying:

> Have you never yet noticed what terror the souls of those who have been foully dealt with strike into the hearts of those who have shed their blood, and what avenging powers they send upon the track of the wicked?"[33]

Observe that guilt is not mentioned. It seems it is irrelevant. Foremost is the fear on the part of the slayer that the slain Other will torment and probably kill him or her.

From the age of Homer to the classical age (roughly 1000 to 300 BC), "curse tablets" were placed, for vengeance or other purposes, on Greek graves. The specific identity of the dead, Johnston says, was of little concern to the practitioner placing a curse tablet; by the fourth century BC you could invoke the dead "for almost any reason, and particularly to harm others."[34]

The polluting force of the murdered corpse in ancient Greece could be brought about by the dead themselves or else "set into motion as soon as the crime of blood occurs."[35] The language here echoes the Nuer-Effect in Sudan, as described earlier, in which the spirit of the slain automatically enters into the body of the killer.[36]

Suddenly, a profanation that seemed to me so extraordinary that words failed—namely, breaking into a cemetery in western Colombia to thwart the magical use of the body of the slain to slay the slayer—seems normalized, or at least made less strange, by this material from ancient Greece.

But that in itself is strange. Why should two strangenesses cancel each other out? And why should the accounts from Africa, Australia, and the Amazon not have done so, as far as I was concerned? Am I a prisoner of colonial prejudice, extolling the exotic character of the "primitive" while slotting ancient Greek societies into another category altogether, that of the Venerable Classics? On the other hand, does not their venerability close the classics and their spirits off from us and make their weirdness banal, amounting to a second burial, so to speak?

Plato and cemeteries in western Colombia surfaced recently for me when a judge sentenced Alex Murdaugh, a legal eagle from a highly respected South Carolina family, for the murder of his wife and son in 2021. I quote from the *Washington Post*:

> Murdaugh, dressed in a brown inmate jumpsuit, gave a blank look as he exited the courtroom at around 10:05 a.m. Before he was sentenced, he maintained his innocence.
>
> "I'm innocent," said Murdaugh. He then addressed his wife and son, whom he referred to as "Paw Paw." "I would never hurt my wife, Maggie, and I would never hurt my son, Paw Paw."
>
> During the sentencing, the judge said that Murdaugh would have to deal with the conviction and consequences of the murders "in your own soul."
>
> "I know you have to see Paul and Maggie in the nighttime as you attempt to go to sleep," said the judge. "I'm sure they come and visit you."
>
> When the judge asked Murdaugh if he has a hard time sleeping, Murdaugh replied, "All day and every night."
>
> "And they will continue to do so and will reflect on the last time they looked you in the eyes," replied the judge.[37]

So, maybe Nuer-Effects are present, or potentially so, even in the USA, even in a courtroom, heartland of Rule of Law, not Lore. The judge's language is unforced, homey, yet dramatic, befitting such an effect—except for one important consideration. His discourse comes from a shocked moral position, whereas accounts of the cemetery break-ins suggest, rather, the logic and realpolitik of remorseless war, meaning gang warfare.

As for Plato and his ancient Greece, I'm not sure if he is coming from a moral standpoint or if the Nuer-Effect he describes is a quasi-physiological impact flowing from the slaying itself. Most likely the latter. And post-Plato, consider Cain killing Abel, at which point the Lord exclaims, "Hark! Your brother's blood that has been shed is crying out to me from the ground which has opened its mouth wide to receive your brother's blood, which you have shed. . . . You shall be a vagrant and wanderer on earth."

Until I had to reckon with the Nuer-Effect, I thought of these words, and biblical language generally, Old or New Testament, as essentially metaphoric. But now I don't, or if I do, it's with the understanding that metaphor is physiologically active and, on further consideration, raises the question as to whether there is any language or utterance that is not metaphoric?

The Break-In

4 The Break-In

It's like a ladder, says Walter Benjamin at one point in his essay on the storyteller dealing with the crucial role of death, the story as much as its teller descending into the earth and ascending into the heavens, back and forth. That is one way of thinking about *narcorelatos*, this up-and-down movement, from the heavens down to corporeal interiors and up again.

This ladder came to mind when I came to town a week after a gang, so I was told, had scaled the newly built wall surrounding the cemetery to destroy a corpse during the revels on New Year's Eve 2014. I tried to picture the scene. Fireworks roaring in the sky. Mannequins of old men representing the Old Year, with baggy trousers and stomachs full of gunpowder ready to explode. Police in riot gear firing tear gas into the more turbulent parts of town. And amid all this mayhem, a fresh corpse stolen by a gang, then chopped up and set afire to prevent its corpse magic.

The gangs formed in the late 1980s when drug trafficking and much else took off in Colombia, including sweeping lifestyle changes and rapid growth in paramilitary, army, and guerrilla violence. In that decade about six thousand members of the Unidad Popular political party, connected to the FARC guerrilla, were assassinated, one by one, directly or indirectly, by the army claiming it was killing members of the guerrilla.[1]

My sense was that by the 1980s a sizable fraction of young people in the sugar plantation zone were loath to accept traditional values of work and authority. No longer would they dig ditches, cut sugarcane, or work as domestic servants like their parents. The town and surrounding region were no longer peasant. Young people had become lumpen prole/lumpen peasant as the plantation regime redesigned the region's infrastructure and the meaning of landscape and life.[2]

By 2021 confidential police reports showed the town's murder rate was close to 80 per 100,000 people and I was informed that most of this consisted of inter-gang killings, meaning adolescent boys killing each other. Other sources put the hiomicide rate even higher at 116/1000,00 for the same time period. To put that in perspective, the national murder rate for Colombia as a whole around this time was 25/100,000 according to the World Bank. Compare also the alarm in the USA, where the national murder rate has "surged," as the phrase has it, from 6.0/100,000 to 7.8, while in Washington, DC, it is, at the time of this writing, 23; in Detroit, 41; and in Baltimore, 58.

In western Colombia, the commercial sectors of the town and the local landowners were also organized in "gangs," though of course they were not labeled as such. It is these that call the shots, whether it be stealing cattle, stealing cars, coercing the remaining peasants to sell their farms, corrupting local government, infiltrating gangs of the young to use them as paramilitaries or, contrawise, paying gangs of killers to come and *limpiar* ("cleanse") the town, sometimes using photo IDs supplied by the army and police.[3]

The *limpieza social* is a major homicidal force in Colombia, a kind of "popular justice" in the absence or weakness of state protection, covertly supported by the army and the police, alongside the indifference or active involvement of the general population. That, combined with killing of gang members by each other, probably accounts for more deaths than the guerrilla, army, and paramilitaries *combined*, yet is of little or no concern to the populace or media. In fact, it tends to be celebrated, and the youngsters themselves contribute mightily to the death toll by way of their internecine warfare. Overall, this amounts to an ongoing slaughter of poor Colombian adolescent boys and young men by each other as much as by paramilitaries and police.

The first gang that I knew of in the sugarcane town on which I focus was created around 1992 and called Las Mechas on account of the long hair of its male members. It was led by the mysterious Nemecio and is remembered as an impassioned cult. By 1997 I was hearing of forty-seven gangs, including an all-female gang called Las Pirañas, although some people said there were only ten, the discrepancy giving you an idea of the confusion and blasting volume of hearsay. When Nemecio was killed, apparently by a nephew, I was told his followers went crazy, stampeding through the

town. In the hospital's emergency room, they screamed at the nurses and doctors, "If you don't resuscitate him, you're dead. We will kill you too." His corpse was carried around town in an open coffin visiting the homes and hangouts of gang members. A story later circulated that his bones had been secretly unearthed from the cemetery and taken to the outskirts of town, to the neighborhood called the Invasion, a highly mythologized zone of nastiness and poverty. There, I was told, the bones were *arreglados*, "arranged," subject perhaps to much the same treatment as I suppose the church gives the bodies or body parts of its saints. I knew nothing at that time about corpse magic and may have gotten the story wrong, that in fact his remains were worked on so as to kill his killer.[4]

I see in my notes that an old friend of mine, who had gone to Nemecio's home in search of a revolver, told me his house was full of "porcelain"— ceramic panthers, tigers, and the like. This bizarre detail intrigued my friend, no less than it intrigued the taxi driver overhearing our conversation, who wanted porcelain panthers too.

A friend of mine grew up in a street on the edge of the Invasion and against all odds became a psychologist working with government agencies in the town involved with gangsters. He had an intimate knowledge of the kids there. In 2022 he described to me seven recent gangs: Los 23, with more than two hundred members; Los Dandys, with forty to fifty, whose age starts at ten; the gang headed by "Fosforito," with forty; Los Galleros, with thirty; Los Escaperos (named for a street called "El Escape"), with twenty; the gang headed by "Miquito" (the Little Monkey), who supposedly is embittered by the fact that he is ugly as sin; and the gang of eight called Los Ocho Grandes, headed by Danielito in the barrio of Los Altos de París (part of La Invasión), whose main aim, my friend says, was killing gangsters, as they, Los Ochos Grandes, opposed stealing and killing!

The gang economy is one of stealing any and everything, selling drugs in small quantities, and working for the police, the army, paramilitaries, and the guerrilla. Many gang leaders have been killed by other gangsters and many are in jail.

"Tienen mucha mística," my friend emphasized and maybe overemphasized. They are deeply into magic, he said, wearing amulets and Christian crosses, while some walk in the street shirtless, bodies covered in oil that makes them bulletproof. I myself have never seen that. "The only way of killing them is through asphyxiation," he added, a detail that would mesh with the notion that bulletproof men can only be killed by machete or that the magic of "arranged corpses," corpses prepared to kill their killer, can only be destroyed by fire or machete, not by guns.

GANGSTER BURIAL

Before I tell you about the break-in, I have to tell you how some of the gangsters had ritualized burial in the cemetery, as I got to see it once in the late 1990s, before the priest and police put a stop to it.

Not the dead man's family but his fellow gang members carried the coffin into the cemetery, the occasion charged with excitement, high fashion, a boom box, and the firing of guns. It was a military funeral with full honors.

Outside the cemetery, an uneasy crowd gathered as if mesmerized, but ready to flee at the slightest sign of danger, like a school of fish darting hither and thither. What was the danger? I was not told. Fear of an attack by a rival gang? Possibly. But that's probably too rational an explanation.

Strangest of all, gang members stood shoulder to shoulder atop the cemetery wall, which was then only six feet high. Some people tell me they

ENTIERO DE UN MALANDRO

stood there to deny other gangs access. But is it not also an inspired and inspiring ritual, defying the gods and invoking new ones?

"It is defined by excess," wrote Carlos Mario Perea in 2007, describing gangster funerals in the three Colombian cities where he did fieldwork (Bogotá, Barranquilla, and Neiva). The funeral is the only ritual gangsters have, he says, because death squads and police force them to otherwise lie low, quit their tattoos and ostentatious behavior. Much is made of the coffin, which is passed around between gang members and may have graffiti inscribed on it. Liquor and cocaine are consumed, music (as of mariachi bands) fills the air, and the church, as Perea puts it, disappears, as does the barrier between life and death. Mastery of the funeral rite confirms these gangs' mastery of violence and terror, and over death.[5]

But not for long. In 2008 I was stopped by two fearful women friends from entering the cemetery during another gangster funeral. To my immense surprise, police, not gangsters, stood shoulder to shoulder on the wall! Were they there to prevent the gangsters' standing there, as the gangsters may have blocked out rival gangs? Were the police themselves eager to slip into a new role as guardians of the dead, policing spirit trafficking, assuming the choreographic maneuver invented by the gangsters? A new vibe was evident. Was it accompanied, I started to wonder, by a new sacred geography?

All of which helps explain why the priest, an energetic, acerbic, middle-aged, white man in this majority Black town, built his thirty-foot-high concrete wall around the cemetery to prevent gangsters from performing their rites. Not only was he from the town, but his extended family included several priests and, as I soon found out, at least one builder who had a contract to rebuild the cemetery on a stupendous scale.

The cemetery takes up a complete block. That's a lot of wall, and bear in mind that most of the town's buildings at the time were half the height of the new wall. Can you imagine walking on the streets alongside the wall, dwarfed by its immensity like the woman in my photograph? It's war! A new kind of war, fought not with guns but with spirits, good ones like the priest's versus the not-so-good ones of the dead gangsters.

You can think of this cemetery wall as the Egyptian pyramid of the Colombian southwest. Not even cocaine mafia bosses such as Pablo Escobar with his escaped hippopotami now wallowing in the swamps of the Río Magdalena built anything approaching this.

But . . . but because corpse magic is performed on the corpse *before* it gets to the cemetery, the wall *cannot stop corpse magic!* What the wall does—or was intended to do—is prevent flamboyant gangster burials and access to the bodies of corpses aimed at killing the killer. But the wall, if anything,

only makes the "arranging" of the corpse in the privacy of one's home more secure. In any case, it would take more than a wall to stop gangsters intent on disinterring a corpse. They seem highly motivated despite their access to apotropaic magic.

THE BREAK-IN

Indeed, on New Year's Eve 2014, some gangsters scaled that mighty wall, dug out the coffin of a rival gang member buried the day before, and then destroyed it.

I arrived a week later. Some people said the coffin had been doused in gasoline and set afire. Others told me it had not been burned but that attackers had fired shots into it. Others said they had hacked the corpse to pieces with machetes. I felt the malice. I felt the desperation. Think of pumping bullets into a coffin holding a fresh corpse. Try and picture the bizarre funeral pyre casting light and shadows over adjacent graves as New Year's revels proceed outside the walled cemetery with life-size gunpowder-filled mannequins representing the Old Year ready to explode at midnight.[6]

It was said that the gangsters destroyed the cadaver to prevent its corpse magic. They feared it had been "arranged" to kill the killer. but most people I spoke with were startled and reticent, as if in discussing this we were trespassing into realms mere mention of which was dangerous, realms which Bataille, following Émile Durkheim, would call "negative sacred." In more ordinary diction, we had entered the realm of profanation—the dark side of the sacred, *not its absence*, for desecration is but another form of the sacred.

One thing that stood out to me was how contagious this force of the transgressed taboo can be. Even to talk about it is to utter words charged with cosmic threat and disarray. People with whom I spoke seemed uneasy, as if caught on the wrong foot. I once read in a short text by Umberto Eco that ugliness, unlike beauty, arouses visceral effects. The facts claimed us. Yes, it was ugly!

Sympathetic magic—if that's the term—is also, and remarkably, present in the way the killer dies when dying from corpse magic. An old friend from the Pacific coast told me that once the vengeance magic takes hold, the killer cannot sleep and dies from insomnia. She could have been quoting Plato who said more than two thousand years ago that the soul of the slain enters into the memory of the assassin, causing all manner of distress. Recall Macbeth: "Methought I heard a voice cry 'Sleep no more! Macbeth does murder sleep.'"[7]

Quite a few people told me that the killer, thus subject to corpse magic, dies of madness. He cries out in his sleep, he wastes away. Still others said that in his insomniac delirium, the killer continually sees the victim's face. That certainly gets me wondering how US police sleep, given the number of folk they kill.

MULTIPLE REALITIES

I asked more people about the break-in. A middle-aged white immigrant to this nearly all-Black town, owner of a store and a successful novelist, suggested that corpse magic was "African" and wondered about "voodoo." This thesis found support in an article in Colombia's leading newspaper, *El Tiempo*, written by Carolina Bohórquez seven weeks after the break-in. She quoted experts from the nearby University Valle in Cali. "It is African," she was told, a "syncretism" of Catholicism combined with "African Ancestors."[8]

That's the first I'd heard of African magic or African religion being practiced in these parts, but then blackness excites those sorts of ideas among non-Black people, especially in the media. Just as Santería and Palo exist in Cuba and Vodun in Haiti, "logic" implies that young black gangsters in western Colombia would be motivated by "African" ideas, would break into the cemetery and extract cadavers. But the history and everyday lives of slaves in Colombia was distinctive, as are the popular religions and magics today. I myself have yet to come across "syncretism" or Vodun or Santeria.

The journalist was told of other criminal exhumations of cadavers elsewhere in the country: some six years before in Tulua, sixty miles to the north; in 2014, in the port of Buenaventura; that same year, in the Cementerio Central of Cali, where the archdiocese claimed the exhumed body was burned. In 2012, also in Cali, the remains of two siblings buried twelve years earlier had been stolen. And so it goes.

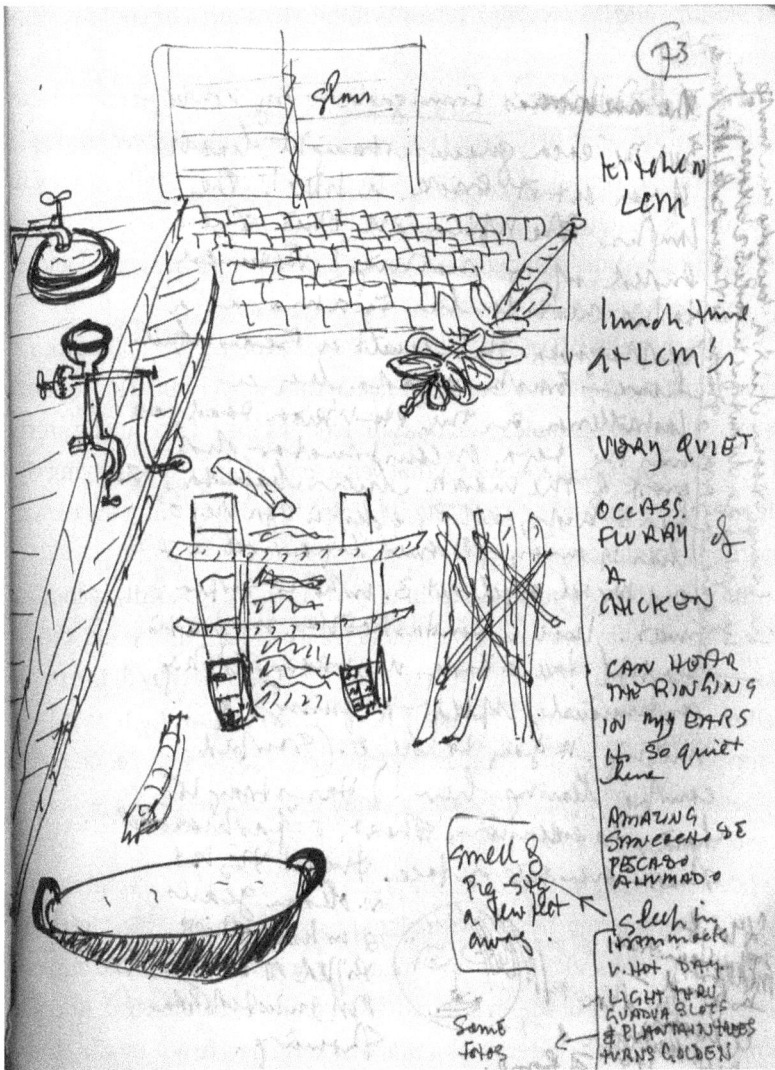

A seamstress friend winced when I asked about the break-in. *Bastante delicado*, she said. She didn't want to talk. Which was strange. She had never been like that. A schoolteacher friend had never heard of such an occurrence and wondered if it originated outside the country. But on reflection he had heard of bones found in the cemetery being used for sorcery, especially the phalanges of the hands and feet. Thinking further, he recalled hearing of a photograph of the killer placed in the coffin so that the victim could take revenge. It was as if, once he started he couldn't stop, even though at first he was mystified.

I had often heard about the cemetery as a source of small bones used for sorcery. This was held to be shocking and transgressive, yet strangely nobody really seemed to care much. There was a certain chill when you entered the cemetery, a sense of foreboding, which you quickly brushed off, and I sometimes wondered if people there were up to no good, looking for bones.

Out in the ruins of peasant farms on the edges of the sugar plantations, friends told me they'd heard of the attack in the cemetery. But they weren't keen to linger on the topic, which was unusual, as they are normally pretty chatty. They did tell me, however, that vengeance magic required tying the big toes of the corpse together. They had also heard of stuffing the ears or the mouth of the corpse with a paper bearing the killer's name.

But while they seemed confident imparting this supposedly recondite information, they seemed unsure as to whether such things existed. It was strange. It was like they were reading from a script they didn't really believe. It gave the phrase "make believe" new meaning. I felt as if they were detached from their bodies or that I was watching someone speak underwater. Then again, they seemed somewhat indifferent.

So, what sort of knowledge is this?

I decided to talk with Teófila. She is about my age, had a cerebral thrombosis three years ago, treated with plant medicines, made a good recovery, has numerous grandchildren and great-grandchildren flowing in and out of her house, some of whom sleep with her in her capacious bed. And she is much sought out, she says, as a *vidente,* a term new to me, by which she means she is clairvoyant. She counts a bishop and several priests among her clients, as well as killers. There is a lot more to tell, about her charm, lucidity, and intelligence, as well as the fact that she comes from the headwaters of the Timbiquí River on the Pacific coast (a river I visit once a year, COVID aside) and has lived here in the sugarcane town for fifty years. (See my drawing of the village on page 18.)

I was stunned to learn that the corpse defiled in the cemetery was that of a nephew of hers (although she could not recall his name), that the gang that broke into the cemetery and destroyed his corpse went a week later to the nearby village of Guachené and unearthed another corpse, beating it to a pulp, she said. There in her nightgown on the edge of her bed with its rumpled sheets, she provided a vivid reenactment.

Guachené, as I recall it in the 1970s, was a rich hub of peasants cultivating cacao, plantains, coffee, yucca, mango, papaya, oranges, mandarins, and lemons. Now, however, the town is a depressing, mildewed rural slum.

There I spoke through an iron-barred window with a maid in the nuns' home, who, goggle-eyed, confirmed with much brio the story of the cemetery break-in. She was around fifty years old and it seemed it was the most thrilling thing that had ever happened in that town, at least to her. But in fact, this small place had seen a surfeit of violence the past decade.

Together with the anthropologist Alhena Caicedo, who had done fieldwork in Guachené, I visited the cemetery with a local schoolteacher who has lived there all his life. The cemetery was at the end of town with a low fence on the side of the main road and consisted largely of graves dug in the soil, not rows of concrete ossuaries. The teacher explained that what was left of the corpse was found by a bus driver passing at sunrise. It had been unearthed and destroyed, the teacher told us, because it was thought to be "arranged" with vengeance magic.

Gang warfare and revenge killings abound in this village, he said, noting that the mayor himself had facilitated several *limpiezas* of gang members, meaning the hiring of paramilitary types to kill them. And here I was, trying to square that with my memories of a sleepy little place of peasant farms, abundant cacao, and not a sugarcane in sight when I first visited in the 1971, arriving on the roof of a rural jitney. A year ago, the mayor was assassinated.

Looking back, you could say sugarcane was the first drug to come this way, opening the floodgates to other sorts of drugs on their way to the USA, especially the marijuana grown nearby for the past five years by indigenous people on the steep slopes of the mountainside of the Cordillera Central, now in good part carried down the Amazon to Brazil.

At night from afar you see the mountain with lights twinkling like diamonds on black velvet. In truth, these are electric light bulbs suspended above marijuana plants so that the plants will grow even at night, such is the economic imperative that has indigenous peasants monocrop an entire mountainside, just like the sugarcane plantations using machines and wage labor carpet the entire valley floor below.

However, some indigenous groups are bitterly opposed, as you can see in a large mural on the school wall in the mountain town of Toribio depicting a man up high manipulating indigenous people as puppets below.

On the town hall is painted:

If we stay silent, they kill us
If we talk, the same.
So we talk.

At night on the valley floor in a car from the airport, the driver, a friend of twenty years, excitedly pointed out those far-off twinkling lights as we ourselves were flanked by fires in the sugarcane fields set to burn the undergrowth prior to harvesting the next day.

On both sides of us, the burning cane fields turned the night purple while the light bulbs on the far-off mountainside made it look like an illuminated tapestry as the marijuana grew another inch into the night sky.

Floodlit by sheet lightning, clouds scudded across the turbulent sky. My friend the driver spoke of rumors of Afro-Colombian gangs in the flatlands, such as the gang "Cinco y Seis" in Guachené, readying, at the behest of the sugar plantations, their next assault on the indigenous group coming down the mountains known as *The Liberators of Mother Earth*.

Such a name!

For decades they have had a motto: "We are not the owners of the land. The land owns us." And they yank out the sugarcane to grow food. The young indigenous man showing me these crops lost his eye in one confrontation. His brother was captured by a gang from Guachené, taken to a schoolhouse, tortured and killed, his mother tells me. The army has built a base close by, while fervent appeals ring forth in the media on behalf of the plantations concerning the sacred right of private property.

5 *Fetishistic Fastidiousness*

As the twilight crowd milled around the plaza of the sugarcane town where the cemetery break-in occurred, the husband of an old friend I have known since 1970, when she was ten years old, told me that he has seen a victim of corpse vengeance magic wither unto death.

Later I wrote that into my notebook, but only now, five years later, do I stop and wonder and wish I could talk to him once more. That's how field-work is, at least mine there and then. Looking back, you think you were not curious enough. You were not inquisitive enough. What's the backstory? But your mind froze. There is no more to say. Stop being so nosy. In fact, there is now a chilling term in Colombia that covers this, *extractavismo académico*, or "academic extraction," likening anthropology to corporate gold or coal mining. Anthroplogists beware! Institutional Review Boards beware! The times they are a-changing.

What also happens is that you hear the most amazing things but uttered in such a matter-of-fact way that you pay little attention. You disenchant them because they didn't come at you in glitzy lights.

"When the killer got to hear there was a black thread tied around the big toes of the corpse," the singer's brother told me, "he decided to stage the cemetery break-in."

Why did people keep mentioning this bizarre detail, tying the big toes together with black cords? What on earth could that be for? Was it the meaningless detail that in its fetishistic fastidiousness flagged the more significant magical onslaught for which the corpse had been recruited? Was it a response to some arcane symbolism of the body focused on the toes in relation to some hallowed kabbalistic scheme?

In the tiny gold-mining village of Santa María at the headwaters of the Timbiqui, a Pacific coast river that I first visited in 1972, the young man taking me upriver by canoe over roaring rapids says in response to my question that nobody there knows how to perform corpse magic anymore. But when I arrive, my host, who at first says that's correct, goes on to tell me what's involved in such abundant detail that I have to wonder if corpse magic has really ceased.

My host has heard that corpse vengeance magic can involve the following: placing a mirror under the feet of the corpse with the reflecting surface against the soles; leaving the corpse clothed in what the person was wearing when killed, with the formal burial clothes placed on top of that; writing the name of the killer on *papel pergamino* (fancy paper used for wedding or birthday invitations), which is then placed in the mouth of the corpse; or someone in the bereaved family praying and talking with the spirit of the dead person. But she has never heard of tying the toes together.

The adult son of the woman who lives in the house opposite where I stay was murdered in Buenaventura in 2001. It is rumored that she then employed corpse vengeance magic, but it did not work. She would never talk of this for fear that the killer's family would kill her, so I am told.

As for the murdered son's four brothers, three of them killed each other, one by one, after his mother's failed attempt at corpse magic, and the fourth was executed by the FARC guerrilla, following a vote by the villagers at the command, or was it merely "a request" by the FARC? There are no resident police. Occasionally an army helicopter flies overhead.

The young mother of one of the dead brother's five children tells me without a moment's hesitation that Yes! corpse magic exists, and it involves a mirror and tying the big toes together.

End of story.

Back in the sugarcane agribusiness town, Regina Carabalí gave me a blow-by-blow account of the latest cemetery break-in. With their large leaves shredded by the attack, the plantain trees in her backyard looked like broken windmills. She did not talk, she whispered, which, for such a large, strong-voiced woman, was disturbing. She can't sleep out of fear of the gangs. This is the second time the cemetery has been broken into, she says, and a cadaver attacked to prevent vengeance magic. The previous time was eight years ago.

Regina is what I would call a cemetery junkie. By now she must think I am too. She knows a great deal about the cemetery and the mortuary practices of the church. Her sister is the principal singer in the church, and Regina sings beautifully too. I saw her sister late one afternoon in August 2016 by the side of the priest in the cemetery at the mass that is supposed to take place on Mondays for the spirits of the dead—as if with these visits he is infusing the church with the power of the dead. As Regina's sister's song floated over the gravestones, it seemed he was trying to reclaim sacred space from the gangs as well. I take this attempt to refashion the house of the dead to be also a refashioning of the Catholic church in the face of strong competition from evangelical churches and the stigma of sexual abuse by priests (not that the evangelical ministers are any better).

SO, WHAT DOESN'T THE PRIEST KNOW?

Not only did the priest build the wall in an attempt to stop gangsters' making their own funerals, he also disinterred the corpses laid to rest in the earth of the cemetery to move them to the new concrete ossuaries. By the time I met him, there were few graves in the ground. Bereft of its dead, the soil looked parched and forlorn. Meanwhile, at a furious pace, row upon row of ossuaries and *bóvedas* were being built. The ossuaries are for bones retrieved from graves after four years. The *bóvedas*, much larger, house entire bodies in coffins.

What before had been a somewhat minor element in the cemetery was now, after the new wall, its predominant feature. Like filing cabinets they were, these *bóvedas* and ossuaries, concrete walls stretching one to two hundred feet. Once bones or a coffin are inserted, the cemetery staff cements the space closed and the bereaved affix the name, maybe a message, and frequently a photograph of the deceased.

Cynics saw in this feverish construction a crass attempt by the church to make money and make death more of a fancy consumer item. Others pointed out that the cemetery space, although large, is limited, and it makes sense to go vertical, like high-rise buildings in a city taking the place of one- and two-story houses.

Be that as it may, I think what's also happening in the cemetery is a tidying up of death, amounting to a regimentation of the corpse population. Amid violence and rampant neoliberalism, here at least, in one of the most homicidal towns in the nation, a stand is being taken on the side of order if not of the living, then of the dead.

What's more, tidying up cadavers resonates with the pattern of agribusiness monocropping: regular rows of sugarcane stretching from here to eternity replacing the higgledy-piggledy of peasant farms with their entangled trees of different sizes, shapes, and colors stretching into the sky.

The new order could also exemplify the Church's determination to be the sole recipient of the power of the dead through a system of "sacred plumbing" whereby the negative sacred of the corpse nourishes the positive sacred of the Church. In this conception, put forward by Georges

Bataille, the church-corpse confluence is a sacred-making mechanism and not merely a transformer of matter into spirit.

On this reckoning the Church is the principal receptor of what we could call corpse magic—not the specific vengeance magic prepared by the family working on a slain corpse but "corpse magic" in the more generic sense as an instance of the magical potentials of death that empower the Church.

When you step back and think about it, the current rationalization of the cemetery is a revolutionary advance. If death and the dead are a privileged source of magic, and the cemetery a source of sorcery, then "cleansing" and rationalizing it is an act aimed, to my mind, not at the elimination of corpse magic but at its more efficient management as a religious resource.

There are now no headstones planted in the soil. Their place has been taken by rows of concrete boxes arrayed like the cargo on container ships. That revolution in shipping changed the shape of ships (not to mention the world economy and the rise of right-wing populism). Today, cargo vessels themselves resemble giant containers, big boxes pushing against the waves when not stuck in the Suez Canal or ramming the Baltimore bridge.

But today in the plantation town, thanks to the priest's innovations, burials are not really burials, not in the earth, anyway, but interments in concrete. The dead are filed like folders in a bureaucrat's office or prisoners in their cells, the cemetery itself a fortress, thanks to the new wall. Cemetery and cement turn out to be more than lexical connections.

In his office next to the church in the town's central plaza, the priest spoke to me from behind iron bars. It was unnerving, to say the least, this barred office of God so emphatically separated from the public.

Barely a century old, this town of ex-slaves is laid out on the standard Latin American colonial-derived grid plan: a central plaza with the church on one side and the mayor's office on the other. The cemetery is nine blocks away, not next to the church as was common in colonial times.

The priest built the wall around the cemetery, he told me, because gangs would attack each other during burials. As for vengeance corpse magic, he patiently explained that it involves black cords stretched from the right big toe to the left index finger (*dedo del Corazón*/finger of the heart) and the right big toe to left index finger, forming a black cross.

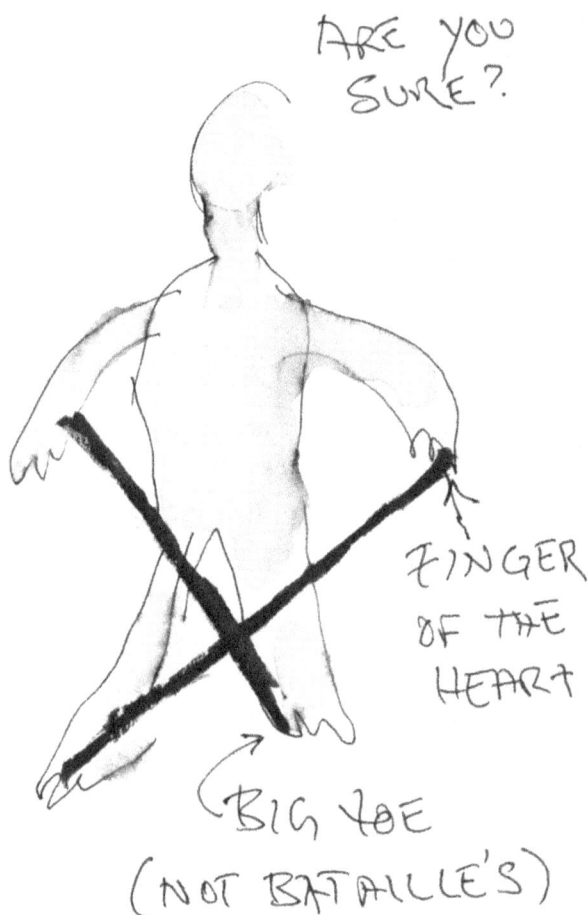

ARE YOU SURE?

FINGER OF THE HEART

BIG TOE (NOT BATAILLE'S)

Are you sure? Yes, he is sure. People come to him to bless the cords! And vengeance magic using the corpse has happened several times here, he assured me.

As our conversation proceeded, I was struck by how sensitive he was to spiritual politics in the indigenous zones in the adjoining mountains. Gone are the days of planting a church on top of a heathen temple and baptizing natives by the thousands (as the Protestant churches still do), wafting incense along with the magic of Latin prayers. Now the attitude seems to be if you can't beat them, join them. Gesturing to the Cordillera Central rising behind us (with its pervasive monocropping of marijuana), he says,

"The indigenous people in the mountains accuse the Church of having tried to destroy their culture by attacking their religion. Now they are forging ahead, reclaiming their own religion, and new doctrines emerge." He seemed enthusiastic, as if indigenous people had in fact reinvigorated the Catholic Church, making me wonder, Who is appropriating who?

What to make, then, of a discreet photograph I was furtively shown recently of a middle-aged indigenous woman in the mountains of the Cordillera Central who had been killed by her son-in-law. She was flat on her back, her hands tied together by the thumbs, the thick black cords forming an extravagant black bow that dominated the photo. The effect was foreboding and frightening. It was as if the bow occupied the entire picture.

My ever-observant friend Ariel Arango, who has spent time in those mountains, told me in an ever so casual way that yes, he has heard about corpse magic, albeit done another way. A seed of *chacruna negra* is implanted into the flesh of the assassinated person's thumb so as to kill the killer. He made it sound almost routine.

As for the valley floor, where we were standing, the priest implied that a religious revival was happening within Afro-Colombian culture too, albeit of less intensity than in the mountains. This was news to me and I wondered whether, with his stupendous wall and elaborate reconstruction inside the cemetery, he might inadvertently be stimulating vengeance magic. By reacting so vigorously against the magical use of the dead, was he not affirming its potency? As for his being asked to bless black cords for use in vengeance magic, was he pulling my leg? Or did he live in a world in which Black sorcerers and white priests rub shoulders with the dead?[1] He seemed more at home in the cemetery than behind the bars in his office, keeping track of the money owed for ossuaries and *bóvedas*. In the cemetery he was a man possessed, a twitching bundle of nervous energy out to change the spiritual landscape.

I spoke with a young man in black overalls whose job was to unearth the remaining graves, from which, after four years, the bones would be removed to a "common pit" unless someone paid for them to be put in an ossuary. A group of anxious-looking people watched him closely. He swung his pick into the black earth. Under the burning sun, he stood in the grave shoveling out gobs of earth, which the onlookers then took in their hands to examine, searching for bones of a family member, perhaps a mother or a son. It's hard to imagine anything remotely like this in the Global North.

I peek into a small, half-completed brick building that will be one of the priest's gems, mandated, he says, by the national government. It is what he calls the postmortem room and already contains the remains of a few unearthed corpses. There is a strangely discolored head, skin intact, mottled red and green with a horrible grimace. It looks alive. Are those eyes actually glowing in the darkness? How can that be after four years in the ground? Can the dead be rationalized, or is this grinning face a sign of the limits to reason, like Goya's *Caprichos*? Am I seeing things? Am I being seen by what I am seeing?

To be seen by what one sees in the Space of Death is the fear Ulysses felt in visiting that space, when "blanching terror gripped me—panicked now that Queen Persephone, queen of the dead, might send up from Death some monstrous head, some Gorgon's staring face!"[2]

CHRIST'S CORDS OF WHEAT AND GRAPES

Three years after talking with the priest, I came across a copy of an exquisite painting made in 1469 in the studio of the German artist Friedrich Herlin. It displays a bone-thin, fragile, almost naked, standing Christ. Stretching from the stigmata on the dorsum of his feet to the stigmata on the palms of his hands are two slightly bowed "cords." The one stretching from the left foot through the right hand is a vine laden with bunches of grapes, while that from the right foot through the left hand is a slender stem of wheat.

There is a wonderfully erotic tension in the way these "cords" compose and balance the image. Their taut, vibrant lines curve to frame Christ's torso, as if the energy of his death, with its promise of resurrection, is bound up in their bowlike form enclosing him as in a womb.

Carolyn Bynum, in whose essay on Christ's body I found this wonderful image, interprets the wheat and grapes as signs of sustenance that Christ, like a mother, provides the faithful.[3] But this is also spiritual bread and wine, meaning flesh and blood.

Anno·dm·M°·cccc·lxviii· starb der erbar Paul straus
am durstag zu mut vasten· der sele got genedig sey·

Armed now with the priest's description of the corpse magic cords transversing the corpse, a description that strikingly parallels this fifteenth-century German depiction of the crucified Christ, might we not want to add something more to the idea of Christ's beneficence, namely the provision of homicidal revenge?

THE DAZZLE OF THE ASSASSINATED'S SHADOW

Early on in chapter 1, I cited the 1961 essay on death rites in the Chocó by an anthropologist from there, Rogerio Velásquez, in which he cites the use of cords on corpses as routine. Velásquez tells us that when someone dies, a strong string is tied around their right leg. Sometimes the thumb and ring finger of the right hand are tied together, or the right arm is connected to the left leg. In the case of murder in which the murderer has fled, Velásquez was told that a twenty-cent coin is placed under the tongue of the corpse, which is placed face-down.[4] Or else one ties the large toes together to ensure that the assassin cannot move because thanks to the machinations of a sorcerer, the shadow of the person killed is now covered in a baffling dazzlement.[5]

BUENAVENTURA INTERLUDE

If the Chocó featured strongly as a source of corpse magic according to people in the sugarcane plantation town in the interior from where I report, so did the port of Buenaventura on the Pacific coast south of the Chocó. I recalled that in May 2001 in the sugarcane town, a storekeeper I knew slightly, aged twenty-eight, was shot dead through the liver in front of his children. His body was then shipped by his father to the port of far-off Buenaventura, where, it was rumored, his relatives performed corpse magic on it so that the killers would be unable to flee town and would be sitting ducks for the paramilitaries who, that very month, were systematically killing young gangsters as part of a *limpieza*, or "cleansing," paid for by some of the town's businesspeople in contact with an "office," as they called it, in Cali.

This attempted magical immobilization of the storekeeper's killers is precisely what Velásquez had described in 1961 in the far-off Chocó as forcing a killer, frozen by the victim's shadow "dressed in dazzlement," to "surrender to justice."

Buenaventura comes across in rumor and reputation as the concentrated essence of malignity combined with real magical realism. It is the largest port in Colombia, rife with drug trafficking, extortion, paramilitaries, and criminal gangs. And it is also the hub for Black communities north and south along the Pacific coast. Along with cocaine, money floods the port, while the violence of the state-assisted paramilitaries in the time of the Uribe government has given way to other kinds of paramilitary gangs. Buenaventura has been in the news for over a decade now for its "houses of pique" or "chop houses" on the mudflats by the sea where rival gang members enact vengeance: bodies are tortured and quartered, and the body parts dropped over the side in plastic bags to drift off at high tide past the mangroves. Picture that! Black bags like buoys bumping into ships, then sinking into the depths.

So it is said and said often. Although how it is said is another matter. In 2019 my twenty-year-old friend from one of the coastal rivers, strong and smart, now working in construction in Buenaventura, would speak of it only in a whisper and cautioned me to silence even when we were walking outside with no one else in sight.[6] At one time, the authorities claimed to have dismantled fourteen such houses.

Is the chopping in the chop houses the same as what happened to the corpse whose mutilation in the sugar-town cemetery I have discussed at some length, but magnified? *In other words, were the corpses chopped up to eliminate their vengeance magic?*

* * *

I hadn't been in Buenaventura since the 1980s. When I returned in late 2019, the weather was not the humid pestilence I remembered, and a *malecón* with elegant cafes and bars stretching along a half mile of waterfront had come into existence, as had some small office towers.

On my taxi trip to the main cemetery, accompanied by a longtime Black friend of mine who lives on a coastal river, the driver recounted how, four months earlier, a corpse had been unearthed from the cemetery and burned. His story was that a killer, feeling ill, suspected that the corpse of his recent victim had been "arranged." So, he took the next step and stole the corpse, presumably to annul its magical power (meaning chop it into small pieces).

It was likely people from the Chocó who had performed the corpse magic, the taxi driver told us. Though Buenaventura is commonly touted as the heartland of sorcery, he invoked a remote, forest-based Other to explain this instance of sorcery and violence—and I am pretty sure that in the Chocó, people would direct the same opinions toward Buenaventura. Magic and violence are always Other and reciprocal.

By long-standing tradition, the Chocó is seen from the outside as a sorcery powerhouse. This reputation is now layered with a new ferment of riches combined with horror, namely the mercury-polluted Chocó rivers running through the no-holds-barred violence of cocaine trafficking and gold mining. This surely adds to the sense of what we might call "mercury-sorcery," a pestilential force aroused by the mix of ecocide, homicide, and gold, as symbolized by mercury poisoning—the shaking human body followed by death due to incurable neurological damage.

Think of mercury as a figure of sorcery; the way it swirls, the way it glistens, the ease with which it vaporizes, the ease with which it attaches itself to gold or silver, sinking those metals to the bottom of the pot, then, when the pot is heated, vaporizing into the atmosphere leaving only the precious metals (hence mercury's other name, *quicksilver*). Think not only of mercury's toxicity but of the manner by which it destroys the nervous system of plants, fish, animals, and humans.

Small wonder mercury played such a leading part in alchemy and during the Spanish colonial period was a crown monopoly. Small wonder that the Roman god Mercury was an intermediary between mortals and gods and was himself a god of commerce and trickery just like the great trickster Hermes, the Greek god from whom he was derived.

The young guard at the cemetery told us he was new to the job, replacing the previous guard, who had been shot but not killed by the corpse thieves the taxi driver had told us about. A lame guitarist hanging out in the cemetery, making a living playing for the bereaved, told us that at one time several bodies would be removed at once, taken to a now abandoned road that had led to the interior, and, I assume, there destroyed.

Is it any wonder that sorcerers from Buenaventura feature in my *narcorelatos* concerning corpse magic in the interior, whether in making it or counteracting it? And could it be that all assassinations occur twice over, the slaying of a living person necessarily followed by the slaying of the corpse in case it has been prepared for corpse magic?

6 *Who Does the Killing?*

It is a curious fact that both the killers and the sorcerers who practice corpse magic against the killers are widely held to be *costeños,* meaning African-Colombian cane-working migrants from the far-off Pacific coast or their locally born offspring. This incestuous coupling of killers and killers of killers points up once more the lively relationship between the living and the dead, the slayer and the slain. While killing by gangs is physical, revenge killing using corpse magic is mystical. Yet the two are linked, the latter, as it were, extending the energy of the former, taking advantage of the mystical bond killing creates between the quick and the dead.

In fact, the *costeños* are scapegoats, victims of the narcissism of minor differences as locals stereotype them as they themselves, being Black, are stereotyped by non-Blacks. It is obvious that gang members, especially in the hamlets, are not *costeños.* As for the stigma, it comes from vague ideas about sorcery and magic being prevalent or stronger on the coast.[1] And like all such stigmas, it is double-edged, bearing both positive and negative force, attraction no less than repulsion and fear, nowhere more so than among those people who live in or close to the barrio known as the Invasion at the eastern limits of the town pressed up against walls of cane.

In the highly confidential 2020–2021 police reports to the Ministry of National Defense, complete with photos and videos, this barrio is considered the most dangerous in this dangerous municipality. To my mind, it condenses the Faustian contract with which the plantations secured their lock on land and labor, creating, among other effects, the devil contracts that neophyte cane workers from the coast were said to entertain in the 1970s.[2]

It seemed to me that the stories told then of workers' devil contracts highlighted the fairytale properties of the market economy and, in addition, were rooted in *dépense*, in the joy of "going over the top," the love of stories of extremity and of what Norman O. Brown, echoing Bataille, called "too muchness."[3] In my opinion today, decades later, *this is also what the gangs and gangsters stand for*, no more so than when on New Year's Eve 2014 they burst into the cemetery to disinter and destroy a corpse they considered magically aroused. They hacked it to pieces. They doused it in gasoline. They consumed it in fire.

Thus, the stories of *costeños* making devil pacts in the cane fields may have passed away with time, but they live on in the aura of the gangsters' transmuted "too muchness," and specifically the too muchness of corpse magic chronologically associated with agribusiness and its consequent lumpen-proletarianization.

Corpse magic is as new as it is ancient (witness Christ's corpse, witness ancient Greece). What makes its newness new in the zones I describe is that the magic channeled stems, in my opinion, from the energy aroused by the overall destruction of landscape, by the upending of forests, land, and rivers, not to mention the torque of the thriving gang culture and *limpiezas*.

As we shall now see. *Like sacrifice, destruction animates what it destroys.* Corpse magic can be seen as an attempt to take the destruction done to the body and inflict it back onto the killer, the actual bodies of young men in gangs, as well as the body of the land.

THE SCENE OF THE CRIME

Early in September 2020 I received a five-minute video that had gone viral in Colombia. It was sent me by my law professor–anthropologist friend in Bogotá, Juan Felipe García. Set amid fields of sugarcane, the video was a response to the killing on August 11, 2020, of five Black teenage boys, ages fourteen to sixteen.[4] It is said they had set out to fly kites in the late afternoon breeze that blows strong and steady in August. The bodies were described as tortured, burned, shot dead or killed by machete.

A week or so later in response to a national outcry some men were apprehended, including, according to police, a sugar plantation watchman who had been patrolling that sector. Yet the brutality and scope of the killing seemed utterly disproportionate to the boys' stealing some stalks of cane, as the police alleged. Nor, as many people I spoke with, did it seem convincing to dismiss the murders and torture as punishment for *vicio*, for their being no-account kids smoking dope, killed as an act of "social cleansing."

Let us take into account the context as living force, as a person in its own right. For is not the scene of the crime a causal factor? The neighborhood in which the youngsters lived, Llano Verde, lies several miles to the north of the sugarcane town with which I am mainly concerned. It was built as a model settlement for refugees from war and for guerrilla fighters who had chosen peace. Many came from the Pacific coast, and like the rest of Cali's huge slum, Aguablanca, Llano Verde has many people of African descent displaced by violence from rural areas, looking for shelter and the advantages of city life.

Llano Verde is said to be beset by gangs and outside groups vying for control of drug trafficking and protection rackets. (So what's new?) A friend recently arrived in Aguablanca described to me ten years ago gangsters brazenly beating down the front door in order to take his terrified step-kids' sneakers. The stores and supermarkets I personally know in Aguablanca are owned by whites from Antioquia. They do their best to kill thieves and killers (am I really writing this, like this? Can it be true?), hiring paramilitary types or other gangs to do so, the net effect of which is the creation of a sullen street culture with razor-sharp edges of anxiety and alertness winding through the hot silence.

To my mind what makes the video Juan Felipe sent me extraordinary is that it rises above the predictable rumors of gangs and drugs to focus on the sugar industry.

* * *

The title is *¿Quién Los Mató?* (Who Killed Them?), and in answer to that question its centerpiece and main "actor" is a dark brown coffin set

squarely in the sugarcane fields, which at times you see close up and at other times from the sky, looking down such that it appears as a speck in a sea of sugarcane.

As the video focuses in you see that the top half of the coffin lid is open, exposing the face of a young Black man, a living Black man. Trapped in his tomb, the whites of his eyes scan back and forth as if looking for escape. While he sings, the leaves of the sugarcane on either side wrap back and forth over the coffin like a loose shroud.

With this the story shifts from the individual murderer, gangs, and white storeowners paying off killers. It shifts to the context, by which I mean the agribusiness racial system.

There is an answer to the question "Who killed them?" And the answer provided here is the sugarcane, meaning the sugarcane industry, which is made clear in the lyrics, concussive and smart such that you can't help smiling at the wit amid death combined with this staged death of the living corpse in its coffin.

We have moved on from gang warfare. We have moved on from *costeños* and the ghetto of the Invasion. All of that is now enclosed within the surround established by the chorus of women in the video singing their elegiac counterpoint to the harsh rap. They mourn the wound inflicted on the earth that is our mother.

Here's my insight, or rather my question: Is not all of this a rendition of what I call corpse magic but involving the land itself as assassinated corpse?

Years ago, as I described earlier, young gangsters buried their dead amid music and the shooting of guns while their comrades stood on the cemetery walls. Later, on New Year's Eve 2014, members of one gang scaled the heightened walls of the cemetery to fight off corpse magic by destroying the corpse of a rival whom they had killed. A week later, the same thing happened fifteen miles away in the cemetery of the small sugarcane slum town of Guachené, close to the Cordillera Central where live indigenous people known as Nasa, some of whom, the "Liberators of the *Madre Tierra*," whom I have already described, yank out the plantation sugarcane so as to cultivate food and do so under principles of share and share alike.

And today, some nine years later, the young video artists of *Who Killed Them?* invent and perform a corpse magic resurrection of the assassinated youngsters who were flying kites in Llano Verde. They resurrect these deaths while resurrecting our dying earth, as if the corpses are the same.

The video may not kill the killer who through corpse magic would be writhing in his bed at night unable to sleep, *but it gathers those elements of corpse magic in an act of singular genius*, planting the coffin in the cane fields, the face of the living corpse exposed, singing truth to power in exploding rhyme as the whites of the eyes swing back and forth awaiting redemption:

Pumping out fear and leaving corpses
This monster of the cane fields
Which instead of sweetness leaves death and quicklime.

When I asked Juan Felipe about these last lines, he replied, without knowing much about my interest in corpse magic, that the whiteness of sugar is here transformed into that of quicklime, applied, as in Greek tragedy, to the unburied corpse to prevent the spread of plague.

7 *Realignment of Landscape*

Does not the new wall around the cemetery coalesce changes that have been brewing for decades? It is as if the dead have long been restless—all the dead, not just the victims of gangster and paramilitary predation. Karl Marx alerted us to the importance of the means and mode of production in changing the ideas dominant in an epoch, but rarely except through metaphor and sarcasm did he include the dead. When the chips were down, however, Walter Benjamin did just that, playing his anarchist and Kabbalist cards, as when he wrote in his last text, "Theses on the Philosophy of History," that in the current state of emergency not even the dead would be safe from the Antichrist. Is that what motivated our friend, the priest, to undertake his infrastructural works in the cemetery, to protect or, should we say, control the dead, so their magic would flow churchward?

But who or what is this Antichrist? Is it the same as the antagonist portrayed in the video *¿Quién Los Mató?*, namely monocropping sugar plantations eradicating the groves of trees that constituted peasant agriculture following the abolition of slavery in 1851?[1] Like enclaves of rain forest, these groves absorbed heavy rains, curtailing flooding and sustaining moisture in the dry seasons. Sugarcane requires large drainage ditches and irrigation, ultimately the product of hydraulic engineering, like the damming the Cauca River, inspired by the model of and advice from the Tennessee Valley Authority, which opened the valley further to agribusiness in the name of progress.[2] It makes you swallow hard to see old photographs of paddle steamers unloading cargo in the town before the sugar plantations took over, such was the volume of water in the river back then, in contrast to the malodorous remnant today, although heavy rains subsequent to climate change are altering that.

There are aesthetic dimensions to this as well. The colors and tangled forms that made up a peasant farm, with its intense, three-dimensional

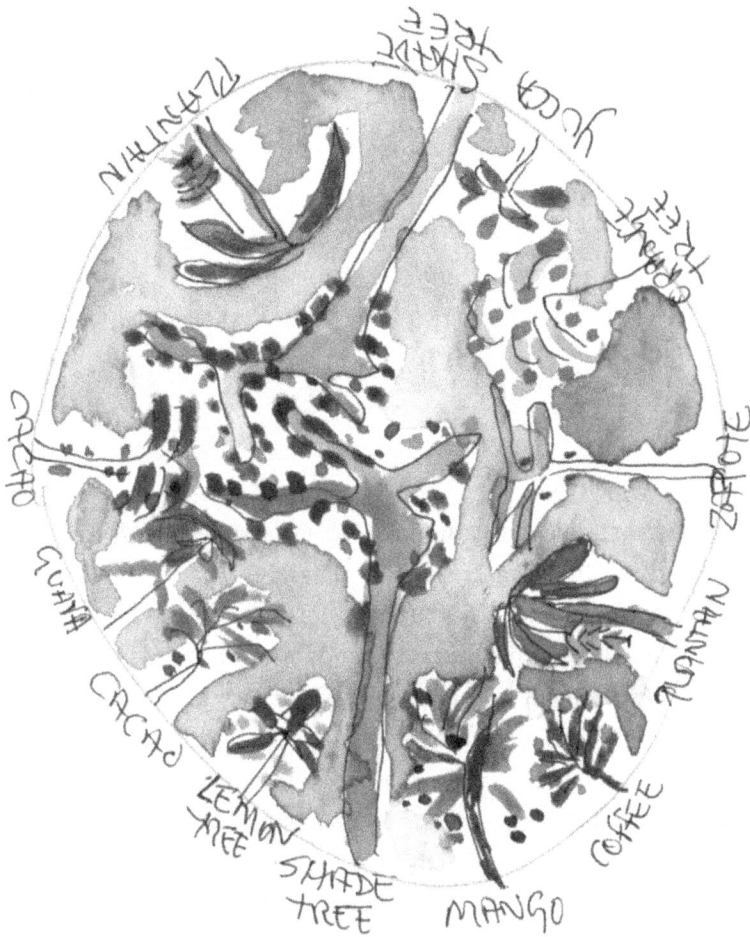

PEASANT FARM

PURE IMMANENCE

heterogeneity, are lost in a valley now converted into squares and rect-
angles suited to the head-on domination of nature obedient to a rectilinear
cast of mind.

To compare the peasant farm with the sugar plantation is to contrast
Baroque with Newtonian worlds, living nature with dead matter conceived
of as mass and velocity. To walk along the paths winding through the

COSECHA CACAO

LUIS
CARLOS
MINA

shaded peasant farms connecting house to house with their flowering gardens was to walk backward through time. To walk along the roads serving the plantation fields and the bedraggled remnants of peasant farms today, though, is to take your life into your hands as I've been reminded again and again of gang predation the past few years. The now shadeless roads stretch in long straight lines, choked with dust stirred up by tractor-trailers laden with sugarcane destined for the mills every ten minutes or so. Even at night. The billowing dust clouds, to one side, and the gangster kids, on the other, mean you can't walk anymore. More's the pity as every now and again, you come across a burst of color from a meticulously cared-for flower garden in the remnant of a peasant plot side by side with a few straggling cacao trees and plantains coated with dust like an impoverished museum registering past glories. Over the decades, I never once saw a bird or animal in the cane fields although I was told there were snakes.

For millennia the now-extinct volcanoes on either side of the valley spewed ash, enriching the soil from which sprouted verdant forest and animal life. You can see monkeys swinging from vines hanging from majestic trees in lithographs in the French weekly *Le Tour du monde* depicting the valley in the late nineteenth century. The texture of the meters-thick black earth, heirloom of volcanic ash and the forests that nourished ex-slave peasant farms, is now shredded by the deep plows of the plantations. Where there are still peasant groves, you may come across large holes that, if not filled with water, display the stratigraphic history of this explosively fertile land. These holes result from desperate farmers selling their topsoil to brick factories. What is more, increasingly the owners of the holes have allowed people, for a fee, to dump waste—probably toxic—into them.

Nevertheless, the kids are happy swimming with the lily pads in these holes. "The farm was sold for a hole," peasants would say glumly with a bitter smile. Wry humor was the last resource, but it could not be sold.

When you walk through middle- and upper-middle-class suburbs of Cali with names like El Jardin—The Garden—famously home to cocaine traffickers and their aggressive offspring with their new redbrick houses and apartment buildings, you realize with a shock that the buildings are made of soil that came first from the immemorial labor of volcanoes and second from ex-slave peasant cultivators forced to sell their soil, the basis of their livelihood, like people forced to sell a kidney in clinics in Cali for a flourishing international trade of dubious legality.

CENTRIFUGALITY

If forest and waterways have changed so fundamentally, what of the town and its cemetery? What of the sense of space and time, given the new dispensation of kids killing kids in a labyrinth of no-go zones as the pressure cooker of agribusiness and rural slum life tightens?

The earlier *centripetal* model of social space—focused on the sacred center of church, state, and cemetery—has given way, as I see it, to a *centrifugal* scheme fanning outward to the periphery of the ghetto of the Invasion, to the town's slaughterhouse, and to the spread of the sugarcane upending forest and rivers. Just as the cemetery is now secured by a mighty wall, so too the dying peasant farms are boxed in by a wall, the wall of sugarcane, repository of their afterlife, while all around reality has been hollowed out by new epistemologies and ontologies of speed, space, and time.

HETEROTOPIA AND GENIUS LOCI

Violent death marks a place and gives it power, as when people die in an automobile or motorbike accident and a shrine is erected at the spot. The place of violent death becomes its own graveyard, pulsing with pagan energy. The place itself bears the wound, we might say, traumatized like the human body.

Often in Latin America you see shrines built by truck drivers along highways, assemblages of flowers, disused headlights, and perhaps a photo of the dead driver. States, too, build monuments to fallen soldiers, as with Saddam Hussein's Victory Arch, consisting of two mighty swords grasped by bronze replicas of his forearm, plus five thousand dead Iranian soldiers' helmets; or Carabobo, in Venezuela, where a granite mountain of corpses provides the state with its necessary quotient of corpse magic.[3] On a smaller scale, far from highways and roads, ascending a mountain path on foot in Colombia, you might come across a cluster of small crosses set by the wayside as a memorial to a group assassination.

In a village, one part mestizo, one part indigenous, in the Sierra Nevada de Santa Marta studied in the 1950s by the anthropologists Alicia Dussán and Gerardo Reichel-Dolmatoff, there existed an abundance of holy sites.

"In general," they wrote, "all topographical features such as mountain peaks, hilltops, caves, large boulders, springs, cascades, lakes, swamps, and deep ponds in the rivers are sacred places."[4] They go on to say that any bizarre feature in the landscape is thought to have hidden significance.

The authors cluster these sites into categories. First are those where mythical or historic personages, generally shamans, are said to be buried and where offerings are made. Then there are places not where a shaman lies buried but where his spirit lingers. Such a place is considered enchanted by evil spirits, and no offerings are made. Other sites are "where monsters dwell such as horned snakes, black dogs, or mermaids. Thunder and song come from these places. Often rain or lightning suddenly appear and the figures continuously transform."[5] Giant trees planted by ancient shamans constitute other sites, as do gates that have to be ritually passed through to gain entry to the village. Still other sites are associated with wandering spirits of recently dead persons doing penance.[6] Reading all this, you cannot but wonder at the impoverishment of what, for want of a better word, I will call "the modern imagination" of spirits of place in relation to death.

What then of the bodies by the bridge over the Río Cauca, three miles from the cemetery in the town upon which I focus? Are these not "bizarre features in the landscape," to borrow Dussán and Reichel-Dolmatoff's phrase? Might they not also "have hidden significance"? Might there not be thunder and song along with lightning and continuous metamorphoses?

Consider Michel Foucault's idea of *heterotopias* that, like prisons, lunatic asylums, brothels, and cemeteries, are set aside from places we tend to regard as run-of-the-mill normal.[7] The passage of time since the Middle Ages may seem to have secularized geography and social spaces, yet, insists Foucault, all "these are still nurtured by the hidden presence of the sacred." His list extends to gardens, colonies, and ships. Strangely, to my mind, he does not mention automobiles (let alone Global South motorbikes) as heterotopias, though the strangeness of automobiles is rendered fulsomely in Foucault's France in Jean-Luc Godard's 1968 film *Weekend*, based on Julio Cortázar's story "La autopista del sur."

What then of the sacred sites nurtured by the dumped roadside corpses of the assassinated, or those sacred sites of the *no-go zones* of danger and death in the town and adjoining countryside? Are these not heterotopias also, "nurtured by the hidden presence of the sacred"? Or does Foucault miss the point here? Is it not the hidden presence of the sacred that's at stake, but the construction of destruction, of the negative sacred, that makes these sites heterotopic?

A map of this new sacred geography would connect the dots between violent deaths in a landscape come to life with "little god-spots," each with its guardian spirit or genius loci. As Leopold Bloom travels by carriage to the cemetery in Dublin, his mind is busy fashioning just such a map, grounded in real places, their histories, and their often-comic idiosyncrasies.

But for most of us most of the time these little god-spots are not obvious, not manifest as thunder and lightning, nor as mermaids, black dogs, or horned snakes. But does that mean the little gods, as I call them, are not there humming in some layer of reality from which corpse magic draws its magic? From there, horned snakes emerge.

8 God-Spots and No-Go Zones

We talk freely enough of "the spirit of a place," paying little if any attention to that troublesome word, *spirit*. We usually mean "spirit" in the sense of a "feel" or of our intangible sense of a place.

And what of genius loci, a strange expression for our day and age, defined as the protective spirit of a place? Does it not suggest something stubbornly pagan in defiance of Enlightenment norms, something counter to freeways and tunnels blasting through landscapes where once paths twisted among trees and zigzagged over hills, or through poor neighborhoods in the USA, Black or white but especially Black? Does the Brooklyn-Queens Expressway have a genius loci?

But then is not the automobile, God's gift to America and America's to the world, in and of itself a genius loci, the one most suited to modernity? Take the beautiful cars of the US inner city: shiny Cadillacs held together with such love, Mercedes, Teslas, BMWs, and Audis that along with clapped-out Datsuns double as tombs as they are stopped in full flight by police.

One of the most charming properties of automobiles is how they make children out of adults whose favored toys they are, whether in real life or in films such as *Bullitt*, with its famous chase scene. A new lexicon emerges, apparently technical but actually magico-formulaic; the two cars in that scene, both 1968 models, being described (off screen) as a Ford Mustang GT Fastback with a 390-cubic-inch, 325-horsepower V8 engine and four-speed manual transmission, pursued by, then pursuing, a Dodge Charger 375 hp, 440 Magnum V8.

Marissa Tomei put this sort of language brilliantly into courtroom speech in her film role as an unexpected automobile guru from Brooklyn in an Alabama courtroom in the hilarious 1992 film *My Cousin Vinny*.

Then there is James Dean in *Rebel Without a Cause*, caressing and being caressed not by a girl or a boy but by his car, until he eventually dies in his Porsche driving too fast across the desert into the setting sun in a meticulously scripted sacrifice. Tell me the automobile is not a spirit, the *genius locus* of modernity! Tailpipe emissions killing the planet are part of its spiritual endowment, as are its weird sexual excitements. J. G. Ballard made a hit with his 1973 novel *Crash*, later a film, based on the premise of sexual bliss occurring with automobile accidents.

And now in Colombia the automobile can become your coffin, as with the young man, wrists tied, body stuffed in his trunk by the bridge, every inch a monument. A surreal one, too, when compared with the advertisements for automobiles charging over hill, over dale, with a wondrous damsel at the helm. Instead, we have the damsel transmogrified, scrunched into the trunk as a male fetus. You dream all your young life of owning an automobile like people in the dreamland that is the USA, but you end up dumped in its rear end, evoking thunder and lightning, mermaids, black dogs, and horned snakes at the entrance to the village.

Even in our godless times, memories of childhood allow of such specters, as when Walter Benjamin in his 1930s memoir of his Berlin childhood recalls sculpted deities as spirits of the place over the entrances to courtyards and buildings in Charlottenburg he walked past with his nanny.

Did not Benjamin base his famous Arcades Project on the idea of the *genius loci*? His childhood awareness of Berlin's guardian spirits continued as an adult in Paris, where he found them in the decaying arcades brought to his attention by Louis Aragon, who saw them as wonderfully apt subjects for Surreal exploration. The catacombs of Paris also provided Benjamin with a pointed example. "One knew in ancient Greece," he writes, "where the way led down into the underworld. Our waking existence likewise is a land which, at certain hidden points, leads down into an underworld—a land full of inconspicuous places from which dreams arise."[1]

As I trace the archaeology of sites of dumped corpses in and around the town of my preoccupation in western Colombia, what do I end up with given that most times these sacred sites are not marked as such.

Embedded in secular reality they emit a vibe amounting to a public secret of the soul, here one moment, gone the next.

NO-GO ZONES ARE SACRED SITES TOO

Of all the sacred sites, I think those of the town's no-go zones are the most sacred and contribute the most to the new spiritual geography of decenteredness. I recall two decades of being lectured to, admonished, threatened, and implored on bended knee not to go to the eastern end of town. Each step I took in that pestilential direction I felt I was walking into a gale.

For a long time I downplayed these warnings until early one evening in August 2008, I bumped into a smiling young man in the center of town whom I did not recognize. Turned out that as a kid in the 1970s he had lived opposite me where the two rivers bordering the town converge. I asked why his right shoulder was covered with a plastic shield. It looked like a prosthesis. The arm was swollen and paralyzed. His right eye was closed. He told me he was shot driving a horse and cart past the Invasion. He had a young steer trotting behind that he was going to kill for market next day. He is a butcher like his father.

Three adolescents came at him. With a shotgun he killed one. A gang later killed the other two, saying he was *"buena gente."* He smiles and I realize again how much I'd underestimated that end of town. But then I don't go around driving a steer.

Added to those no-go zones is the sugarcane itself, bringing to mind those sacred sites in the Sierra Nevada "where monsters dwell ... rain or lightning suddenly appear and the figures continuously transform." In the cane fields, however, it is something else, something less figural and more atmospheric. It is the nighttime sky lit purple and red with flames crackling through the undergrowth while during the day black columns of smoke drift skyward like after an aerial bombardment. Eeriest of all is the *utter sameness* of the environment bereft of human habitation and trees from one side of the valley to the other. Not even monsters can live there.

Any map showing this negatively sacred landscape would be like a Jackson Pollock painting, with spidery lines and splurges of red that crisscross the territory with stab wounds and bullet holes. Congealed shapes of timeless time linger on street corners as assassins plotting revenge sit and wait and wait some more.

In the good old days, the sacred came laden with poetry and oracular wizardry as in the Bible, Homer, Dante—although what you might call the real sacred is what you see through Regina's one-way black glass window looking onto the stiller-than-still street as the killers on the corner wait their prey. They have all day. And the next. And they must know we are watching. But do they care? We are part of the scene too. They know me well. (Not like the six fourteen-year-olds who came at me at the Rio de Arzobispo in Bogotá the other day with murder in their eyes. Otherwise nice-looking kids.)

Carlos Mario Perea devotes the beginning of his excellent account of street gangs in certain cities in Colombia to what he sees as their defining feature and innovation, namely what they do to time. Gangs disorient and fill you with fear, he says, because they stand on the street corner doing nothing. They have abandoned time. They have found another way of inhabiting the city.[2]

My friend Regina laid out the history of revenge killings that led to this particular scene being acted out as the killers awaited their victim. She knew their names, their families, their murdered kin. Most of all she could trace the links, each murder leading to the next. Yet she was so voluble, her speech so rapid, that it was impossible to capture the details that passed in a blur. No doubt about it, though. This waiting on the corner is a sacred rite, real and deadly. These corners are "hot zones" in which multiple realities bounce off one other, secrets abound, direct talk is rare, innuendo excavates language, and the sacred lunges from dark corners now equivalent to those sacred sites in the Sierra Nevada.

In the mountains of the Cordillera Central to the east of the cemetery of which I speak, indigenous community leaders are being assassinated. I hear the same about the traditional healers, too. The landscape itself seems to suffer this and act as witness. Traveling in a car with sociologist friends from Cali up the mountains to the small town of Toribio, you are told in fearful tones not to mention certain topics, *not even in the car*, as if the mountains have ears. In towns such as Suárez (on the Cordillera Occidental) or Toribio (on the Cordillera Central) there is a double language, the said and the unsaid. Higher up the slopes of the Cordillera Occidental, monstrous men guarding coca fields are everywhere as coca cultivation comes our way north from Nariño on the border with Ecuador. These men threaten local peasants who do not want to grow coca or are ambivalent. With their cell phones, the coca mafias can contact labor contractors all over Colombia to hustle up kids to pick coca leaves at little more than a day's notice. What most arouses their ire is concern for human rights and for the environment, especially from indigenous communities where forests and rivers, *paramo* and lakes, are increasingly presented as spiritual entities because of this very threat and such spiritualization may generate political capital.

THE NEW SACRED AXIS

Before the gangster burials in the cemetery, the sacred axis of the town, as I fancy it, ran north-south, from the cemetery to the town plaza, where stands the church to one side and the Palacio Municipal on the other. But now, by my reckoning, it runs instead from the cemetery east to the ghetto called the Invasion that the police dare not enter, from there north to the bridge over the river, and west to the slaughterhouse by the river where amid offal and sanguinary odor buzzards sit unsteadily on the wall flapping their wings for balance, recalling the gangsters standing shoulder to shoulder on the cemetery walls during the burial of their comrades, who were then displaced by police doing the same.

The new cemetery wall thwarts the gangsters' choreography, their lining up like buzzards at the abattoir, but that does not prevent so much as boost the new orientation of sacred space emerging from agribusiness, drugs, and homicide.

Indeed, the spectacle of the wall signifies a cosmic shift in the maps charting the sacred in everyday life. Recall those mariners' maps of centuries past, showing half-real, half-imagined contours of coasts and inlets, lonely headlands and dangerous reefs. Seafarers knew of shoals and changeable winds, tremendous tides and winter storms. They filled the unknown with chimeric creatures: giant lobsters and whales attacking ships, griffins and human horse-fish, one-eyed kings, one-breasted Amazons, and the monster that swallowed Jonah. Lusty sirens, personifications of the winds, admired themselves in mirrors, and sailors told each other stories not unlike *narcorelatos* about the Marvels of the East. With these maps of wonder and discovery in mind, jump forward to our age of reenchanted space that differs from the old days only in that the monsters are real and more deadly.

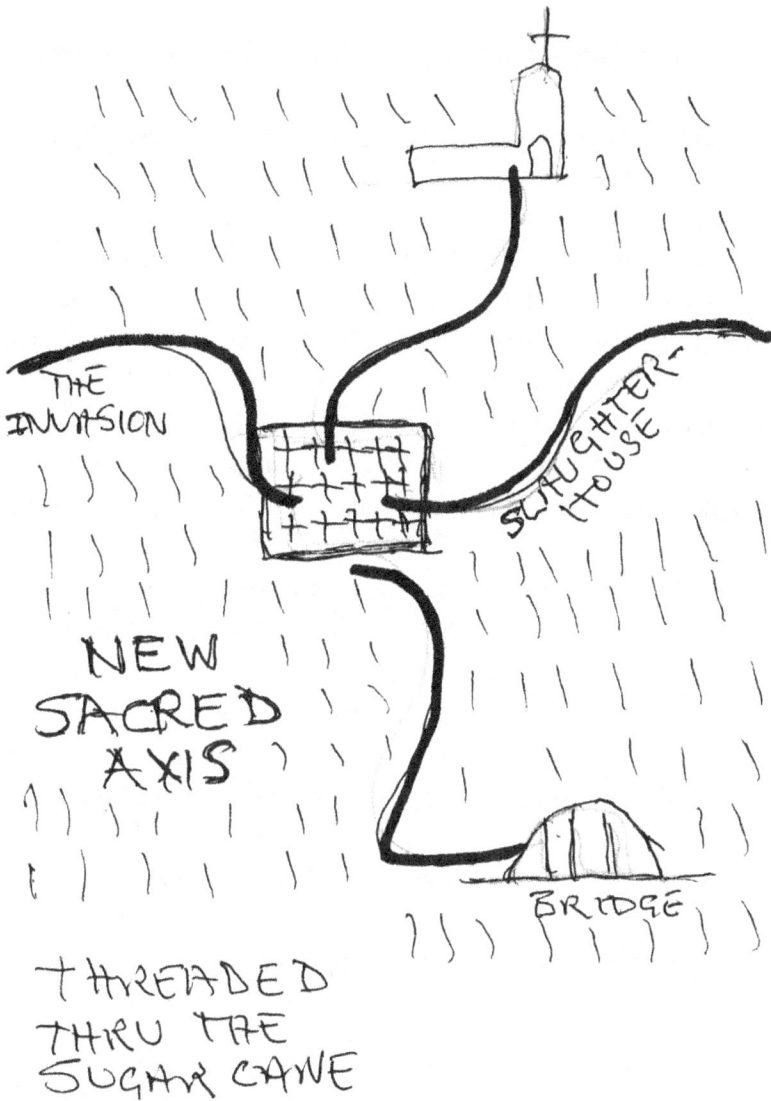

THE
INVASION

NEW
SACRED
AXIS

SLAUGHTER-
HOUSE

BRIDGE

THREADED
THRU THE
SUGAR CANE

That is how I think of the automobile by the bridge with the body of my friend's cousin like a fetus in the trunk. This was a warning and a spectacle, like those staged by state or municipal authorities who used the gibbet to display executed criminals at the city limits in Europe and its colonies.

In the 1990s and the decade following there were many corpses left by the roads leading into this sugarcane town. Some people told me of corpses with their lips or eyelids sewn shut, understood to be a warning to informers. Others said this apparent mutilation was not real but an effect of bodily decay. Yet the fact that some people interpreted it as a message—a message involving mutilation and grotesquerie for theatrical effect—is significant, whether intended or not.

Is this not, then, part of a long-standing practice of corpse display, especially on the part of Church and state, that includes the gibbet and Crucifixion—a display, in the case of Jesus, replicated by the Church a few centuries after He became a god? The corpse display is so obvious that today we don't really see it, and presumably have not for centuries, because the ancient sign of the cross became the Sign of the Cross adorning the interior walls and defining the architectural configuration of churches.[3]

If you're irked here by my use of the word *magic*, try *art*, as in "corpse art" instead of "corpse magic." Think of the magic of the state rearing up like the gibbet festooned with a rotting corpse setting passersby aquake. The art in that, like a neon sign at the crossroads, a billboard of retribution for high crimes like treason and piracy permeated with the stench of decay.

Eventually the Enlightenment suppressed the display of criminal corpses. Now, in most of the USA, capital punishment is hush-hush, secreted behind prison walls. But in the town I am concerned with in Colombia during the decades in question, 1990–2010, another art of display took its place, and that is what we might call the "real law" hard at work with its murderous art of "crucifixion," with corpses dumped by the bridge while others float by in the muddy current unless their bellies have been punctured so they sink out of sight. It's all so modern now. Not a cross resplendent with a corpse but an automobile doubling as a tomb, or a river become a freeway for assassinated bodies, while meanwhile in the USA, like nowhere else in the world, as far as I know, the automobile has become the major site for state assassination.

9 *From Corpse Magic to Corpse Montage*

Suddenly it becomes easy. We evade the pitfalls of *magic* and become acolytes of something that is nowadays even more fashionable—*art*. Consider the photomontages I saw in the cemetery of Buenaventura in December 2019, where several bodies were said to have been recently stolen. The facades of the niches housing the dead are about thirty inches wide and twenty inches high, each with a space at least two inches deep, into which people insert images and adornments. The facades thus become puppet theaters of a sort, venues for spirit-art dedicated to the dead, mourning, and memory.

Facade displays were sold next to the cemetery by a woman vendor who purchased them in the town of Buga in the Cauca Valley and had them transported over the mountains to the port of Buenaventura. The ones I saw contained photographs of the deceased, sometimes at different stages of life, within vividly colored dreamscapes: sapphire blue rivers with tropical foliage, for instance, or close-ups of brilliantly colored flowers on which the deceased appeared to float. Some included biblical texts, and I saw one, in December, in which Santa Claus was pictured bearing gifts. In these images the dead person seems alive yet ethereal, living-dead, buoyant in landscapes of life folded into the afterlife. Corpse magic aimed at killing the killer is surely not very different from this.

Current images owe much to Photoshop technology, but montage has been practiced by Colombian street and studio photographers for over a century. In the street, the photographer develops the negative using a small pail of chemicals he carries with him, makes a print and inserts it into one of several paper backgrounds chosen by his client, then rephotographs the composite. Voila! There your dear departed is, surrounded by angels, romance, filial piety, or a fairytale scene. As you wish.

Outside the Cementerio Central in Bogotá in November 1985, where a crowd assembled on Mondays, multiple copies of an astonishing montage were for sale. It consisted of two conjoined images—a color photo of thirteen-year-old Omayra Sánchez, trapped for three days until she died in the water and rubble of the volcanic eruption of the Nevado de Ruiz in Armero, much featured on TV news. Joined to this was a photo of the pope, as if he were right there next to Omayra, blessing her with his right hand.

BURDEN OF DREAMS

A fine example of a street photographer creating montages like this occurs as the end of Les Blank's 1982 film *Burden of Dreams*, which concerns the making of Werner Herzog's film *Fitzcarraldo*. Blank's film ends with several street photographers set up close together in a dirt street of what could be a small Peruvian town. One of them takes a photograph of Herzog's face and develops it with chemicals attached to his tripod, and we see in the black-and-white reversal of the negative the unreal face of Herzog, his eyes glowing like lanterns. Then the photographer asks Herzog which frame he prefers, inserts the photo into that frame, takes a photo of that, and Voilà! There is Herzog surrounded by jungle plants and flowers with parrots in the corners and a scroll above saying, *What do I have to say to tell you that all my words mean I love you?*

Two more ornately framed photos follow, one of Blank himself, and one of Maureen Gosling, his film editor. Such is the finale to this great film paying tribute to another great film, *Fitzcarraldo*, by means of the most elemental photographic technology, namely the fairytale art of montage.

This ending to Blank's film accomplishes at least three tasks. First, it presents as capstone the role of montage in practically all filmmaking. Second, it presents Blank's entire film as an homage to Herzog's film. And third (and most important for our purposes regarding cemeteries and spiritual geographies), it suggests an ongoing enchantment that is not an end at all but endless, which is what those Buga facades accomplish in the cemetery in Buenaventura as the life eternal.

MONTAGE AS DECEIT

We might posit a fourth task, beyond the scope of these films but adding to the burden of dreams. I am referring to what I take to be the widespread use of montage to deceive us—especially prevalent in today's photography of war and violence, where, so I am informed by war photographer Malcolm Linton, situations are often staged as in the infamous Robert Capa photograph of a militiaman being shot dead, arms flung outward as if from the impact of a bullet, during the Spanish Civil War.

In Spanish "montage" is *montaje*, the predominant meaning of which is "trick." What Capa gave us in Spain was staged, a deceit intended to convey a truth. One curious thing about this is how, given photography's reality-effect, we feel extra cheated when we find out the photographer faked a shot. In Colombia, on the other hand, *montaje* sums up a common practice associated with violence, business, and politics, what in the English-speaking world is today now glossed as "fake news." There is no reality outside of it. Fakeness is all there is.

Let us review the etymology of *montage*—a French word that today has many meanings: to climb up, to climb on, to mount, to assemble, to increase, and, of course, to juxtapose unalike images thar have something in common.

In sixteenth-century France, montage meant to *assemble*, as in clockmaking or printing. In the eighteenth century, we find the sense of *mounting* a theater production, followed in the early twentieth century by its application to film editing, or should we say manipulation, as with Sergei Eisenstein and Dziga Vertov.

John Heartfield's practice of photomontage, abutting one image against another, was manifestly political; some of his best-known work appeared, for example, on the covers of the German antifascist, procommunist magazine *AIZ* in the 1930s. Heartfield did not set out to deceive. He was upfront with the constructedness of his montages, pungent, witty, scornful, and at times terrifying assemblies, often depicting and satirizing fascist leaders and incorporating text from the right-wing press.

My understanding is that Heartfield's work was as much about montage as it was montage.

The *Historic Dictionary of the French Language* concludes its genealogy of montage by claiming that from cinema the word *montage* spread into the visual arts to "describe the process of producing a single work by combining several elements." But what Heartfield achieved by juxtaposing the capitalist press with his imagery was to expose and play with the conceit of journalistic neutrality. Montage was not an assembly like a clock, not just a technique, but a fabrication that showed the fabrication of reality.

Hence the Problem Facing the Writer

The question facing me is this: if killing a corpse impacts
logic and language, isn't that impact likely to be greater when
death is denied? And in turn isn't that likely to be made even
greater when what is denied is secretly admitted? And still
more, what if the corpse killed has been animated so
as to kill its killers?

10 *How to Kill a Corpse*

Writing and talking about the dead is made difficult by the taboos aroused, especially in the case of killing, yet may not writing in so charged a field flex language in interesting ways? Can I take for granted the sense of words if the commonplace denial of death is challenged not only by actual death but by the riddles of corpse magic? Then, like an oil spill, language spreads its rainbow hues.

I believe that is one reason why, as I kept asking about the cemetery break-in, people are often without words or speak strangely, as if they were underwater, then suddenly find their tongue.

I keep thinking of those old peasants on a high mountain range in Colombia in *The People of Aritama*. Nursing their ailments and gnawing hunger, feeling neglected by younger people, by their family and by neighbors, these old folk would curse them out. "Just wait till I die," they would mutter, threatening spiritual retribution.[1]

I like the story. I like it because it seems to present an uncomplicated, matter-of-fact notion of death and the afterlife that is almost casual while endorsing the power of the dead to exact revenge. How feisty and mean the spirits of the dead come across in the muttering of these old folk on the mountain. But elsewhere in Colombia, as in García Márquez's Macondo in the hot northern lowlands, or in accounts I have read of the mystical visions of paramilitaries, spirits of the dead are a pitiful lot, desperate for human company, a drink of water, or getting their mutilated bodies put back together again. Like beggars, they be, with long memories. This same pathetic image is presented by Fustel de Coulanges in his discussion of the dead in ancient Greece and Rome.[2]

Pathetic, they may be. But nonetheless scary. They form a flitting multitude giving vent to a "strange kind of screaming sound that made me turn pale with fear," says Ulysses, making sure to perform his animal sacrifices, draw his sword, and keep the dead on the far side of the trench he has dug filled with sacrificial blood.[3] But on that high mountain where live the people of Aritama, the dead come across eager for a fight, confident they will win or at least score some satisfying victories.

While it's one thing for old peasants laid low by arthritis and neglect to mutter threats about the revenge they will take once dead, it seems quite another to write about the dead in my academic, middle-class world in the Global North, where the dead don't exist. You die, decompose, and are gone. Sad but true. Or almost true.

For all around my home in gentrifying Brooklyn's BedStuy are storefront churches, African American and Latino, at least one per block, in many of which, I believe, the dead play a significant role and ghosts are (almost) no strangers, as in Tony Morrison's *Beloved*. Then there is the governor of New York, Kathy Hochul, who talks with her dead mother, while the other Democratic Party contenders for the governorship say they believe in spirits and the afterlife. As for the shadows of academia that I inhabit, do not the dead play a mighty role in the guise of endless books in libraries and in the genealogies of ideas? Engraved deep in stone on the wall of my university library, stretching from one side of the building to the other, are the names of illustrious dead white males stretching back more than two millennia. Yes, it is a library. But it's also a mausoleum with its dead holding court in the underground stacks. It is strange down there amid the antiquated shelving and even older elevators, weak lighting, and silence as heavy as in a catacomb.

In *Hope Against Hope*, Nadezhda Mandelstam's memoir of her life in the Soviet Union with her poet husband, who was one of the millions who died in work camps in the late 1930s, she recalls how he and his close friend, that other great poet Akhmatova, could "somehow bridge time and space when they read the work of dead poets. With them it meant entering into personal relations with the poet in question: it was a kind of conversation with someone long departed."[4]

Susan Sontag says something similar, as I recall, that when she writes that she envisions a genealogy of dead writers before her as if alive.

But the rest of us? Do we converse like that? Seems unlikely. But then I have to admit that when it comes to the dead, all bets are off. Despite its finality, death is not the end but the beginning, the beginning of uncertainty that may undermine yet renew thought itself, and hence writing too.[5]

A BLUNT SHOVEL

It is said that action speaks louder than words. That's certainly the case with breaking into a cemetery to steal and destroy a corpse. Anything seems possible as we blast through taboos, pushing aside any dead shaman we read about in *The People of Aritama*, knowing that exhumation and corpse destruction has a long history.

Take the case described by the twelfth-century English monk William of Newburgh concerning the corpse of a man who had done much evil in life but was nevertheless buried in a Christian graveyard.[6] With the aid of Satan, his animated corpse would leave its grave at night and, followed by braying hounds, wander through the village till dawn. After this corpse had killed several people, villagers unearthed it from its surprisingly shallow grave and found it "swollen to enormous corpulence, with its countenance beyond measure turgid and suffused with blood." When corpse was stabbed with a blunt shovel, a great stream of blood flowed, after which the corpse was dragged to a pyre. But it would not burn until the body was opened, allowing someone to reach in and extract the heart. Then the body was successfully consigned to the flames. Killing a living person seems simple by comparison, as we see vividly in the case of Bram Stoker's *Dracula*, written seven centuries after William of Newburgh's chronicle.

Killing a cadaver seems an assault not only on the dead but on logic. Killing what is already dead doesn't make sense. But language can take us to that Other world, the language of story parsed as documentation and now as history: There's the bluntness of the shovel used to split open the corpse like a *piñata*. There's the surprisingly shallow grave, the corpse ballooned with blood, its resistance to fire until the heart is wrenched out. All this flamboyant detail is thrown up by the fathomless illogic of killing the already dead. It is this same exuberance that allows the story to flow like that copious stream of blood, an ecstasy of corporeal exudate.

My question, then, is this: if death jolts language, and if killing a person jolts language, how much more so does killing a corpse?

Earlier I expressed surprise at the gangsters' hacking to pieces a corpse suspected of being the vehicle of magic and then setting it afire. How, I asked, could such crude physical destruction trump the wiles of magic? But after reading William of Newburgh I am less perplexed. And I recall my old friend Teófila, the epitome of serenity and gentleness, recounting the destruction of the corpse unearthed in the cemetery of Guachené. She was not an eyewitness, but she narrated the events with, initially, the magisterial calm of the *vidente*, or seer, that she is. But that calm evaporated when she described the cadaver being torn apart. There in her bed with her grandchildren and great-grandchildren she broke into a violent gestural language, mimicking the savage violence. She laughed, as well, but questions lingered at the corners of her mouth.

DEAL WITH DEATH, AMERICA!

If killing a corpse strains credulity, how much more might that be the case in a culture like the Global North where death occupies a troublesome no-man's-land. A recent article in the *London Review of Books* tells us that the book under review, on the arts of dying, begins with a paradox: "we talk incessantly of death, but can't say anything about it because it has no being."[7]

Online I once heard Alan Ball, producer of the acclaimed TV series *Six Feet Under*, set in a Los Angeles funeral home, say, "I think we live in a culture which works to deny death exists," and he talked, as I recall, of his show's having taken death "out of the closet." What I most recall was his glowering at the camera bellowing, *Deal with death! America!*

Today scenes like the one described by William of Newburgh are part of the (new?) genre of death porn, exciting and uncanny but, at the end of the day, not something that would make you grab a blunt shovel and head off to the cemetery.

In the Global North when someone close to us dies, our words can feel cliched and trivial. The most eloquent statement I heard after a succession of tributes to a friend's dead father recently was the thud of the first shovel-load of dirt hitting the coffin. But when my artist friend Carolee Schneemann died near age eighty in upstate New York after a long illness, an ad hoc memorial was organized two days later, not in a funeral parlor but at a friend's house in the woods. About twenty-five people turned up. We stood in a circle. Things were stiff. There was no plan. But then people started to tell funny stories about her, the scrapes she had gotten into and gotten out of, sexual escapades, her wit, her grace, adventures of one sort or another, many of which reflected humorously or sheepishly on people in our memorial circle. It was as if she hadn't died and was there among us laughing. Ted Hughes has a poem about Sylvia Plath being present that way, like Ariel hovering over the flickering flames of her birthday cake, years after she died (for which he is often blamed). The stories we told about Carolee were stories that opened up life and changed us all as we spoke and listened. And there was no stopping them. I can see why Walter Benjamin thought death spurred storytelling, even if we weren't sitting around a deathbed but were gathered after her death. The authority of death is at the very source of the story, he claimed, and I think that is evident in my story here.

Toward the end, an elderly fellow slowly got up off the floor. It took a while. Joint by creaking joint. He reached into a plastic shopping bag and pulled out a paper plate and what looked like three eagle feathers. Around the circumference of the plate was hand-written an elegy that he read, turning the plate while holding the feathers, which he waved slowly back and forth. When he finished reading, he thrust the feathers into the sky: "Go Carolee! Go!"

Spontaneously like that, he freed her soul.

What do I mean, "freed her soul"?

Now there's a cliché! I think it evokes the fear we have of dead souls or of our feeling of inadequacy as we deny them or struggle with the ambiguity of believing and not believing in them at one and the same time. The outflung gesture with the feathers provided a pathway through those contradictions, granting permission for the dead soul to wander freely in our midst and for us to welcome her and feel her, yet nevertheless recognize the distance. Vinciane Despret draws attention to the expansion of the dead person that such a gathering of storytelling mourners creates, while bringing us close to that person. Social science, she claims, tends to ignore these stories because they imply that the dead exist like living persons who feel and socialize.[8]

GO CAROLEE GO!

There are many ways to deny dying and the dead. The most obvious is its erasure through medical care in a hospital, although I am told that prior to COVID long-term trend in the USA seemed to be reversing, with more dying people opting for death at home.

Ensconcing death in a hospital has come with the weakening of an older custom of people gathering around the bed of the dying person. Much was made of this by Benjamin in the 1930s, it being his idea that the shift to dying in the hospital or isolated in an old folks' home spelled an end of storytelling. But during my recent hospitalization in Manhattan I noticed some eight family members and friends were gathered in the room next door around the bed of someone (I took to be) dying.

And then there is judge Ivan Ilych as described by Tolstoy. He is taking his time dying, our not so old Ivan. And it is painful. There is the illness clawing at him, but equally painful is his family hovering like vultures and on top of that the clerks from the law courts jockeying for favor. What's a dying man to do? I think the judge would prefer a bit of denial and being left alone. In this story, Tolstoy saw death head on. It was ugly.

Could Benjamin's claim have been influenced by the *ars moriendi*, the Catholic Church's aid to dying? Prescribed in the fifteenth century as a means to align one's death with Christ's death and resurrection (which parallels my approach to corpse magic), the principal idea was that sin had to be confronted, confessed, and thus disposed of. There were instructions for family and friends as well. Woodcuts were made such that images of the "good death" could be circulated. It seems fair to say that death was not denied but magnified, theatricalized, and scripted, as if life was naught but a steady preparation for death, its tumultuous and most significant climax.

Benjamin saw death prior to his time as providing a quasi-theatrical stage for storytelling (something we shall see in more detail in chapter 14 where I discuss the death watch). In his 1936 essay on the storyteller, however, it is not biblical images but the face of the dying person that provides the screen by which this is accomplished, as it is the face which expresses events in the dying person's life that passed unnoticed even by the dying person.

Phillipe Ariès tells us it was common to assume that the life of a dying person flashed before his or her eyes at the moment of death. But that was before what he sees as the modern transformation of death in the West, a shift from "tamed death" to the "wild death" that came with death's being denied.[9]

When death changes like that does anything happen to storytelling? Does it die too? That was Benjamin's thesis in 1936, implicitly confined to Western Europe. Closer to us and our time, the novelist and critic John Berger tells of being by his father's side, and drawing his face shortly after he died. "As I drew his mouth, his brows, his eyelids," he wrote, "as their specific forms emerged from the whiteness of the paper, I felt the history and the experience which made them as they were."[10] In the context of the Global North's denial of death today, this would be the exception that makes the rule.

THE DENIAL STORY

Here is the denial story as I understand it: Once upon a time we were accustomed to death. Once upon a time we had protocols and formalities. We had a script, and we were close to death as a physical thing. It was all around us, with massive mortality rates, especially for children and women in childbirth, especially amid incessant wars, ubiquitous sorcery, and rampant plagues. Being largely a rural society, we frequently saw animals being killed and probably killed a few ourselves. We had our rites, hymns, music, clothes, and prayers. But then came the Enlightenment, and confusion reigned. Death became more physical than metaphysical, and it became physical in a new way, with the corpse transformed into a miasmatic germ bomb, something "unhygienic." Death became toxic.

It seems a paradox that as death became more material it became more frightening and repellent, taboo in ways that create blankness, as if denial is but an admission that there is no meaning to death (and hence life). Thank God, then, for Jessica Mitford and Evelyn Waugh and, behind them, tender jokes about corpses and death.

This picks up on the theatrical space between death, the denial of death, and the denial of that denial. The elaborate funerary performances with long faces and angels strumming harps and guitars that Waugh delights in, and us with him, are the result of our not knowing what to do with death, our being rendered vulnerable and open, as it were, like newborn babes. For now, in the Global North, as in the time of Waugh's novel, the script is a morass of hypocrisy, as if modernity is a leaking tub when it comes to death. A friend told me he attended a funeral service in a church in Sydney and for a few bewildering moments thought he'd walked into the wrong service. "I didn't recognize whom they were talking about," he told me. For a moment I didn't understand what he was saying.

Is this the denial of denial, this pantomime in the form of Waugh's embalmed and beautified corpses? Is the denial of denial inevitably wildly funny? Could that be why Ariès calls modern death "wild"? But then, as Bakhtin would have it, the "seriocomic" or the carnivalesque has been around a long time, more than two thousand years of what is called *Western* history. I put my money on Bakhtin.

Listen to Leopold Bloom talking to himself in *Ulysses* sometime in the second decade of the twentieth century, as James Joyce plays with Homer's two millennium-old text. Bloom does okay and more than okay with stories of death rattling through his skull as he rides clip-clop in the funeral carriage to the Dublin cemetery. Is he denying death? Are his thoughts reactions to that denial? Or is he "pre-denial" in the long-colonized society of Ireland, which I guess even in Bloom's time barely made the grade into the Global North and still believed in leprechauns?

My point is that death as something more than organ failure is *not* denied. When push comes to shove, as Thomas Laqueur emphasizes with such elan, no corpse is left to rot in a field, now or at any time in the past. *The dead body is not a germ bomb but a taboo bomb*, and no amount of secular stricture can change that. If the body is left to rot, all hell breaks loose, as in Sophocles's *Antigone*, as relevant now as it was when first performed two millennia ago.

One of the corpses Laqueur considers is that of Karl Marx. Ardent followers of this Enlightenment prophet insisted on being buried by his side in Highgate cemetery in London.

Today, to my mind, this is a cemetery like few others. Its graves lie amid towering trees, ferns, bird cries, and damp forest smells drawing on the rich mulch of the dead. At one point on a well-trod path are a crowd of tombstones at ground level dwarfed by the leonine head of Marx brooding over the expanding flock of corpses below. Some of these tombstones seem like mere nameplates lying on the ground that have fudged their way into the charmed circle, such as a sharp-elbowed student leader I recognized whose harangues were prominent among the Trotskyists where I studied in London in the late 1960s.

It seems to me that people buried close to Marx wanted their corpses to imbibe something spiritual from his corpse, the same as in the cult of the saints millennia before. We visitors to any grave may be granted a bit of spirit exchange too. Such an act emphatically denies the denial of death. We may deny death. But we also deny its denial. "Go Carolee! Go!"

ONLY DUST AND MEMORY

Do the dead exist in a physical or quasi-physical way, or are they nothing but dust and memory? And what if the dead are dead because of assassination, in which case their souls cannot rest?

I am reminded of meeting Fabiola Lalinde of working-class Medellín, whose politically active teenage son was disappeared by the Colombian army in 1983.[11] Years later his remains were found. She spoke of repeatedly dreaming of him, as did her neighbors. Note that in the Spanish language one does not dream "of" but "with." She became a leading human rights activist, translating that of/with into political action.

Dreaming of/with the dead is an artifact of language that seems appropriate when I try to assimilate the of/with world of the assassinated dead. But how do you do this for people who, like me, are pretty much infested by the denial camp, which has plenty of tricks up its sleeve?

I think of BedStuy, Brooklyn, where I sit and write. Do the neighbors and people mulling things over in the local park dream of/with the victims of police and gang killings? Is not Black Lives Matter the outcome of such dreaming on a vast collective scale? Can the *of* become *with*? That would seem what is necessary for justice.

Perhaps this was the wisdom or at least the questions that history threw at me, namely the shock in early 2015 of the cemetery break-in? That was transgression sufficient to leave me in a vacuum in which neither belief nor disbelief mattered. What mattered was transgression inciting that "shipwreck in the nauseous" that allows corpse magic to emerge.[12]

And what if my readers are secretly believers, their denial of death actually a smoke screen? What if my readers, as I imagine Laqueur's, are liars, and they too believe the dead are more than dust and more than memories, as the acolytes who whirl around Karl's grave and the towering trees in Highgate cemetery replicate the cult of the saints?

That is Laqueur's position, that death and the dead are at our elbow despite widespread denial. His seven hundred-page tour de force is dedicated

Agosto 20, 2022   9:10 Am

Reading LLL
in Spanish

to showing us just that, its overflowing abundance testimony more to his enthusiastic interest in the topic than the requirements of proof. But what of the denial of denial, something we do unthinkingly every day?

If we listen carefully to our everyday speech, we might notice how we slide between layers of ambiguity and exploit that function of language in relation to the dead. This is what Vinciane Despret does with great calm and subtlety in her book, translated by Stephen Muecke as *Our Grateful Dead*. Laqueur provides history and analysis thereof in abundance, while Despret, the philosopher, meditates on stories that have come her way in Belgium concerning the dead today as they visit people in dreams, in premonitions, and via other channels. Each story she hears from family, friends, and the occasional anthropology book is a story that *weaves together layers of belief and disbelief*, depending on how much the storyteller trusts her to respect the story. The dead seep into the intricacies of plot-making, grammar, and turn of phrase, not to mention gestures of body and face, all of which is what gives life to the dead by means of what, at one point, Despret calls "ontological tact." At another point, she describes such speech as "doing ontological acrobatics, but never in huge leaps."

Which brings to mind the dead husband who performs such leaps, returning at night to have sex with his wife, as told to me recently by a Spanish friend, a story the wife, her aunt, told her when she was twelve years old.

AN ENLIGHTENMENT PERFORMANCE OF CORPSE MAGIC

Given Laqueur's statement that no corpse is left unritualized, and Despret's attention to the subtleties of contemporary beliefs and disbeliefs in the dead as living beings, what are we to make of deliberate assaults on the sanctity of the corpse?

In his 1958 film *The Magician*, set in early modern Sweden, Ingmar Bergman has a proudly materialist medical doctor rolling up his sleeves to perform an autopsy on the corpse of a magician whom he believes to be a fraud. The autopsy is to take place in the dimly lit attic of the prince's castle, where the magician has just pulled off a marvelous trick in front of a select audience including the doctor and the local police chief. The trick consisted in having the coachman, a veritable giant, tied up with invisible chains. This so frightens the coachman that, when released, he turns on the magician and kills him with his bare hands in front of the audience, then flees. The police chief—who has been deeply humiliated by his wife, whom the magician had earlier hypnotized—orders an immediate postmortem when the doctor announces the magician dead.

Alone in the attic with the corpse under a sheet, the doctor scans his notes prior to cutting open the body, only to have the notes strangely whisked from his hands. Other disturbing events follow—strange sounds and moving objects. An amputated arm appears on the desk.

Perturbed, the doctor lifts the sheet covering the corpse and gasps. It is not the body of the magician. It is the corpse of the coachman, who, after being magically chained and unchained, has hanged himself in the laundry room of the palace.

Trying to remain calm, the doctor tells himself he is either dreaming or losing his mind. He crawls on the floor. He loses his glasses. Two boots appear; someone is walking, but all we see are these black boots pacing slowly back and forth crunching the doctor's glasses, those symbols of Enlightenment. The doctor sees only black bars and slats of light as he tumbles down the attic stairs, eventually realizing that the magician is not dead and has switched the bodies. Ontological antics indeed!

Corpses, we might note, seem made for storytelling. We might note, too, that here it is the magic not of the magician but of the Enlightenment that is hard at work on its favorite ready-to-hand material, the human corpse. All in all, we don't quite know what to believe. Is science magic? Is it the other way around? Whatever we might conclude, the magician's brain has eluded the doctor's scalpel, as have the illusions of film, the ultimate medium of the spirit world.[13]

11   *Reenchantment*

The subtitle of Philippe Ariès's book *The Hour of Our Death* promises "a history of Western attitudes toward death" since the Middle Ages. The tension invigorating his text stems from what he sees as the revolutionary change from intimacy with death to its fearsome nonexistence, bringing to mind a not uncommon observation that the repression of death is to our time as the repression of sex was to the nineteenth century. Today, free spirits that we are, we don't even call it death. The word is taboo. We call it "passing," as if to the adventure that is life we add a postscript. Banish the D-word with its horrid clanging, like the closing of a prison cell. I am reminded of the town dump I use in upstate New York. Except it's not called that. It's called the "transfer station." Like "passing," both deal with corpses.

In Laqueur's assessment, despite hard-boiled Enlightenment materialism, respect if not fear of the dead is a constant and as near a universal as you can find. But surely the Enlightenment "wildness" that Ariès emphasizes regarding death is also true and indeed explains the motivation and necessity for Laqueur's book? Hence my dilemma, the dilemma facing the writer: how to address something universal but denied, and not only denied but "wild"?

Fear of the dead and respect of the corpse may endure over millennia, but that does not mean there have not been significant differences over time and place. Laqueur reiterates the persistence of respect for the corpse. Ariès, on the other hand, emphasizes the radical alteration in attitudes brought about by Enlightenment. Both seem right.

But here's the rub. Is it not the case that the Enlightenment's disenchantment of nature actually reenchants death and the corpse, albeit in new ways? In the battle against superstition, is not another form of superstition recruited?

Victor Frankenstein's enlightened teacher in Switzerland, as portrayed by Mary Shelley early in the nineteenth century, takes up cudgels with missionary zeal against alchemy and Renaissance magicians like Agrippa. The result? After days and nights spent in charnel houses and vaults, using the most advanced sciences of the day, Frankenstein delves deep into the scientific form of corpse magic and creates a monster.[1]

In his history of sexuality, Michel Foucault pursues a parallel idea, that exposing the secrets of repressed libido added to its secrecy.[2] In allowing sexual discourse full throttle, sex became a more powerful and enticing secret. Does not the same apply to death and the corpse? Does not their disenchantment bolster their reenchantment?

On this count, enlightenment turns out to be part of the bundle of tricks inherent to what we might read about initiation into secret societies and to what I think of as shamanic logics for dealing with sorcery and spirit attack. I am referring here to the conundrums involved in unmasking as a means of remasking and of disenchantment as a means of reenchantment in which revelation of the secret adds to its concealment.[3] By the same token, enlightenment is most effective where it creates its own taboos, namely taboos against taboo, by which I mean taboos against the mystical notion of taboo, which, however, entail their own, unstated mystical elements, as pungently addressed in a variety of ways by Nietzsche, whose ideas must have been foremost in Foucault's mind in writing his history of sexuality.[4]

Yet reenchantment cannot be a return to the past but, rather, its incorporation. Denial of death amounts to a continuous back-and-forth of disenchantment and reenchantment. We could think of this as a dialectic, but a more fitting image would be a patchwork or mosaic.

In the Global North, we may not tell stories about the vitality of the corpse as the planets whirl around the sun that is the corpse of Karl Marx, but the facts speak for themselves in the tranquility of birdcalls and the odors of the damp forest mixed with what in Enlightenment language we call his "remains."

HENCE THE QUESTION FACING THE WRITER

The question facing me is this: If killing a corpse impacts logic and language, isn't that impact likely to be greater when death is denied? And isn't it likely to be even greater when what is denied is secretly admitted? And further still, what if the corpse killed has been animated so as to kill its killers?

You can think of this back-and-forth of disenchantment and reenchantment as a laminated thought operation analogous to making an omelet, or should I say, *omelette*, which I learned to do in "the French way" from Elizabeth David. One hand moves the hot skillet with the beaten egg back and forth horizontally over the flame. The other hand, using the back side of a spoon, gently rotates the surface of the fragile egg mix producing the desired fluffy sponginess. Let's say taboos regarding death are the back-and-forth, and the Enlightenment taboo of taboo the gentle, fluffing rotation. Voilà! Our current dispensation. Add filler.

In my opinion, taboos concerning the corpse, and certainly the taboos of taboos, loft language. The taboos and the taboos of taboos form barriers, but they also uplift. They censor speech but enthrallingly so. We may avoid saying "dying," but "passing," however fatuous, at least leaves open the door to life after death, strange and spooky as that life might be, rattling the bars of the cage of certainty. "Passing" lets you have your corpse and deny it too.

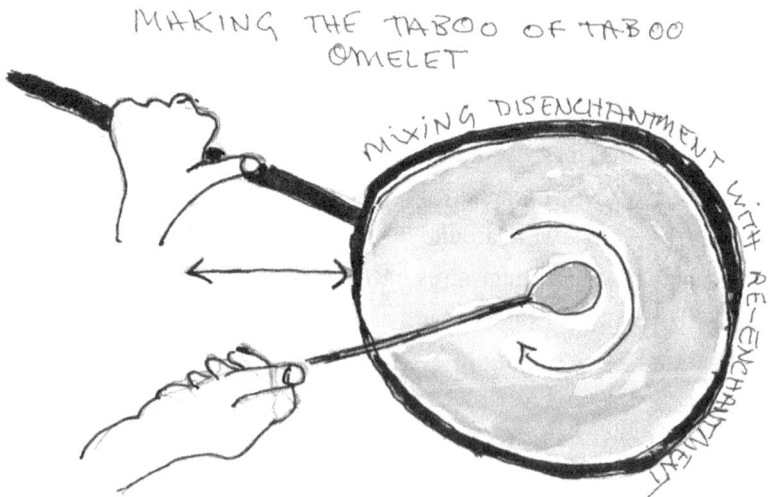

MAKING THE TABOO OF TABOO OMELET

MIXING DISENCHANTMENT WITH RE-ENCHANTMENT

KARL MARX, COMMODITY FETISHISM, AND THE SPIRITS OF THE DEAD

Perhaps surprisingly, to view the situation thus is to endorse Marx's idea of "commodity fetishism," which at one point he likened to then-current European colonial ideas of the "African fetish" as something made by man but attributed to spirits or gods. Against this he posited what he thought of as a materialist, nonspiritualist theory of value based on labor. He also memorably drew a parallel with spirit seances in Europe, Britain, and North America, in which people purported to awaken and receive spirits of the dead, spiritism being a growing fad at the time he was writing *Das Kapital*.

But instead of heaping scorn on benighted commodity fetishists, including ourselves, let's try something else. In keeping with Marx's sarcastic humor and Enlightenment edicts of disenchantment, how about we practice mental jujitsu so as to reenchant the fetish or, better put, allow it to realize its fuller potential? For Marx this would require social and economic revolution birthing a new and different economic structure such as communism or at least what in the USA today is called Democratic Socialism—it's a question of how you make the omelet.

By this I mean taking the fetish to new extremes of liveliness where dead things like corpses become endowed with life, hence divinity. Think of the upmarket prostitute played by Catherine Deneuve in the film *Belle de Jour*, lying faux-dead in her shuddering coffin, opening her eyes for one forbidden moment as her client, fetishizing with zeal, jerks off below.

Spiritism was of widespread interest in Marx's day, and it could be said that the spiritualists' séance provided him with a golden opportunity to explain his insights about the labor theory of value and the fetishism of commodities. Therein "Capital is dead labor," he wrote, "which, vampire-like, lives only by sucking living labor, and lives the more, the more labor it sucks."[5] Think of Count Dracula, who notably sexualizes this scheme by sucking blood from the necks of beautiful upper-middle-class women in London some thirty years after Marx wrote about vampires.

On this reckoning, capital is neither dead nor alive but both. It is a living corpse—like the corpse "arranged" by the corpse magician to seek vengeance against its assassins. "Commodity fetishism"—that star in the Marxist pantheon of ideas—is indubitably corpse magic, and what's more, to the extent that the living corpse sustains capital, we are all stockholders. What, then, would a socialist democratic revolution do?

Was this question uppermost in the mind of Diego Rivera when he painted *Frozen Assets* in 1931 at the height of the Great Depression?

This painting shows a skyline of Manhattan skyscrapers below which, laid out on pallets on the floor of a windowless gray room are inert bodies, all the same, in endless rows. They seem like corpses. Could it be a gigantic morgue? Beneath these "frozen assets" of the worldwide Depression, in a third, subterranean layer, sits a lonely scribe at an office desk, as if keeping a tally of the bodies above. Behind him is a wide, arched doorway with a metal grille; behind it, a guard and the door of a vault. Perhaps these layers are heaven, purgatory, and the inferno, but the more salient connection, it seems to me, is the corpse magic by which the world of the skyscrapers, like the church, lives off the life-in-death below.

René Magritte, a longtime member of the Belgium communist party, has a similar but simpler painting hanging in Belgium's national art gallery. Below a flat horizon, a dark landscape occupies a narrow band at the bottom of the canvas; above is a moody Belgium sky.[6] Like the sugarcane fields in western Colombia, there are no people, animals, trees, or dwellings. But as Magritte's title, *Hidden Labour*, indicates, the land is anything but natural or neutral. As with Rivera's frozen bodies, the brooding mass of land is the repository of dead labor or, should we say, capital, like the land the sugarcane plantations occupy.

What strikes me about the Magritte painting is how different it is from his most familiar works with their impeccable surrealism, cold, clinical, conceptual, and enigmatically comic. But *Hidden Labour* is where surrealism disappears and something heavy and expressionist takes its place with terrible simplicity.

Let us take another look at the fetishism that Marx, in a comic mode saw as providing the mystical infrastructure of capitalism, the salient feature being that thing and spirit hang together as reification and fetishism, two sides of the one coin. Think back to Rivera's frozen assets,

HIDDEN LABOUR

MAGRITTE

down there under your Manhattan floorboards, ready to reanimate, or the eerie silence of Magritte's Belgium landscape, perhaps whooshing past the train window, not a person in sight except for the labor perhaps visible in the curve of the hills where human history and environment unite. Could a sorcerer have envisaged a more propitious situation than this zigzagging metamorphosis of things in which disappeared death reappears, as Rogerio Velásquez says regarding the cadaver, like an errant star aloft on a fiery path?

DANCING NAKED WITH ANGELS ON THE GRAVES

Let us stand on the shoulders of the sorcerer and take the long view of the western European corpse the past two millennia, for is not Christianity itself a leading instance of corpse magic? Paramount here is its founding story, namely the Crucifixion. A humble carpenter is killed by leaders of his own people in concert with the colonial state, following which his corpse is resurrected as a god. In fact, he was a god all along, it turns out, but instead of vengeance his message is love, although in Nietzsche's crabby view, this love was vengeance anyway.

For a long time, then, and not just in a cemetery in western Colombia, corpses have been active agents in social life. They disappeared but found new life in, for example, Halloween, children's books, Disney animations, and Hollywood comedy, to mention but the lighter side of the macabre. We might note that these examples, largely the province of the modern child, are in many respects a repository for what was once adult reality.

Today we adults enjoy the enacted fantasy of Halloween vicariously, via children, dispensing with its disturbing possibilities. (Though "trick or treat" retains the threat of vengeance.) That is not so much denial as a performance of the adult's imagination of the child's imagination, and vice versa. With its dancing skeletons, ghostly ephemera, bats, vampires, and bleeding body parts hanging from the front porch, Halloween is not so much a safety valve, as social scientists would have us believe, but a mnemonic and pathway to the spirits of dead people.

I came across a wild story provided by E. Louis Backman asserting that starting at least by the fourth century after the birth of Jesus, there was dancing over graves led by women in both southern and northern Europe.[7] They were dancing with the angels and the spirits of Christian martyrs, which is to say with those cruelly killed for their faith. The choreography, says Backman, was like that danced to the dead in ancient Egypt, which, according to many authors including Plato, accorded with the movements of the planets. Imagine, if you can, being a naked woman dancing over a buried corpse in parallel with Saturn passing through the orbit of Mars.

It is a measure of the distance we have come that dancing on a grave would now seem the height of disrespect. That reaction has to do not only with modern Western ideas of death but with the idea that dance is transgressive, or potentially so. That was not the case for the first Christian millennium, nor for many centuries thereafter. Yet today you can chant in a choir, levitate as a monk (as Blaise Cendrars extols), but dare not never ever dance in graveyards.[8]

If we consider how communion with the dead in many places outside Europe involves trance, dance, and spirit possession, it is truly remarkable, if not frightening, how stillness, corporeal rigidity, and silence in the presence of the dead or the spirits of the dead became the norm in much of the West.

However, to say that dancing on the grave was not uncommon is not to say it was not marked by transgressive force and danger. They coexist, this desire and this danger, which is Durkheim's and later Bataille's point about the sacred as overwhelmingly a force of attraction *and* repulsion. For according to Backman, the dances were said to be lewd and erotic, with the dancers often naked and drunk. In vain the church passed ordinances against this from the fourth century to 1777, when the last edict was proclaimed.[9] That's fourteen centuries, a major chunk of Christian time.

Let us pause a moment to take this in.

The first point I wish to make is what a shock it is to read of this transgression as a founding moment of Christianity. It unsettles. It is exciting too, and the reason I call for a pause here is to allow what I call an "applied anthropology of shock" to reframe and resituate the enormity of what I call corpse magic and to give it a genealogy.

Second, I wish to underline the fact that initially the dances were not for any old corpse *but specifically for the corpse of a person deliberately killed.* I am here referring to the corpses of the "cult of the saints" killed, and killed most cruelly, for their Christian faith. It was this that made them saints. Being killed, as was Jesus, is well nigh essential for hallowed status. How different, according to Nietzsche, from the ancient Greeks, among whom it was victors, not victims, who were gods. The exaltation of the victim as a source of sacred power comes with what he called the world-transforming power of resentment (what he termed *ressentiment*), based on cunning and double-dealing.

Third, as regards Christianity, for at least fourteen hundred years it was not unknown for funeral rites to involve revelry, sex, dancing, and games. On this account, Dionysian bacchanalia thrived at the core of early and later Christianity (as it does in transmuted form in Evelyn Waugh's satire of a Los Angeles cemetery, *The Loved One*).

Backman notes that the edicts of the church against such graveyard rites object particularly to the following:

> The dances occurred at night
> Sometimes the people were naked
> Sometimes they wore masks
> They beat on drums
> There was much laughter and derision
> They sang devil songs, that is to say magical spells, as well as indecent
>   ditties, all of which were songs for dancing
> There were ball games, arrow-shooting, and stone throwing
> Drunkenness and fornication were common[10]

What shocks history (and anthropology) holds in store for us! Readers in the Global North: go to your nearest cemetery, close your eyes for a moment, and maybe you can see people whirling like planets over the graves. And what a shock to read Frazer of *The Golden Bough* claiming, in *The Dying God*, that the origin of the Olympic games lies in contests held in honor of the dead.[11] Imagine reintroducing funeral games today—the hundred-meter dash, pole vault, and two-hundred-meter freestyle alongside burial and perhaps whispered requests of the dead to win a gold medal. Respect for the dead human body may be universal across time and space. But how that respect is expressed is another matter.

Caution reminds us that these transgressions are known to us only through proscriptive edicts and may represent less people's true actions than what was going on in the imagination of the church fathers. But such dancing could well have been happening, and even if not, what went on in the minds of the holy fathers provides evidence of the imagination required for what I call corpse magic.

In his 1973 lectures on changing attitudes toward death in the West since the Middle Ages, Philippe Ariès presents a similar if less erotic picture of the dances Backman describes. In 1231 the church council of Rouen, for example, forbade dancing in cemeteries or churches. In 1405 another council forbade dancing, gambling, mummers (masked actors), jugglers, theater, musicians, and charlatans. The situation seems pretty much the same as late as 1657. Then, at the end of the eighteenth century, cemeteries were relocated outside the city or at its margins (as they had been in ancient Greece and Rome). Still, the question lingers. Why did the dancing stop? The late eighteenth century seems a grim time for the European corpse. Something momentous was on the way.

CORPSE DEFILEMENT

A genealogy of corpse magic would be woefully incomplete without mentioning the startling role of corpse defilement in Europe. In early modern France, for instance, when the populace was fiercely divided between Protestants and Catholics, the latter exhumed, then drowned or burned their enemy's corpses, or threw them to the dogs, dragged them through the streets and, cut out their genitals and internal organs "which were then hawked through the city in ghoulish commerce."[12] So much for turning the other cheek.

Thomas Laqueur relates how, when the Catholics returned to power in England after defeating Cromwell, bodies were dug up in what he deems acts of revenge. In three days in 1661, twenty-one bodies were unearthed from Westminster Abbey, including those of Cromwell's granddaughter and his ninety-year-old mother, and dumped in a pit in a nearby churchyard. Two days later the bodies of Cromwell and the two others who had condemned Charles I to death were, as Laqueur puts it, "ripped from their desecrated tombs" in Westminster Abbey, taken face down on sleds to Tyburn, hanged, decapitated, and flung in a pit below the gallows while their heads were displayed in different places.[13] Note also Bruce Lincoln's description of the exhumation and display in July 1936, during the Spanish

Civil War, of thousands of long-buried corpses of Catholic priests, nuns, and saints.[14]

Colombia, too, has an overwhelming history of corporeal defilement, as in the massacres involving mutilations of living and barely dead bodies since the era of *La Violencia*, from 1948 to the present. (Did mutilations only begin then? Seems unlikely.) Right-wing paramilitaries with covert and not so covert police, military, and other government support, local or national, have been especially active in this regard since the 1980s, when the US War on Drugs (meaning also the war on leftists) began. As attested in June 2022 by the Colombian Truth Commission their activities have been known to the US government via the CIA since the early 1980s. Bolstered by billions of dollars, provided initially by the Clinton administration, the paramilitaries are well known for their massacres of villagers and subsequent defiling of corpses.

In our age of the screaming power saw the mutilators do not seem to feel the need to give their depredations fancy names, as in the earlier *Violencia* with its poetry of the "necktie cut," the "monkey cut," the "flower-vase cut," and so forth. In our time, the "power-saw cut" suffices.

In any event, exhuming the body of a rival gang member and burning or otherwise destroying it seems to have a long history. Why? Because the corpse is a charmed object. If I initially doubted the efficacy of destroying the corpse as a means of preventing corpse magic aimed at slaying the slayer, I now acknowledge the long-standing tradition of corpse defilement. Imagine Cromwell's body being dragged through the streets face down. Imagine his granddaughter's and his mother's corpses exhumed and dumped.

You can't argue that that was normal for those times. The point is that corpse mutilation was and is transgressive—not normal—and that is why it was done.

12 *Corpse and Temple*

The history of the corpse in the Global North is architectural: at first a snug togetherness of corpse and temple, then, in the wake of the Enlightenment as cemeteries were built on the outskirts of cities and towns, a yawning separation.

This separation coincided with other sorts of spatial dislocation, like the expulsion of slaughterhouses from cities at roughly the same time, followed by the creation of art museums and venues for haut couture taking their negative sacred place, as we shall see.

THE BODY OF THE CHURCH

The corpse is an existential part of the church, as fundamental as its stones and mortar, only more so.

Vampirelike, the church inhales the odor of the corpse and exhales the Holy Spirit. In Bataille's terms, the negative sacred of the corpse becomes, in an endless cycle, the positive sacred of the church. This fantastic alchemy converts the corpse into sacred splendor, and how much more, I wonder, is this likely or unlikely to be the case with the supercharged corpse of someone who has been assassinated?

After about 1800—the dates vary by city, town, and state—this physical connection between church and corpse in Christendom diminished, but the magical connection, if anything, was enhanced. The corpse was henceforth buried in cemeteries outside the city, away from the church. It was defined as unhygienic, a source of disease—a notion that, though disputed by medical experts, has remained firm. The open, gardenlike space of the new cemetery was thought of as an antidote to the purulence of the corpse, a healing space with flowers and trees and soft breezes, each body set apart from the rest, supposedly to minimize contagion and affirm the individuality of the dead person. It sounds like US suburbia. In Dostoevsky's story "Bobok—From Somebody's Library," much is made of this individuality; the interred corpses argue with one another, allowing Dostoevsky ample opportunity to relate their subterranean polyphony to what could not be said during life.

To sum up: for more than a millennium in the West and for three centuries in its colonies such as Colombia, corpse and temple formed a physical unity. The rich lay inside, everyone else, outside but still near the church—although in the colonies, I doubt that included African slaves, freed slaves, or indigenous people. Both inside and just outside the church walls, cadavers were clotted together cheek by jowl, their miasmic sublimity infiltrating the stones of the temple. It was a marvelous system of sacred plumbing, a two-way, push-pull apparatus one might compare with the famous "double pelican" system of two glass retorts used by alchemists transmuting matter into spirit, lead into gold.

The Latin word *sacer* means both pure *and* impure, *impure* here being not simply the absence of the pure but its empowered negation. Similarly, the corpse is disturbingly sacred. Exuding the holiness of the negative sublime, the corpse augments the wattage of the temple. The temple needs the corpse as much as the corpse needs the temple. A win-win situation. The purity of the church depends upon the impurity of the corpse. They feed off one another. It is an infernal machine from one point of view, a blessing from another. Christ's Crucifixion and Resurrection are an instance of this mutuality. Corpse magic aimed at killing the killer is another.

It is not that the corpse is made wholesome by the church, not at all, but precisely that, because of its horror and repellent status, the corpse "charms" the church, adding to its life-force, just as does Christ's naked and mutilated corpse hanging on the walls.

GEORGES BATAILLE'S CORPSE

Then there is Bataille's corpse, not to mention the corpse of Mary Magdalene, or at least a purported digit thereof.

Let me explain. Artist and magus Jesse Bransford told me of the time he visited the Romanesque basilica in the hilltop village of Vézelay in

Burgundy, France, three hours from Paris, where reposes one of the great basilicas of Christendom, a starting point for the Crusades, including the pilgrimage of Richard the Lionheart to Jerusalem, an early version of Christian Zionism.

Jesse was excited at the prospect of seeing the relic of the finger of Mary Magdalene in the crypt, but when he got there was disappointed. You can barely see the finger amid the gold and dazzling light surrounding it, but Jesse made out, he thinks, a diminutive brown phalange, repulsive in the same way as Bataille portrays the big toe in his famous essay of that name.

But other discoveries lay in store. To his surprise he found a plaque in the village commemorating a house where Georges Bataille lived and was told that his body lay in the graveyard several hundred meters from the basilica. Thus, in his mind and in his story the two relics, Mary Magdalene's finger and Bataille's body, kept each other company, a bit like the push-pull apparatus I described earlier.

Truth to tell, Bataille's corpse has become a sacred relic too, as much as Mary Magdalene's finger. In 2021 I too made the pilgrimage to Vézelay, with filmmaker Carolina Saquel. The plaque Jesse saw was affixed to a humble house where Bataille lived with little of the gorgeous view of the surrounding fields with which most of the village, floating in midair, is blessed.

As we walked in search of Bataille's grave I was struck by the size and beauty of the basilica rising, as it were, out of the earth. "Exuberance is beauty," wrote Bataille as the epigraph to *The Accursed Share*, a line he took from William Blake. Searching for the graveyard, we passed through a grove of tall trees like a fairytale forest with no underbrush. It was a threshold to the azure beyond as if, for a moment, the sea itself was within our reach, rolling over the graves.

Eventually we found Bataille's grave, simple in the extreme, a concrete slab on top of a slightly larger slab with Bataille's name and dates of birth and death inscribed so discreetly on the vertical side at the foot of the slab that the barely legible name seemed of no account. Such minimalism seemed inappropriate for the theorist of *dépense*, but the wild red poppies on the ground around made up for that. Nature asserted itself also by mottling the slab with cloudlike patterns of black fungus. Two small cairns

Red Poppies

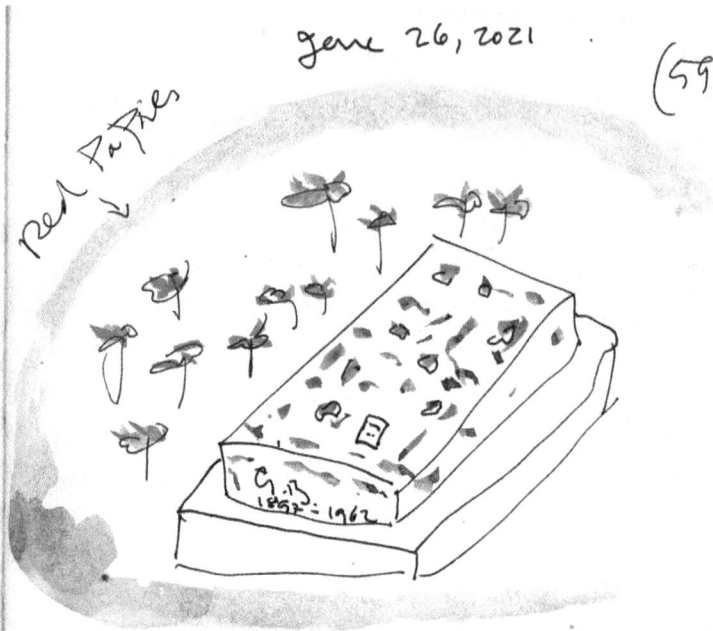

Morbid Fungi white, grey, black
Black, grey, a white cat patrolling!
Simple Notification at foot of grave;

2 small piles of stones
(one on top of both;
L'Impossible
les Editions de minuit.

of stones lay on the grave, the lower one atop Bataille's book *L'Impossible*, published by Les Editions de Minuit in Paris in 1962.

Close to the church as it is, Bataille's grave raises the question as to what extent the new laws prohibiting church-side burial were accepted. Did friends and family of the dead comply? There is a fine story from Bogotá, where for two centuries after the European invasion of the Americas, colonists and their offspring were buried in the precincts of the church. But early in the nineteenth century this changed. The president succeeding Símon Bolívar, namely Francisco de Paulo Santander ("The Man of Laws," 1792–1840), had declared his support for the new laws banning the deposition of corpses in or by the church. Yet his widow secretly unearthed his body from the new graveyard on the periphery of Bogotá and placed it in her home.

TABOO OF THE TABOO

By the late eighteenth and early nineteenth centuries, then, the human corpse had become taboo in a new way, both in Colombian law and in Paris. Its ontological character changed. Now it was matter, but matter out of place, as symbolized by its geographic displacement. And it was matter itself spiritualized—dead matter made all the more strange and scary when deprived of hocus-pocus.

This paradox forms the backbone of Max Horkheimer and Theodor Adorno's *Dialectic of Enlightenment*, their argument being that in negating magic, Enlightenment created new forms of it, as in the extreme case of the ceremonies and race fantasies of the Third Reich.[1]

Less dramatically, their argument amounts to the claim that to overcome magic's prescientific thinking, and so open the door to science, another form of magical thinking was required. This is why I invoke "the taboo of taboo," the need for the magic of science to supersede the magic of magic.

And this is why Horkheimer and Adorno refer to the Enlightenment as "mythic thought turned radical," in effect borrowing from Nietzsche's sustained questioning of the purported value of truth over error.[2] We could also invoke Wittgenstein's claim, in his critique of Frazer's views of magic in *The Golden Bough,* that we have magic embedded in our language, akin to Nietzsche's view that language depends on unrecognized metaphor. (Listen to the last sentence you spoke or wrote and figure out what in it is not based on metaphor.)

Thomas Laqueur plays an Enlightenment trick on Enlightenment, presenting a "back of the envelope" calculation of sources and annual amounts of "organic waste" in London around 1840.[3] The waste that was human corpses came to two thousand tons, while living humans excreted almost a hundred times that in feces, plus 160 to 225 million gallons of urine. Then there was animal excrement: 118,00 tons of horse manure, 52,000 tons from cattle being driven to market, and yet more from pigs trotting to the slaughterhouse. That's 370,000, tons of waste, not counting human urine or pig feces—nearly two hundred times as much as human corpses by weight—most of which was not whisked away in sewers but left in open cesspits. The horror aroused by the allegedly unhygienic human corpse, in other words, had a great deal more to do with the spiritual meaning of the corpse than with its matter, the epitome of "mythic fear turned radical."

THE CATACOMBS OF PARIS

One of the most spectacular instances of the taboo of taboo was the placing of millions of human corpses under European cities in imitation of the burials along the Appian Way in ancient Rome, from which the word *catacomb* is thought to derive. What happened in Paris can be seen as a harbinger of the hygienic revolution Foucault would call "biopolitics." It is also a dramatic instance of corpse magic in the literal sense of that phrase, making crude corpse art out of human skulls and long bones;the hygienic component and the mythic-aesthetic component went hand in hand.

Héricart de Thury, the designer of this underground funereal art, was a scientist, General Inspector of Quarries from 1809 to 1830, and an aristocratic member of the court of Charles X. It was under his direction that the mass of bones removed from the malodorous surface of Paris became underground monuments in disused underground quarries that had supplied the stone to build the city.

Thus we could speak of a fourfold historical movement: (1) distaste at the heaps of corpses putrefying aboveground that sparked a hygienic impulse prior to the political revolution of 1789 and was perhaps its harbinger; (2) massive killing during the Revolution, adding to the already formidable corpse population; (3) mythological incentives, if not necessities, for the Revolution to take advantage of the horrors of the corpse and the autochthonous powers of the underworld; and (4) a mix of science with royalty in the immediate postrevolutionary period in the figure of the General Inspector of Quarries himself.

In Paris, the construction of the catacombs coincided more or less with the formation of cemeteries on the periphery of the city—as if their aboveground pastoral innocence required an antidote, something deep and dank, more deathly, we could say, and more essential than birds and sweet-smelling roses.

In the fourteenth and fifteenth centuries charnel houses, depositories of corpses ("charnel" from the Latin *carnis*, meaning flesh), were built along the walls of the Cimetière des Saints-Innocents in the center of Paris, where the market of Les Halles would later rise, and still later that apex of high culture, the Centre Pompidou. With its exposed air shafts and skeleton, you could surmise that the Pompidou brought the underground of death to the city's surface in a sublimatory flourish. As corpse magic gave way to corpse art underground, so it eventually surfaced as fine art aboveground, as Bataille had suggested with his tongue-in-cheek "dictionary" entry in *Documents* regarding the beheading of royalty and the conversion of the Louvre palace into an art museum as a necessary consequence.[4]

Murals of the Dance of Death known as the *danse macabre* were painted in the cemetery of Saints-Innocents. Side by side with this vision of skeletons dancing their hearts out, all manner of commerce, including sexual, was transacted in the graveyard. It was a miniature city within the city in which sex and death were interchangeable and mutually energizing, a significant backdrop to the Revolution or at least to the movie one could make about it.

This confirms Ariès's notion of people's familiarity with death at that time, a familiarity that had persisted in Christendom for more than a thousand years. These "cities of the dead" within the city enjoyed economic benefits, he tells us, thanks to the Church, which made money from lodging the corpses. People built houses and actually lived there while others came to gamble and dance.[5] In his book *The Funeral Casino*, based on fieldwork in Thailand in the 1990s, Alan Klima portrays something similar, the frenzied gambling that could occur at funerals, on the one hand, and the Tantric Buddhist public display of the rotting corpses of nuns for prolonged meditation in Buddhist temples, on the other.[6]

In Paris between 1787 and 1814, six million corpses, mostly from the Cimetière des Saints-Innocents, were placed beneath the city in the disused quarries. These twenty-seven years coincided with the French Revolution, during which time four cemeteries were made for the victims of the guillotine. You would have to search long and hard to find symbolic connections as striking as these. The geophysical translocation to underground caverns strikes a chord with the idea of social revolution, especially the French Revolution, as both cosmic and chthonic in its reach, abetted by the revolutionary cults, their language and imagery no less than the flow of blood and severed heads.

You might ask why the prerevolutionary dead in the Cimetière des Saints-Innocents could not have been transported elsewhere and deposited in mass graves outside the capital, in the newly created cemetery of Père Lachaise, for instance? But no! Today, as we walk the streets of Paris and sleep in our beds, make coffee in the morning and ride the metro, there they are, the prerevolutionary and revolutionary corpses, a mere sixty feet beneath us. Not even a stone's throw away—you have just to let it drop.

SLAUGHTERHOUSE ART

Like the displacement of the dead from the city to the catacombs and to cemeteries, so the slaughterhouses of Paris and other European towns and cities were displaced to the periphery at roughly the same time. Out of sight and effectively out of mind, today the meat people eat, the world over, especially in the USA, comes from nowhere. The unceasing killing of animals is rendered invisible. But why?

In a series of jaw-dropping interventions between 1929 and 1931 in the journal *Documents*, Georges Bataille inserted mischievous "dictionary" entries. Neither in alphabetical nor any other order, they were often accompanied by eye-catching photographs. One such entry was "Slaughterhouse," another, "Museum." The former contained the radioactive observation that although a French abattoir at that time did not require religious rites as in other countries or at other times, it was nevertheless *cursed and quarantined like a plague-ridden ship* because "the sacred horror of killing an animal is *not acknowledged*," an idea that would surface twenty years later in Bataille's discussion of the animals on the walls of Lascaux.

Sensitive to Bataille's observation that the geographical displacement of the slaughterhouse and the decapitation of royalty occurred at about the same time, Denis Hollier drew attention to the conversion of the king's palace, the Louvre, into an art museum where, as Bataille would have it, the victorious bourgeoisie could stroll on Sundays, purifying themselves with art. "At the heart of beauty," mused Hollier, "lies a murder, a sacrifice, a killing (no beauty without blood). The origin of the museum, says Bataille, would thus be linked to the guillotine."[7]

As for my own city of New York, the same mythic scenario has unfolded in the Meatpacking District on the west side of lower Manhattan. Was a time, few respectable citizens ventured into its streets, full of huge trucks, prostitutes, and gargantuan bloodied men carrying sides of beef and hogs. Then, almost overnight, with a whisk of neoliberalism's fairy wand, all that disappeared. What took its place were the new Whitney Museum, high-end clothing stores, expensive restaurants, clubs, and an elevated park, the "High Line," inspired without (as far as I know) accreditation by the Coulée verte René Dumont in Paris.

René Dumont was an anticapitalist ecologist, hardly the ethos you'll find along the High Line winding its way through the heartlands of High Capitalism. Similar sleights of history occur throughout the surrounding forty-four transformed acres: *Meatpacking District* appears on doorways and windows of opulent palaces of consumption. "Meatpacking"—a curious if not sinister moniker, conjuring the work of ghouls sorting, assembling, and preparing barely dead animals for market. Yet signs bearing the word are everywhere—the older and hence more authentic the sign, the better—as art and fashion seek to benefit from the corpse of the old and the dead animals much as the church, prior to the nineteenth century, derived a charge from the corpses beside it.

Shop windows in this restored Meatpacking District are themselves art museums, extensions of the Whitney, only the art is a little cheaper. "Anthropologie" is one such store, "Rag & Bone" another. The district's hardscrabble past is not so much eradicated as incorporated, its infamous, cursed and quarantined character reclaimed as edgy fashion. The procession from the slaughterhouse to your designer jeans with their artificial holes and your visits to modern art in the Whitney is not such a long march.

Bataille's slaughterhouse essay was published with five full-page photographs by Eli Lotar of a slaughterhouse on the outskirts of Paris at the park of La Villette, known by butchers as "Blood City." As if to ram home the sacred horror, not only of killing animals but of what the displacement of the slaughterhouse meant to the spirit of the city, the photographs emphasize the blood- and grease-smeared trail of carcasses dragged to the exit. One iconic image shows the white forelegs of cattle cut off at the knee, neatly placed in a row by an exit. It was the ultimate symbol of displacement: ready to trot but now cut off at the knee.

With the slaughterhouses now on the periphery of the city, the people of Paris no longer heard the lowing of cattle, the bleating of sheep, the squealing of pigs. Nor did they inhale the stench or have to step carefully around strange liquids seeping onto the street as kids were rushed past. All of that disappeared. The world turned a corner, squeaky clean. We have, since then, separate realms: in the one, fables, children's picture books, and cartoons showing frolicking lambs and dewy-eyed cows; in the other, a lamb chop sizzling in the pan.

Before, if you were rich and could afford it, you might recall, when you bit into a steak, the smells and sights of the slaughterhouse, if only subliminally. As a kid you might have seen the animals driven to slaughter, as Leopold Bloom describes in Dublin. But now the steak tastes different. No longer is it part of a Wagnerian *Gesamtkunstwerk*, or "total work of art." Today the killing is elsewhere, and the lamb, steak, or pork chop in the supermarket comes sanitized and sealed in styrofoam on its petit diaper.

TABOO OF TABOO AS APOTROPAISM

So far I have journeyed back in Western corpse-time to confront our fears, our denial, and above all our Enlightenment culture of taboo of taboo. I have paid special attention to instances of corpse magic that confront or engage that taboo of taboo. This is *not* to negate the taboo of taboo, an impossible feat, but rather to appropriate it. What that entails is the applied anthropological maneuver of outmaneuvering one form of magic with another. In other words, an exercise in apotropaism, meaning magic that blocks magic.

This is not to explain or reduce belief and behavior to something more basic. To the contrary, it is like moving along the signifying chain created by corpse magic, by its pathos no less than its horror and estrangement, even its humor.

Could it be that by so doing I am entering the ranks of corpse magicians, no longer the neutral observer but caught up in the melee, adopting an activist role? Perish the thought. Am I urging on the ensorcelled corpse so as to slow down the slayers, if not stop them altogether?

That would seem right.

But then would that not merely perpetuate the cycle, the cycle of *apotropaica*, as the killers sharpen their magical defenses so they can outmaneuver corpse magic and continue their killing sprees? My mind flashes back to my bodyguard, beholden to San Benito, lighting a candle each morning on waking and praying to the souls in purgatory for protection.

Or maybe my motivation comes from what I have already described, an anthropology of so-called primitive societies wherein it is reported that the slain inhabits the slayer, stupendously so in the case of the Arawete in Brazil, cited by Viveiros de Castro, who quotes Heraclitus as epigraph, thereby opening his account to ancient Greece, hence foundational aspects of Western belief as regards the mystical consequences of murder.

If so, how is it that these consequences disappeared?

Have they disappeared?

To the extent those foundational aspects still adhere, what would it take to reinstate them as forceful and living energies in the bodies of killers in the USA, especially but not only the police killing three people per day? It's a naïve, even stupid question. But I can't help wondering.

Reading this, I realize that this question too is an attempt at reenchantment, that this text unspooling before you is exactly that, noting that disenchantment and reenchantment circulate through each other's shadow, most especially and decisively in the shadow cast by the assassinated human body. Did not Rogerio Velásquez, in his study of the rites of death in the Chocó in Colombia sixty years ago, state that a magician can work on the shadow of the corpse of an assassinated person so that it dazzles and thereby freezes the assassin?

Is that what I am inspired or victimized by?

Any connection with Chocó-like worlds or with ancient worlds foundational of the West, I conclude, is not to be understood as linear or crooked or spiraling, whatever, but as a montage or mosaic in which pasts exist as medleys laid over the present such that the tension between them cracks like unused joints.

CORPOREAL KNOWLEDGE AND THE ART OF DYING

Susan Sontag writes, "We no longer study the art of dying, a regular discipline and hygiene in older cultures, but all eyes, at rest, contain that knowledge. The body knows. And the camera shows, inexorably."[8]

So we know without knowing we know.

Camera and body, alive or dead, are one. What sort of knowing is that? Is it resonant with the slain inhabiting the slayer?

That's from Sontag's introduction to Peter Hujar's 1970s photographic portraits of people with AIDS—a drawn-out, fatal illness, far different from the lightninglike assassinations of which I speak, yet similar in the way corpse magic works. If anything encouraged the exploration and innovations of an "art of dying" in the USA in the decades before COVID, it was AIDS. I am recalling AIDS funerals and the waves of collective love and friendship by the dying person's bed. With COVID, by contrast, you were on your own, while with police assassination, the language of law holds center stage and the mayor hands out tax dollars as compensation to the families of the assassinated and the killers go free, part of a day's work.

Tolstoy's story "The Death of Ivan Ilyich" makes clear with what obstacles an art of dying must contend. But Sontag, who had already survived breast cancer with lymph-node involvement when she wrote Hujar's introduction, and who would suffer other cancers, goes on to wonderfully complicate the idea of an "art of dying" by saying that the *body* knows the knowledge behind this art, as does the *camera*.

THE CORPSE AS STRESS TEST OF
ENLIGHTENMENT RIGOR

There is something else to consider here. Could we say that enlightenment itself depends on the corpse as some sort of stress test of Enlightenment rigor, and that if we pass that test, we are free to roam unmoored?

If you can free yourself from superstition and morbid mysticism concerning the corpse and death, you are to be admitted into the corps of resolute freethinkers, as Ingmar Bergman illustrates in his film *The Magician*.

Or take the morgue worker in the now-legendary TV series *The Wire*, calmly eating a sandwich during his lunch break, right beside the corpse of a murdered witness. No sweat. But why show this if not to shock? Is not this lunchtime rendezvous between the living, the dead, and a sandwich all the more shocking because of its calm everydayness?

EXPLOITING FLOW

One way of thinking about the corpse magic I describe in the cemetery is to see it as an act of piracy, intervening in the flow of the dead that sustains the magic of the church.

Corpse magic exploits this flow, channeling it into revenge so as to slay the slayer, while the church, based on the myth and magic of the Crucifixion, tries to channel that magic elsewhere.

Let us return for the moment to Hertz's observation that, worldwide, no amount of ritual can appease the restless spirits of people who have died from violence. But Hertz does not take into account that sorcerers can channel those restless spirits into vengeance. Bearing this in mind, we could read Nietzsche as saying that the spirit of the dead Christ was just such a restless spirit, but one that broke the mold. Instead of attacking his killers, Christ sought to control them by turning the other cheek.

In other words, I am looking at Christianity as a death-cult based on the Crucifixion and also on pre-Christian practices in which the god sacrifices him or herself. Reading Frazer's *Golden Bough* with an eye to its pre-Christian stories and its theme of the *dying god*, I realize it would have been more accurate for its author to write of the *slain god* and to emphasize that Christianity gave this slain god an unexpected future. The ecstasy and violence of sacrifice and self-sacrifice were transmuted with all their force into an ecstasy of non-ecstasy, in Nietzsche's terms an Apollonian hijacking of the Dionysian impulse, meaning a calculated repression of the instincts. This appropriation is now itself being appropriated by evangelicals who, swaying and singing, return to Dionysiac roots that put them in the same register as the gangsters, which accounts for the tremendous popularity of evangelicals worldwide and their decisive voting power in the USA and in Colombia presidential elections.

By having pagan murder grounded in ritual as the origin story for the many volumes of his work, was not Frazer practicing a form of corpse magic, too, returning repeatedly to the scene of the crime in its many iterations?

His inquiry and incitement was the story of the priest of Nemi circumambulating an oak tree with a golden bough in the grove of Diana near Rome, which he himself visited. The story was that when he grew old, the priest was slated to be killed by a younger man, who in turn would be assassinated when he aged, ad infinitum. We might emphasize the sacrificial or self-sacrificial quality of this and follow Mauss and Hubert in locating the origins of sacrifice in the god killing himself. Or we might allow it to blossom out to include the golden bough of the oak, the surging life and decay of the seasons and the round of life itself from birth to death, as does Frazer. But whatever implication we follow, the singular act is the spilling of blood in the sacred grove, making it sacred, which makes me realize that the book on corpse magic you are now reading is indisputably a rendition of *The Golden Bough* and the Bible adapted to present circumstance.

THESES ON THE PHILOSOPHY OF HISTORY

"Not even the dead shall be safe," exclaimed Walter Benjamin in his last text, handwritten on aerogrammes addressed to his Paris address while in flight from the Third Reich in 1940 to Spain, where he killed himself. On almost every page of his "Theses on the Philosophy of History" he invokes the Messiah as a vengeful spirit, albeit an anarchist-trending, Marxist-inflected Messiah bent on vengeance.

While much has been written on the mystical idea of history presented in this text, and to a lesser extent on its anarchist thrust, as far as I know *no one has seen it as a vengeance text*. Yet in its scorn of chronological accounts of history and in its consummate outrage at the German left and 1930s Soviet-style communist doctrine for neglecting payback in favor of a supposedly better future, Benjamin's theses underscore a sense of the past erupting into the present, which alters, no matter how briefly, time understood as an homogenous flow. It is a process in which images from the past converge unexpectedly with images in the present, as in montage.

MONTAGE

A curious understanding of montage empowers Benjamin's text on the philosophy of history. Images are one thing. Images in states of political emergency (as in the USA in the time I am writing in 2024) are something else. They are likely to be saturated with tension and come if not in batches then as pairs separated by a before and after. Hence not images but "dialectical images," not Carl Jung but Aby Warburg's notion of image as a stilled movie entering the body of the perceiver. It is vengeance that maintains an image of the past smoldering like an ember ready to burst into flame, yet elusive and intermittent.

This is relevant to corpse magic, which, after all, is the recent past come alive through the medium of the ensorcelled corpse. It is the image of the slain person that comes at night into the deranged sleep of the slayer making him eventually die of insomnia compounded by terror and madness.

Insomnia seems too balmy a way of describing what is happening here. Not just lack of sleep or being unable to sleep, not just the wearing away of body and soul through fatigue, but the nocturnal state of confrontation of malignity in which the image of the slain burns its way into the being of the slayer, as Plato noted long ago. It is an old story.

PREPOSTEROUS EQUATIONS

Montage is basic to what I will call "preposterous equations" when I overlap corpse magic in a Colombian cemetery with the killing fields of the

USA, specifically the police killing three people per day. I see the overlap not as a cause-and-effect relationship but as co-occurring realities in a globalized drug-engorged universe in which differences and similarities grate together. The magic in one reality (Colombian cemetery) does not so much highlight the apparent absence of magic in the other reality (US police killing) as expand our capacity for thinking about the slayer-slain nexus.

After all, it is not that strange. We think all the time in contrasts and overlays. What is strange, perhaps, on my part, is "freezing" this state of affairs before it gets "straightened out" by more conscious, less imageric deliberation. All I am doing is rotating the kaleidoscope of everyday as well as historical consciousness.

As regards the "calling" of the past into the present thanks to the montage of dialectical imagery, is this not performed daily when something that purportedly happened two thousand years ago is solemnly evoked, as in the Catholic Mass? We eat Christ's flesh. We drink his blood. The remote past is remote no longer. We are catapulted through time and space, where bodies and images intersect to become one with his Crucifixion, transported thus by the church's practice of corpse magic.

Recall that with corpse magic I am talking of more than death and of more than corpse. I am talking of killing and of corpses that are the result of killing, like what happened to the carpenter from Nazareth. It is at this juncture that church and state kidnap the spiritual effluence emitted by the slain-slayer nexus, which becomes, in fact, the continuously reproduced foundation of Church and State. Dramatic and spectacular, the Crucifixion was the transfer point channeling the magic of the state.

In an early essay, "Critique of Violence," the young and anarchistically inclined Walter Benjamin famously distinguished *law-making, state-founding, violence* from *law-maintaining violence*, exploring how they come together.[9] This, as we shall see, is especially the case with murder by police, which, like the Catholic mass, amounts to a continuous merging of myth with the here and now.

But then why did Benjamin harp on the *elusiveness of the images* that history throws our way in states of emergency? Was it because, as montaged images bound to a mystical "now-time," they are bound to what in his 1929 essay on surrealism he called "the body-image sphere," yielding "a profane illumination"?

In other words, it seems that image passes into corporeality, into corpus, into corpse—as with the sorcery of corpse magic.

13 *The Funeral March*

I keep wondering why the priest was worried to the extent of building his cemetery wall, and within it such innovations as an enlarged church, a renovated paupers' grave, a building for postmortem examinations, and hundreds of meters of aboveground concrete slots for coffins. Until COVID hit, the graves in the soil were being emptied out, leaving at least half the ground area bare in the shadow of the mighty wall, which raises the question as to whether the wall was a vanity project, the sort of thing you might find in a novel or a movie about a crazed priest protecting his corpses?

The fact that the priest, a white man, grew up in this largely Black town as part of a family that supplied several priests, one of whom achieved high office in the provincial capital, suggests that he had not only a firm grasp of provincial power and funds but a finely grained sense of local culture. That there was a considerable amount of money involved suggests that others were behind him, that this reconstruction was grounded in politics and social networks, not individual whim.

Nevertheless, I do think the wall was a "vanity project" as strange, in its way, as corpse magic itself. It was religious sculpture, "environmental art," you could say, exactly the sort of thing Bataille had in mind with his notion of *dépense*, meaning spending for the hell of it, the unprofitable, anti-utilitarian, exultant gesture done for the sake of extravagance. It was religion in another key, like Trump's (and then Biden's) border wall.

Or was it the turning of the wheel such that corpse and church, once together, then separated thanks to hygiene, were reunited, the cemetery becoming, de facto, a church, except now with its new works the church was coming to the dead, construing a Church of the Space of Death. Yet the practice of corpse magic would be unaffected by the new wall. Families could still hire or persuade a sorcerer to arrange the corpse in their home as usual before the body got to the cemetery.

What's more, the logic is such that you never ever know if corpse magic was actually carried out. It could be simply a rumor to rattle the killer (and I suspect that's probably true in most instances).

At the end of the day, you have to wonder whether, with its spectacular wall, the church is not amplifying corpse magic? Didn't the priest tell me that people brought black cords to him to be blessed?

SACRED GEOGRAPHY: A PARTICULAR HISTORY

Questioning the motivation for the wall got me thinking about changes in psychogeography whose key moments I imagine as the following: In the beginning, so to speak, we have women dancing naked, singing lewd songs on graves of the cruelly killed in the early Christian period.[1] Then for a thousand years, from around 800 AD till the Enlightenment and the French Revolution, corpses were buried in the church or next to it. The bond between church and corpse, you could say, provided the sacred center of the social world of Christendom and its colonies.

Around 1800, the cemetery is moved from the church to the outskirts of the city, and the same displacement befalls the slaughterhouse.

Like a charmed snake, mourners now walk from the church to the gravesite or else follow the hearse in a car or a horse-drawn coach, as memorably occurs in James Joyce's *Ulysses*. The charmed snake maps out the sacred axis of the town, no longer centered on the physical proximity of church and cemetery. The reciprocal "blood transfusion" between church and the corpse buried in the churchyard, between the pure and the impure as two halves of the sacred, becomes stretched and tenuous as the cemetery acquires relative autonomy.

Yet is not the procession of mourners a lifeline preserving the older intimacy? The funeral procession performs the siphon-function of the corpse transfusing spirit power back and forth between church and graveyard. Corpse and church may have drifted apart, but the funeral march ties them together.

It is a procession as much through mental space as physical, a procession that unfurls the montage principle in grand display. Take Leopold Bloom in *Ulysses*, jostled as the horse-drawn carriage carries him to the cemetery to bury an acquaintance. Joyce modeled *Ulysses* on Homer's *Odyssey*, brought up to date in Dublin with all manner of montaged overlaps of similarity and difference combining texts more than two thousand years apart.

In Homer's book XI, Ulysses, aided by the witch Circe, visits Hades so as to greet the dead and gain advice on how best to find his way home (which is basically what most visitors to any cemetery are doing today, dipping into the underground so as to get home). In Joyce's rendering, the heroic, masculine tone of pre-Socratic Homer is displaced by the mundane and seriocomic as Bloom, our modern "hero," daydreams in the carriage. He is sensitive to the attraction of the corpse, as when he sees an old woman peeping through her blinds as the carriage passes. "Extraordinary the interest they take in a corpse," he says to himself. "Glad to see us go we give them such trouble coming. . . . Never know who will touch you dead."[2]

Suddenly the carriage stops to make way for a herd of cattle and sheep being driven to the slaughterhouse. We recall Bataille's "hygienic" displacement of cemetery *and* slaughterhouse from center to periphery. Tomorrow is killing day. The best cuts are exported, Bloom says to himself as the carriage makes its way through the herd. "Roast beef for old England," he muses, while here the "hide, hair, horns," the by-products of the slaughterhouses, are destined for "tanneries, soap, margarine."

The carriage passes a tavern at a sharp corner where once a "hearse capsized. . . . A coffin bumped out on to the road. Burst open. Paddy Dignam shot out . . . in a brown habit too large for him. Red face: grey now. Mouth fallen open."

In the graveyard Bloom's mind wanders to its sexual allure. He thinks of "whores in Turkish graveyards. Learn anything if taken young. You might pick up a young widow here. Men like that. Love among the tombstones. Romeo. Spice of pleasure. In the midst of death we are in life. Both ends meet. Tantalizing for the poor dead."[3]

Graveyards are sites of sacrilege, for humor as well as sex. The caretaker of the cemetery tells Bloom a story of two drunks stumbling around in the cemetery one foggy evening looking for the grave of a friend named Mulcahy. Eventually they find it. Looking up, one of the drunks sees a statue of Christ on the cross erected by the widow and says, "Not a bloody bit like the man. . . . That's not Mulcahy, whoever done it."[4]

Bloom's mind wanders to the soil. "I daresay the soil would be quite fat with corpsemanure, bones, flesh, nails. Charnelhouses. Dreadful. Turning green and pink decomposing. . . . Of course the cells or whatever they are go on living."

Like my friend Regina musing about worms swarming sui generis in the interior of the corpse, Bloom opines that "they must breed a devil of a lot of maggots. Soil must be simply swirling with them. Your head it simply swurls."[5] It seems like the mind in the cemetery or on its way to the cemetery midst the funeral march also swurls, breeding a devil of a lot of ideas and swarming images. That is to say, there is a resemblance between the richness of corpsemanure and the richness of thought—and something else, something to do with corpse magic and what I call the Nuer-Effect, meaning the insinuation of the spirit of the slain into the body of the slayer.

Before Bloom gets to the cemetery his carriage passes a gloomy house, its garden full of weeds. Here a man had been murdered by his brother, they say, and Bloom's mind turns to people's morbid interest in reading about murder and also to the reading of eyes, to reading "the murderer's image in the eye of the murdered."[6]

Here the eyes of the dead person act as a camera, a spiritual camera, like when Walter Benjamin in his essay on the storyteller says that the expressions on a dying person's face manifest their life, especially aspects of which they were unaware. These expressions, he assures us, provide the authority of storytelling. He does not write here in the singular but in the plural; not look but *looks*; not expression but *expressions*, "a sequence of images," as with cinema:

> Just as a sequence of images is set in motion inside a man as his
> life comes to an end—unfolding the views of himself under which
> he has encountered himself without being aware of it—suddenly in
> his expressions and looks the unforgettable emerges and imparts to
> everything that concerned him that authority which even the poorest
> wretch in dying possesses for the living around him. This authority is
> at the very source of the story.[7]

THE EYE OF THE CORPSE
SHOWS THE MURDERER

Compare this with the idea that we might see an image of the murderer in the victim's eye, affirming the spiritual bond tying slayer to slain, the starting point of my inquiry.

Like film whirring through a cinema projector, Bloom's carriage rolls on to the cemetery, jolting from scene to scene, blending events outside the carriage with scenes within himself. Why! His could be a murderer's eye too! And we are reading his eye now, enlarging before our eyes to become a novel, or should I say "a novel," which, thanks to montage—ancient myths and storytelling plied over modernist inner consciousness and Dublin streets—became the blue-ribbon sacred of European modernism.

14 *Disappearance of the Death Watch*

Why is the death watch now largely a relic in the plantation town of my concern? What does that imply about the changing significance of death?

Could there be a perverse mathematical function at work: as the number of murders rises, death rites diminish? There is terrible irony in the fact that participation in the death vigil is discouraged out of fear of being violated or even killed if one is out at night.

Another reason given for the decline of the death watch is the increased presence of Evangelicals, who have come, over the past thirty years, to constitute perhaps 30 percent of the town's population, and who limit their ritual to the night of the death.

On the first night of the Catholic *novena*, or death watch (as I recall from the 1970s), mourners would gather at the dead person's home, where the corpse was displayed. Women with their rosary beads stood by the body, reciting prayers and singing psalms; the men stood or were seated outside the house, chatting. After the burial, there would be eight nights of smaller gatherings, until the ninth night, on which a larger group again assembled. Looking back with the eyes of the present, I am overwhelmed at the ease with which the women performed this role, making their own church, so to speak, in domestic space.

Now, however, the death watch, which existed in many cultures worldwide, is disappearing or gone in Colombia, its place taken by a one-night gathering in a commercial funeral parlor. How could it become extinct almost overnight?

Death was earlier displaced in Christendom beginning in the late eighteenth century when corpses were moved from the church to the cemetery outside the city, and now the death vigil has been moved from the personal home to the commercial "funeral home" or "funeral parlor," appropriating the name of the room in the home where the death watch used to occur.

In the 1970s the *novena* in the plantation town was lavish by local standards. It had a potlatch quality, with gifts of food and drink bestowed upon the people attending. On the first night, people viewed the corpse in an open coffin placed chest-high on a table in the deceased's house. Candles were lit, small children lifted to view the face. The men moved outside, chatting till the early hours of the morning. Coffee and aguardiente brandy were served every hour or so, as were, before the 1990s, cigarettes. The sense of companionship and even, dare I say, love was flowing and intense. Many people came great distances by bus and slept on whatever they could. The women stayed inside with the corpse until late at night. They prayed. They sang old church songs, some in Latin. It was beautiful and more heartfelt than any church service. In the early hours of the evening, cars passed, as did pedestrians and cyclists. The hallowed space was open to the street. Anyone could wander in.

I recall a *novena* in the countryside in the 1970s for a young woman who had worked as a live-in servant in faraway Bogotá. We walked to the house through the moonless night with candles cupped in large leaves to shield the flame. It felt like a pilgrimage. Mourners emerged in the night from all directions. There must have been more than a hundred people. The night was alive.

In his 1958 book on voodoo in Haiti, Alfred Métraux emphasized the importance of death and burial there, how poor peasants would mortgage their farms, he said, to ensure a decent funeral, as if all life was but a preparation for death. It certainly felt like that into the 1980s in and around the sugarcane town where I was living. Some people suggest that today a death due to homicide is more likely than a natural death to prompt a *novena*. I recall the intense solidarity I felt attending the *novena* in the 1990s for the young man found shot dead in the trunk of his car that I described earlier. I recall also the crowded *novena* I attended for a young woman killed by her boyfriend in 2001, who then killed himself. It was heavy with grief and shock, not to mention maudlin fascination with the crime. The death watch allowed for a true catharsis, for emotions bound to memories to intensify and spill over in ways that a church service could not.

So what happens to society when the *novena* disappears? And what happens to the corpse?

"Nine nights into my death," said terror-stricken Luis Alejandro Velasco to himself early March 1955, of nine nights without food or water on a raft.[1] He had been swept overboard into the Caribbean from the Colombian destroyer *Caldas* sailing from Mobile, Alabama, to Cartagena. He was sure he was dying. He wanted to die. He etched the passing of each day on the side of the raft. When he got to the ninth day he felt that his home in far-off Bogotá was at that moment full of family and friends for the last night of his *novena*. Tomorrow the altar would be disassembled, and little by little, he told the young reporter by the name of Gabriel García Márquez, people would become accustomed to his death.

Of all the desperate nights on the sea, this was the worst. Each wave recalled the moment he was swept overboard. "They say," he reminds us, "that when a person dies they re-trace their steps. That's pretty much what was happening to me, still alive."

Retracing his steps, he felt one moment he was back on board the destroyer, wedged with his shipmates between contraband refrigerators and stoves. With each wave washing over the raft he felt the wave that swept him off the ship. With each minute of his imagined *novena*, his nine days of solitude, fear, hunger, and thirst would return neatly etched, he said, like in a movie.[2]

So here I am wondering about the movie imagined by this living-deadman, Luis Alejandro Velasco, and whether, in the case of corpse magic, the corpse made potent by sorcery deploys the movie of living-death over and over again to kill the killer, or whether the killer does this to himself?

Perhaps it's all up to the corpse, for does not assassination resemble being swept overboard into the sea? Might not a corpse that has been subject to corpse magic be more than simply physically present at its *novena*, which, in effect, is the occasion of its resurrection?

In any event, we might conclude that death ritual has shrunk, except for (1) the procession with the coffin from the church to the cemetery; (2) the gangster rituals within the cemetery, now outlawed by police; and (3) corpse vengeance magic, which offers a glimpse into what the spirit of a freshly killed human being can perform, reliving the catastrophe of assassination as if in a movie.

When asked today, people in town tell me that the *novena* has been abandoned because it is too expensive. But they never said that twenty years ago. Indeed, the whole point was to spend and spend big. Rogerio Velásquez describes the banquet in the Chocó in the 1960s on the first or last night of the novena as including chickens, pigs, and bush animals, liquor . . . and disorder.[3]

People in the plantation town are quick to say that nowadays it's dangerous to host or attend a *novena* as a rival gang may attack—that you are at risk walking or taking a motorbike taxi at night. Commercial funeral homes close at midnight, are thought to provide better security than a private home, and are a lot cheaper than a *novena*.

In my experience, the *novena* was what separated the countryside from the city and the lumpen-peasant class from the urban middle class. I have never heard of a middle-class *novena*. The mere thought to my mind is ridiculous, soulless gatherings in a commercial funeral parlor with long faces frozen in silence. I've had the feeling, possibly exaggerated, that the *novena* I knew would be considered horribly transgressive by middle-class Colombia and that death was more feared by the middle classes because they've lost that ritual, to the degree they had it.

Like the speed-up in everything, it seems people in much of the world have shortened death to an alienating mini-ritual observed in silence. In place of collective rites there is an individualized psychic numbness with little sense of the spirits of the dead activated through song and collective force.

Yet despite Norbert Elias's "civilizing process" and Philippe Ariès's assessment of modern death as a soulless affair, we must acknowledge at the same time an imaginative consumer-oriented approach to death rituals, as if the drama of death cannot be shoved aside no matter how crass modern life has become. The current interest in cremation in the USA and Colombia presents, for instance, another form of "corpse magic." In the USA, cremation offers a variety of fetishes: having your ashes pressed into a diamond, becoming part of a coral reef, being shot into space—marvelously inventive escapes from silent inwardness, far exceeding anything in Evelyn Waugh's novel *The Loved One* or Jessica Mitford's *The American Way of Death*, both written more than a half century ago by British authors reacting to grotesque aspects of America's culture of death.

But none of that matches the florescence of ritual that followed the death of the inner-city gangster in the largely Black town whereof I write. It is as if they not only go together—death and gangsters—but are more morally imbricated than church and corpse ever were. Gangster funerals have given burial new life.

As for Black communities in the USA, Ida Harris writes:

> Black funerals are hands down the Blackest environment known to Black folks, where raw forms of Blackness are exercised—aesthetic, void of dress code, just "come as you are," suited and booted, with colorful, elaborate hats, or oversized T-shirts honoring the deceased; celebration, gospel, grief, rage, repentance, the organ and its sonorous chords melded with guttural chords of the vocalist—it all goes down. For African Americans, the homegoing is the ultimate form of liberation. It is one of few Black spaces that has not been permeated with whiteness.[4]

But it was, she writes, not so during slavery in the USA.

SLAVERY AND BURIAL IN COLOMBIA

From its beginning, the Spanish colony that is today called Colombia was hostile to the *novena* as practiced by slaves from Africa and their descendants. Its prohibition was demanded early on in the late sixteenth century by the celebrated Jesuit San Pedro Claver, "Patron Saint of the Slaves," famous for his hands-on concern for the physical and spiritual welfare of the African slaves then pouring into Cartagena on Colombia's Caribbean coast. It is often stated, surely exaggerated, that over his lifetime he baptized three hundred thousand slaves. Yet he bitterly opposed the *novena* of the slaves for its "deplorable drunkenness, excesses of all sorts, and the pagan rites thus inspired."[5]

What could be more crucial to the slave owners and to the enslaved than the rites of death? Such rites, surely, offered a potent channel for the Church of the whites to assert its hegemony. What's more, as the saint's comment indicates, there was a gut-level repulsion among at least the

Jesuits to slave rites of death—repulsion that was expressed in the 1960s in the Chocó, where the *novena* was cast by the church in an official document as "against civilization and hygiene."[6]

As I sift through possible reasons for the Patron Saint of the Slaves to outlaw the slaves' *novena*, it strikes me that the most offensive reason is the one he stated: that the mourners seemed to be enjoying themselves in their "deplorable drunkenness, excesses of all sorts, and the pagan rites thus inspired." I am reminded of similar behavior in Europe as described by Backman and Ariés in an earlier chapter.

That the *novena* lived on vigorously in the Chocó, as described by Velasquez in 1961, and in the plantation town I describe into the 1980s, strikes me as a great cultural achievement. But today in the agribusiness town, the *novena* barely exists. What's more, it seems that nowadays the *novena* is likely to occur, if at all, only for deaths due to assassination. It is then that the corpse demands more than the Church on its own can deliver. Is that why this book on corpse magic came into being, to make up for the demise of the death watch?

15   *State Execution*

From at least 1500, state execution in England and elsewhere in Europe was thought to create or possibly create magically potent cadavers. The just-executed corpse could be healing, especially, it seems, where the possibility of sorcery and occult influence lurked.

For example, in his story "The Withered Arm," set in southwest England and written in 1888, Thomas Hardy describes a young woman in an unhappy marriage whose arm is mysteriously withering. An old countryman, a conjuror or wise man, tells her she needs to attend a state execution and touch the neck of a person just hanged. It seems he discerns the possibility of sorcery.

"Before he's cold—just after he's cut down," insists the conjuror.

"How can that do good?"

"It will turn the blood and change the constitution."

The day before an execution, she visits the harness maker fashioning rope for the hanging. "'Tis sold by the inch afterwards," he tells her. "I could get you a bit, miss, for nothing, if you like."

Next day, she approaches the corpse, which is supported on two trestles. She feels a gray mist floating before her and can barely see. "It was as though she had nearly died," writes Hardy, "but was held up by a sort of galvanism."

"Galvanism" refers to the inexplicable properties of electricity then being used in medical practice. As in Émile Durkheim's 1912 famous analysis of religion, electricity was a handy metaphor for magical influence. In Hardy's rendering here, a mysterious quasi-electrical force is emitted by the corpse, pushing the woman into the arms of death while also sustaining her.

The hangman uncovers the face of the corpse and lays her "poor cur'st arm across the dead man's neck, upon a line the colour of an unripe blackberry, which surrounded it." She shrieks. The turn of her blood predicted by the conjuror has just taken place.[1]

HEGEL'S DEATH-SPACE

Here enters G. W. F. Hegel, with his *aufheben* obedient to the law of negation, in which concepts generate their contraries such that the negated lies within the embrace of the negating as a ghostly presence. This, together with his idea that each "moment" here enters into the being of the other in a dramatic confrontation that is also an embrace, is pointedly relevant to the hybrid life-in-death coupling I take from Hardy's story. In equating death with the philosophical principle of negation, Hegel wrote the most famous passage in his influential work *The Phenomenology of Spirit*, a statement about what it means to understand something, and how understanding occupies a profound relation to death.

"Death," he writes "is the most terrible thing, and to keep and hold fast what is dead demands the greatest force of all."

Imagine the gangsters at midnight New Year's Eve in a cemetery suffused in this "greatest force of all," holding fast a corpse before destroying it with fire or machete.

Now we enter the gray mist, that space of death occupied by the young woman suspended by galvanism in Hardy's story. Now we enter the mind and chutzpah of the sorcerer readying the corpse before it is buried. "The life of the mind," Hegel assures us, "is not one that shuns death and keeps clear of destruction; it endures death and in death maintains its being. It only wins to truth when it finds itself utterly torn asunder." What he describes here is not a slam-dunk victory over the negative by something positive; rather, "mind is this power only by looking the negative in the face, and dwelling with it. This dwelling beside it is the magic power that converts the negative into being."

Hegel's *Phenomenology of Spirit* can be read as an extended study of corpse magic with the killer on the wrong side of history. Mind and death linger in each other's Otherness for something like seven hundred densely written pages until we reach closure, as kick-started by what I take to be the slaying of the slayer in the famous and famously obscure chapter on lordship and bondage.

Yet, lingering with the negative is likely to be endless. Just as the sorcerer prepares the corpse to slay the slayer, so the slayer, after five or six killings, stocks up on preventive magic such that the cycle never stops, even though Hegel stops it with Napoleon. But that is another story.

Hegel's idea of *aufheben* resonates with this never-ending cycle of sorcery and apotropaism, magic and countermagic.

Interpose yourself into this embrace in the space of death, says Hegel. Don't let the contraries merge, don't let them blend or fuse too fast. Keep the two, the negated and the negating, at arm's length, engaged and engaging (as in this book).

Not easy. Not easy at all. But's that's what philosophy requires and that's where the magic is, facing death and dismemberment, holding fast to the negative all the way—all the way into magic is what he said, as if a screw went loose and his infernal machinery for once stopped short of slamming shut in dialectical closure.

Did he keep to his own advice, urgent as it was? Not really. He wasn't one to tarry with negation. Not that way, at least, writing abstraction heaped on abstraction. Perhaps the magicians and families applying corpse magic are the true Hegelians, or at least "applied Hegelians"? For they do stare death in the face. They do tarry with the negative. They lubricate the unsteady state of being that is the conundrum of the attraction/repulsion of the corpse so as to activate vengeance—which is where their Hegelianism is proudly on display, with the slow dying of the killer writhing in insomniacal terror spellbound by the face of his victim looming in the darkness night after night until, yes! the crazed slayer dies too.

BENEATH THE GALLOWS

Hardy's ensorcelled heroine partakes in a covert transaction with the hangman. But in other instances, access to the state-assassinated corpse was wide open to the public. Spectators ascended the scaffold as if it were a stage in a theater, as indeed it was. In which case, why not extend it a little and appropriate some of its magic, namely the magic of the state as bound to and fructified by the corpse it has just created? After all, the church had been doing this for centuries, like a vulture feeding off the dead buried within and near its walls, not to mention the founding corpse in Jerusalem about which there exists considerable mystery concerning the empty grave guarded, in some accounts, by an angel. Was His corpse stolen or did it ascend, metamorphosing into spirit? Other corpses come to mind, notably that of Eva Peron.

As regards the theatricality of eighteenth-century hangings in London, Thomas Laqueur emphasizes their carnivalesque character, with crowds of ten thousand or more in attendance, as if for a sporting event. He questions whether these events could thus provide the gravitas that was supposed to accrue to the benefit of stately authority. Moreover—as with executions in the USA today—all manner of things could go wrong. Killing is usually messy, far from the cool radiance of Andy Warhol's electric chair silk screens.

Designating the hanged body as "the magic body," Laqueur cites James Boswell, Dr. Johnson's biographer, describing in 1776 a London hanging he witnessed wherein "no less than four diseased persons had themselves rubbed with the sweaty hands of malefactors in the agonies of death, and believed this would cure them."[2] In other accounts, nannies brought children to be touched to ensure their health. This is the passing of life, like passing the baton, from the state-created dead to the growing child. I wonder what it must have felt like for such a child as a grown-up knowing it had been thus fortified—a novel yet to be written?

Bodily substances of the state-executed were in demand for healing and other purposes. In a remarkably researched and engaging book by Kathy Stuart focused on the city of Augsburg, Germany (Brecht's birthplace), from the fifteenth to the end of the eighteenth centuries, these substances were mainly human fat, blood, and skin, the latter being used as a belt when giving birth or to cover books, the fat being a common ingredient in many medicines provided by the executioners.[3]

The executioner and the "skinner" (the man who flayed animals) were like tabooed persons at the bottom of a formalized hierarchy policed by their respective guilds. Not just the lowest of the low, the executioners were the "anchor" defining the system as a whole. Like untouchables in

India, they were avoided because their "pollution" was thought to be contagious, but—and this is what's so important—executioners and often their wives were frequently consulted for healing, much to the chagrin of the university-trained doctors.

Once again, we encounter this bewildering mix of attraction and horror, of finding biopower in the hands of the person who, as a servant of the state, kills criminals and is thus endowed with the ability to cure the living even though, and in fact because, he or she is polluted.

This is one variant of what Roger Caillois saw as that magnetic coupling of king and executioner, existing as a mythic register in France as late as 1939 when he put pen to paper upon the occasion of the death of the nation's executioner, Anatole Deibler.[4] The magical powers of the executioner proved to be alive and well, especially on his death, as parlayed through obituaries in daily newspapers and magazines, where the collective imagination was allowed to roam, seduced by the newsworthiness of the event.[5]

In Caillois's estimation the executioner, as alter ego to the king, is the king's dark side, the embodiment of the implacable violence of the state as spectacle. Like the strands of a double helix, king and executioner complement each other, forming a connection that, through corpse magic, binds society as a whole.

An instance of this is illustrated by the cure for the disease called scrofula, referring to enlarged lymph nodes due to tuberculosis, often suppurating in the neck. People sought its cure through the touch of the king's hands, hence its designation as "the king's evil." But people also sought the touch of the just-executed victim's hand for the same disease.

What is noteworthy is that even in the age of the Republic in 1939, long after the king had himself been executed, the folklore and customs described in Deibler's obituaries sink their roots in the sacred coupling of king and killer. The king may be long gone but his charisma lived on in the majesty of the executioner.

I have via Hardy's story already mentioned the hangman's rope—"sold by the inch," according to the harness maker. Such rope was considered a cure for mysterious illnesses called "evils," which I assume include and probably mainly refer to, sotto voce, sorcery up till the late nineteenth

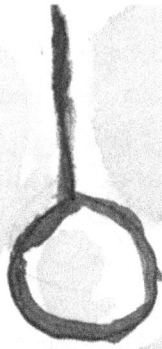

THE LiTtLE GALLOWS MAN

century in isolated parts of Britain. The "hangman's rope" could also apply, not just to the executioner's strand, but to rope used in suicide by hanging.

The spirit of a person who has committed suicide is among those that Robert Hertz singles out as impossible to assuage. The bodies of suicides were not permitted to be buried in Christian graveyards. Kathy Stuart writes that suicides in the Augsburg region could be disposed only through burial beneath the gallows, being burned at a crossroads, or being thrown into a swamp—legendary sites of desacralization.

By the same token, the area beneath the gallows converts polluting force into good fortune. That would explain the story related since at least the sixteenth century in England that, as men were being hanged, they ejaculated sperm that became "the little gallows man." These were mandrakes, known for their beautiful white flowers, and their root was sold as magically potent throughout Europe, into the early twentieth century. It was often human-shaped and dressed in clothes. It was said that the most efficacious mandrakes were those found under or in close proximity to the gallows.[6]

16 *Vengeance and Repentance*

The corpse magic I describe can, as I've continually noted, be thought of as a skewed replay of Christ's resurrection, directing the ensorcelled spirit not toward Christian salvation but toward killing the killer.

The model, though, is the same: a corpse, Christ or an assassinated gangster, aroused from his death-sleep, is charged with a holy mission of vengeance. Christ proceeds with humility and love, the gangster's family with smoldering hate. Some readers may find this more doctrinally acceptable if I suggest that Christ's resurrection might itself be a copy of an older corpse magic that existed in Palestine long before his birth. In any event, vengeance as a fact remains far more popular throughout history than turning the other cheek.

VENGEANCE

In previous chapters I've described the cemetery break-in, the removal of the corpse, and its being cut to pieces or burned. And I've asked how such crude physical actions could forestall what I take to be the wraithlike character of corpse magic.

The logic is straightforward. The corpse is physically *arranged*, as people say, with cords and toe ligatures, a photograph of the killer, special clothing, and so forth. Given that, a logical way of blocking the magic is to disarrange, by physically destroying that physical paraphernalia.

Yet the destruction goes further. Its perpetrators are bent on annihilation and, as I see it, something more: *on deliberately profaning the corpse.* The taboos enforcing respect for the corpse indeed seem stronger than those protecting life, or at least their transgression seems to have a stronger magical effect. Mutilating the corpse, then, is stronger medicine than killing. It unleashes spiritual energy. And it is this, I submit, that trumps corpse magic.

Earlier, I set forth instances of profaning the corpse, as when Catholics unearthed Protestant bodies and vice versa, a notable case being the exhumation and profanation of the corpses of Cromwell, his mother, and his granddaughter.[1]

If killing generates a lively relationship between slayer and slain—the premise on which this book rests—then hanging a corpse (Cromwell) or mutilating a corpse (in the cemetery upon which I focus) would seem to do that in spades. As we say in English, it does so "with a vengeance."

Thus, we confront the "vengeance economy," a delirium of the gift economy turned inside out, reciprocity unbound, infinite, and deadly. Eye for an eye, tooth for a tooth. The obligation to give, the obligation to receive, and the obligation to pay back.

The commonest form of murder in Colombia is classified by officialdom and elsewhere as an *ajuste de cuentas*, which means something like "settling scores." The terrible violence of the "classic" *Violencia* in Colombia, from 1948 onward, with one half of the rural population devoted to killing and mutilating the other half—this too was an *ajuste de cuentas* but on an epic scale. It was more than that, however, since the Conservative Party ran the state and identified with the church. Hence you could say that the *Violencia* was vengeance anchored both in the magic of the state and in the *mistica* of the two political parties involved.

A convulsion of revenge, the *Violencia* swept like a forest fire, spiraling unstoppably for eight years before morphing into left-wing guerrilla formations and drug trafficking to the USA versus US-supported counterguerrilla warfare and War on Drugs rooted in Nixon-era racism and hostility to the anti–Vietnam war movement.

The classic *Violencia*, largely rural, involved extraordinary levels of sadism, matricide, and feticide, as well as artful mutilation of the human body, dead or alive. Strangely, the many attempts at explanation have barely mentioned what seems the most obvious factor—revenge—as if its very obviousness seems to professional analysts and commentators to demand explanations outside of itself. My approach, by contrast, is to hold it fast and burrow in.

We tend to think of revenge as a symptom, not a thing in itself, a means not an end. Yet we know that the thirst for revenge can preoccupy a person, body and soul, and likewise a collective, a nation or ethnic group, prompting them to do the most terrible things and do them incessantly, as we see daily with the Israeli attacks on hospitals, schools, and mosques in Gaza. With good reason, one of the first declarations by the just-elected president of Colombia, Gustavo Petro, on June 19, 2022, was "El cambio no es para vengarnos, ni construer más odios" (The change is not to seek revenge, nor to seek more reasons to hate).

Good luck!

Of the political philosophers, Nietzsche stands apart in placing vengeance at the heart of power. In his view, revenge and resentment play a leading role in history, not least of which is our better understanding of why we avoid revenge as a subject of inquiry.

As often happens, stories of sorcery bring out the essentials.

A friend I have known for fifty years in the sugar plantation town thinks the woman living opposite her is using magic to make her thirty-year-old daughter crazy to the point of death. Her daughter can't sleep, is constantly anxious, and has stopped eating, and Western medicine is not helping. My friend thinks her neighbor is doing this as revenge, saying that my friend, out of envy twenty years ago, used magic to kill her daughter in childbirth.

Maleficent magic is often provoked by romantic liaisons gone awry. One friend of mine, a peasant farmer friend who took part in the attempted invasion of a large hacienda by the Río Cauca in 1971, has now become morose and befuddled, socially isolated, he says, on account of sorcery caused by his philandering. For at least twenty years, he has spent his money on fruitless efforts to counter magical attacks, either by vengeful women he's been involved with or by the very sorcerers he's paid to cure him. Each attempt at a cure, he says, has stimulated another attack.

Another case proved devastating to me. In 1972 my landlady in the plantation town was having a romance with a married man, a truck driver who was also a friend of mine. But things started to go wrong. She didn't feel well. She wanted to get rid of him. She suspected his wife, on the other side of town, was using a sorcerer to get at her as revenge. She brought in her own sorcerer, an elderly fellow from the Pacific coast who sprayed each room with herbal medicine, conducting a *limpieza*, or spiritual cleansing. The spurned lover grew more and more anxious at being rejected and drank heavily. I would see him weeping in the bar by the town plaza late afternoons. Months later in Mexico, I was called by a friend, a Palestinian haberdasher in the town, who told me that my truck-driver friend had shot my landlady dead, attempted to kill one of her two children, and then killed himself. The orphans were taken in by a distant relative and now live in Spain.

From my experience over decades, I know that vengeance tied to envy is how people in the Putumayo region of the upper Amazon, indigenous and nonindigenous alike, understand what motivates sorcery, an ever-present likelihood.[2] How strange it is that in the Global North, especially among its middle classes, revenge and envy seem absent from conscious reckoning other than at an aestheticized distance as a dramatic contrivance for Hollywood and fiction. In day-to-day life, revenge has little to no place, being regarded as uncouth, childish, or primitive. Like death itself, it is denied, or so it seems. (Philippe Ariès, whose volume of lectures given at Johns Hopkins on the transformation of Western attitudes toward death I've repeatedly cited, could have written a parallel volume on the transformation of attitudes regarding vengeance.)

But is the desire for vengeance really gone? I recall a colleague telling me to "watch my back," a chilling phrase, but then he was a keen hunter and surely got it right. Then there were the stories about a female colleague of renown who, generations previous, was rumored to have tried sorcery against a male colleague. Was the story contrived by nervous men? Was it that rare moment when a concealed fear and truth bursts through their armor? Male professors chuckled when they told me this, but it was a nervous laughter—academics are every bit as riddled with envy as are the poor peasants and indigenous people of the Upper Amazon, or the witchcraft and sorcery practicing Azande in central Africa. Perhaps more so.

So here's the question: What makes revenge in the Global North seem uncouth and uncool, restricted to novels and movies? And how has its rejection become transformed into the moral high ground of "justice," "due process," and "rule of law"?

I ask because I am not happy with the notion that vengeance is not cool. In some instances it is cool. The call to defund the police or replace many of them with unarmed community police and restitutive justice in the US following police murders of people of color seems to me a justified act of revenge against systemic police brutality, yet, if labeled "revenge," it is deemed morally inappropriate. It has to be dressed up as "justice" in accord with Rule of Law, as if revenge were not justice but its antithesis. But is not justice a euphemism for vengeance?

Revenge is bad style, even taboo, the prerogative, we like to think, of some "uncivilized" underground: the Neapolitan mafia, Tennessee hillbillies, the Crips and the Bloods in Los Angeles, or the Bloods just down the street from me, guarding/extorting the Yemeni-owned corner *bodega*. Add to this list George W. Bush and Dick Cheney, invading Afghanistan as revenge for 9/11 in what became the longest war in modern history, now being emulated in the vengeance being enacted in Palestine with US bombs.

At the drop of a MAGA red hat, Donald Trump turns viciously on anyone not supporting him. Revenge is his default position. In *Peril*, cowritten by Bob Woodward and Robert Costa, a discarded Trump campaign manager, one Brad Parscale, exacts his own revenge when he says, commenting on Trump's quest to return to the White House, "I don't think he sees it as a comeback. He sees it as vengeance."[3] Maureen Dowd suggested in November 2023 that Trump's leading motive is revenge and that his campaign slogan should be "There will be blood."[4] As Trump and his base geared up for the 2024 election, they were said to be embodying "grievance politics," a euphemism for revenge.

Revenge politics is the heart and soul of "the culture wars," which, as detailed by Thomas Frank in his 2005 book *What's The Matter with Kansas? How Conservatives Won the Heart of America*, connects the dots between conservative business interests and the manipulation of public opinion. Those interests seem to understand that revenge yields as great or greater pleasure than does money, that envy and the promise of revenge render opinion all the more pliable, which is why people consistently vote against what seem to be their economic interests.

Beyond the psychospiritual dimensions of revenge, I need to take into account the weakness of law as practiced in Colombia and Latin America, where only 2 percent or so of homicides result in arrests and even those apprehended rarely serve time.[5] Hemmed in by the wealthy and the army, the state cannot provide justice and therefore people practice revenge, join the guerrilla, form a cartel, or get recruited by a gang or a paramilitary group to wipe out each other. Moreover, in Colombia, people under eighteen—which would include most gang members and FARC dissidents—are classed as minors and cannot be jailed even for murder.

That means that not only are people likely to resort to direct action—to threaten, injure, or kill an offender themselves, or pay someone else to do it. They are also unlikely to go to the state seeking redress of an injustice, because that is likely to backfire.

What is the impact of all this on the magic of the state? Thomas Hobbes encourages us to look at the state as if it was designed to appropriate violence previously practiced by individuals, violence that could well be a manifestation of vengeance. Hobbes emphasized the citizens' surrender of arms, but more basic, I suggest, is their surrender of revenge, which is henceforth to be practiced only by the state. Corpse magic vengeance contests that surrender, as do a considerable number of US citizens.

The picture of society that emerges differs from what political theorists and law professors like to imagine. It is a picture in which it is not the law of the state but the law of vengeance that maintains as well as perturbs social order. Corpse magic is a fantastic manifestation of the imagination of the law of vengeance.

AN OBSTACLE TO VENGEANCE

There is a price attached to revenge, and that concerns what happens to the spirit of the slain and to the spirit of the assassin. Close to the beginning of *One Hundred Years of Solitude*, its author, Gabriel García Márquez, describes the decision a small community takes to abandon their village. They journey over the mountains through the wilderness to found a new settlement, Macondo, which is destined to become the genius loci of Colombia.

The story is this: A fighting cock belonging to José Arcadio Buendía defeats that of Prudencio Aguilar, who, in his rage, insults the manhood of José Arcadio, who in turn kills Prudencio with a spear, shattering his throat. One night soon after, José Arcadio's wife, Úrsula, goes out to the courtyard to get some water and sees Prudencio by the water jar with "a sad expression on his face, trying to cover the hole in his throat with a plug made of esparto grass. It did not bring on fear in her, but pity."[6] She takes to leaving pots of water around the house.

The dead man returns. José Arcadio again confronts him with a spear but this time dares not use it. The dead man ignores the threat and keeps returning. Thereafter José Arcadio never sleeps well. That is Prudencio's revenge.

"He must be suffering a great deal," José Arcadio tells Ursula. "You can see that he's so very lonely."

José Arcadio finds Prudencio in his room, washing his wound. "It's all right, Prudencio," he says to the dead man. We're going to leave this town, just as far as we can go, and we'll never come back. Go in peace now."[7]

I will return to the issue of pity later. Here I wish to point out the role of vengeance, in fact a threefold vengeance: first, that brought about by Prudencio insulting José Arcadio; second, that caused by José Arcadio killing Prudencio; and third, that of Prudencio's eternal return as the pitiful living-dead—not unlike Christ. Except Christ's vengeance had been of another order, refusing the warrior's game for that of humility, love, and equality. You could say that Christ's vengeance was to practice vengeance on vengeance. He was contending with the vengeance chiseled into the Old Testament, which continues apace today, very much so in the Holy Land but also worldwide.

In the book of Exodus, the Israelites flee Egypt, seeking to escape the pharaoh's vengeance. In *One Hundred Years of Solitude*, vengeance killing creates a powerful bond between slayer and slain, and fear or some deep-seated sense of upset drives the community to flee. The dead man's thirst for vengeance, however, is expressed not so much through violence as through his pitiable state on the Caribbean coast of Colombia hanging around jugs of water.

The murderous twins out to avenge their sister's dishonor in García Márquez' terrifying *Chronicle of a Death Foretold* are not so meek. In the few hours the story narrates, you hear them sharpening their knives as details of the narrative emerge. In retrospect, chance encounters, apparently trivial details, and everyday routines snap into place as omens of revenge ministered by fate when their sister is abandoned on her wedding night for not being a virgin. The mystical quality of this conglomeration of events is pointedly that of vengeance coiling itself like a snake ready to strike. Vengeance tightens the randomness of the everyday world into a scheme of good and evil, which, as we have seen in other situations, can lead to the magic of the animated corpse of corpse magic.

RESURRECTION AND REPENTANCE

Corpse vengeance magic leads me to ask if repentance is possible: Do killers ever feel bad about killing and, if so, what sort of bad? This question, however naïve, lies at the heart of my inquiry, alongside another key question: Is corpse magic mainly rumor? Might a victim's family members let it be known that they are considering corpse magic, so as to frighten the killer, even if they will not actually perform such magic or hire an expert to do so? Might it be possible that in fact nobody sets the rumor mill in action, but that the premonition of corpse magic is simply in the air once a killing has occurred?

In short, could corpse magic be more rumor than fact? Might anxiety about corpse magic be more potent than anything actually put into practice? Could the cemetery break-in, for instance, have been caused by no more than the paranoia that follows from assassination? (But then, would there be such paranoia if corpse magic were not a realistic possibility?)

In truth, these explanations are by no means incompatible: yes, corpse magic is practiced, and yes, it is paranoia that kills the killer. To the latter point, the physiologist Walter B. Cannon set forth a theory in 1942 that what he called "voodoo death" is the result of the human body entering into something like surgical shock, a circulatory disruption consequent to an outpouring of adrenaline as part of a fight-or-flight response to fear engendered by a magical attack *or its possibility*.[8]

Or, to take another tack, could it be that there is no such thing as heartless, cold-blooded killing and that, to the contrary, all killing exacts a soul-price from the killer, no matter how callous? That is a big claim and one that goes against much common sense. Most of us, I think, tend toward a bleak view of humanity that holds that people are capable of, if not prone to, violence and evil, and that this inclination grows every day worse. Yet is that not counterposed to a faith in humanity, these opposing beliefs making us the strange creatures we are, fertile ground for magical thinking such as corpse magic?

I feel I could have and maybe should have written this entire book from the viewpoint of the paranoid killer, sensing every twitch in his body, every stabbing pain in his gut, and every shadow that crosses his path as the sign of incipient vengeance magic.

Let me cite a curious story I heard recently: In late 2021 an armed paramilitary group took control of a small nonindigenous state-sponsored settlement of ex-guerrilla (FARC) in the infamous Urabá region in the north of Colombia, near the border with Panama, a blastingly hot and humid area famous for decades for its banana exports via United Fruit and for its endless guerrilla and paramilitary violence. It is an area also through which a lot of cocaine travels.

Assembling the inhabitants, the paramilitaries demanded—can you believe this!—an end to sorcery and gossip: no more *brujerías,* no more *chismes!*[9] This seems more bizarre and more really magically real than anything Gabriel García Márquez could dream up. The story points to what I might call "the two sides of life," or coexisting sides of the real, one side visible, the other obscure or, as we say, "occult."

In 1972 I was speaking with peasant friends living on the periphery of the sugar plantations. An eccentric barefoot anxious man whose name I still recall was running around in circles cussing out a neighbor for *sal* or *maleficio* or something. His words as much as the concepts they pointed to mystified me. Suddenly I figured out he meant sorcery, which to that point I'd known nothing about. In a flash, a whole world opened—a world behind the world, perhaps, or woven into it, in which sorcery and talk about sorcery is mundane, even banal, and yet can be scary serious even if it provokes nervous laughter. It's like talking about cancer or COVID, facts of life but—and this is what's so strange—you have to have a sort of library card, or Rosetta stone, to access this other language that lies between words, in gestures and above all, in meaningful looks. Once you do, it's quite simple. You just slide into this vocabulary and pull faces.

The ex-FARC guerrilla women in the Urabá settlement say that during the decades of war, the FARC *comandantes* (all male) feared sorcery and that contributed to their hostility toward indigenous people.[10] This needs a good deal of unpacking and specification, but recall that indigenous women healers/sorcerers appear baked into accounts of the bulletproofing magic sought by right-wing paramilitaries on the eastern plains of Colombia.[11]

So why did the paramilitaries, at this particular moment, seek to ban sorcery and gossip, *brujerias* and *chismes*, those mainstays of social life? When a fifty-year-old ex-FARC guerrilla woman died suddenly, the paramilitaries blamed her death on sorcery and expelled an indigenous woman from the community, saying she was a witch. Notably, this "witch" had a reputation for helping women magically curtail their husbands' philandering. Since the sex-gender system here, as in the rest of the world, involves much philandering, it would appear that the paramilitaries have their work cut out, no matter how many indigenous sorcerers they expel or kill.

What to my mind is unusual here is that what we might call *folk-law* or *folklore* enters into both *paramilitary law* and paramilitary lore as the sorcery-fearing paramilitaries assume the draconian powers of a state attempting (against the odds) to prohibit sorcery, imaginary or real.

Might we not then conclude that for all the paramilitaries' bravado, for all the killing in cold blood, there is this other story as well—that killing is wrong not only because of the Church or law, not only because of the pain and suffering incurred, but because of lore inflaming the corpse?

This realm is real and unreal at the same time. Witness my old friend, the ever-ironic Raúl, as we walked into town midmorning dodging motorbikes and horse-drawn carts. "You know how it is," he exclaimed with a smile creasing his taut face when I asked him about the cemetery break-in. "One of these guys feels a pain in his gut or can't sleep and starts to think that a *brujo*—you know, like those from the Chocó—has put a spell on the corpse." The way Raúl chuckled you couldn't be sure whether he believed this or not. Bear in mind, he knew many of the killers intimately.

While it is logical to assume that vengeance goes hand in hand with aggression, I keep thinking of the sorrow and self-pity of Prudencio Aguilar, the dead man who, far from trying to kill his killer, adopts the more Christ-like posture of abjection that we could call "passive-aggressive." I keep thinking of how that pathetic stance irritates and eventually drives to despair his killer, Aureliano Buendía, who then moves an entire village of people through the wilderness to form a new village, where their hundred years of solitude will eventually end as the United Fruit Company, a.k.a. "the octopus," takes over, and there is a massive worker's strike and then a massacre by the Colombian army backed by US Marines.

Self-pity on the part of the slain also comes across in stories related by the Colombian anthropologist Claudia Steiner concerning paramilitaries who feel spooked by their victims, become possessed by them, and go mad. Drawing on her own fieldwork and that of her students, as well as articles in daily newspapers, Steiner draws attention to accounts in the early 2000s of paramilitaries said to be possessed by the spirits of their victims.[12]

"Said to be possessed by the spirits of their victims." You read the words but they quiver, then disappear, for what they describe seems too strange for language to bear. But then there's the ready-at-hand alternative, our trade language of anthropology and teenage horror movies with stock phrases like "spirit possession" that don't wobble at all. Instead, the terminology reifies, making the strange mundane except for the glow at the edge.

What does "possession" mean here? Let's go back to my anthropology of slaying and what I have intermittently called the Nuer-Effect, in which the spirit of the person you've killed enters into you. By definition, that qualifies as spirit possession. In the stories that Steiner, her students, and the newspaper articles relate, the *possessed paramilitary killers talk and act like the person they have killed.*

Can you imagine this!

In the body of their killer, the assassinated person pleads for the return of a severed limb or some other amputated body part—and here you might recall the first *narcorelato* I presented, concerning the incomplete corpse of an assassinated young man, disinterred as his different body parts were found and reunited with his previously buried corpse.

But the demand for completeness, it seems to me, is not what's central here. Rather, it is the fact of being possessed by the spirit of the person slain that is devastating to the paramilitaries. These are cold-blooded killers who claim they eat human flesh, even that of a fetus, as part of their training, though it may happen only in stories. Yet it turns out they are vulnerable to the spiritual consequences of their killing, suggesting that the brutality of which they are capable has a spiritual and moral basis. What makes and allows them to devastate, devastates them too.

Think of it! The killer now possessed by the victim, the killer now a twofold being like we read about among the Arawete in the Brazilian Amazon. The dead victim speaks to the victimizer, both alive in the one body. Dancing partners. Maybe having sex with the one wife.

In a story from the vast plains of eastern Colombia known as *los llanos*, a group of desperados freaks out. The callous killers run scared. The spirits possessing them bash them against trees. Addressing one of these maverick spirits, the comandante of the paramilitaries demands:

"Are you of God or the devil?"
And the spirit answers.
"No! They got it wrong. I'm not a *guerrillero*.
I'm a peasant."[13]

FANON'S CASE STUDIES OF GUILT IN RELATION TO VIOLENCE

Born in Martinique, Frantz Fanon was a psychiatrist trained in a provincial French university just after World War II, in which he fought in the French army. He became head of the Blida-Joinville mental hospital in Algeria and, when his alliance with the FLN (Algerian Liberation Front) became dangerous, moved with his wife and child to Tunis, continuing his psychiatric and anticolonial political work there and in rebel training camps in Tunisia and Morocco.

In his last book, *The Wretched of the Earth*, dictated (as all his books were) shortly before he died from leukemia in 1961, he presented fifty pages of case studies on colonial war and mental disorders. The patients were from both sides of the revolutionary divide, Algerian and French, although

Fanon did not speak Arabic or a Berber tongue, which surely affected the clinical situation. His style in these case studies is dry like a police blotter but on occasions, given the contents, cannot but overwhelm.

Noting the prevalence of acute anxiety, agitation, and hallucinations, Adam Shatz quotes Fanon saying that his patients were suffering "the bloody, pitiless atmosphere, the generalization of inhuman practices, of people's lasting impression that they are witnessing a veritable apocalypse."[14] He predicted that the "human legacy of France in Algeria," would be "an entire generation of Algerians bathed in gratuitous, collective homicide with all the psycho-affective consequences that this entails."[15]

I was particularly struck by Fanon's description of psychosomatic disorders, a kind of catatonia in which the muscles contract, making it difficult to climb stairs or walk other than by shuffling, such that "the patient seems to be made in one piece. The face is set but expresses a marked degree of bewilderment." In the absence of a common language, perhaps Fanon was extra perceptive of physical behavior when it came to his non–French-speaking patients.

The text continues: "The patient does not seem to be able to 'demobilize his nerves.' He is constantly tense, on hold, between life and death. As one of them told us: 'You see, I'm as stiff as a corpse.'"[16]

This sense of living the apocalypse, combined with the immobilization of the body, makes me think of the symptomology of what I call "corpse magic," of course, but more profoundly of the Colombian *Violencia* and the unstated war undertaken by the Colombian state with US support since the 1980s. That's an achingly long time. Although this war differs greatly from the national liberation struggle against French colonialism, the questions Fanon poses concerning the character of lived experience, a concept he imbibed from reading Merleau-Ponty and Sartre, are surely germane to Colombia. But these questions concerning generations of country people exposed to and practicing violence in Colombia have not to my knowledge been much posed at the clinical or psychoanalytic level. In their stead lies abundant storytelling, fictional and nonfictional, such as the brilliant work of Alfredo Molano and his tape recorder.[17]

The violence in Colombia is not a "classic" colonial conflict as in Algeria,

Vietnam, or Palestine. Instead, it is marked by intense entanglements of small groups fighting for local control, far different from the bipolar array of colonial and anticolonial forces aligned with race, religion, language, and culture. Which is not to say that these local groups do not frequently have roots in state apparatus such as the army and police, as well as in the wealthy classes.

Fanon regarded colonialism as the key issue and had little tolerance for *négritude* or appeals to tradition, Islam, or orthodox communism. The practice he learned in St. Alban hospital in the south of France in 1942 from the Catalan François Tosquelles, combining Marx and Freud with anarchism, trying to break down the hospital hierarchy, was something he attempted to replicate in Algeria and Tunis. But as I read Fanon and Shatz (his latest biographer) and come across anthropologists and historians of the Maghreb, especially Pierre Bourdieu, who are critical of Fanon's romantic notions of the peasantry, and as I consider his lack of understanding or hostility to the appeal of Islam, I cannot but wonder about Fanon's apparent lack of interest in local magic and spirit-possession cults. Surely these practices, as much as Western psychiatry fused with anarcho-Marxism and Freud, had much to offer, separately or combined, especially before the chemical revolution in antidepressants and tranquilizers took hold in the 1960s.

Which brings me full circle, back to corpse magic, sorcery, and the diffuse character of apotropaic magic (magic against magic), given that Fanon himself cites dramatic cases of Algerians haunted by the ghosts of French people they had killed. One young man was haunted by a French woman he had disemboweled. He "spoke constantly of his blood being spilled, his arteries drained."[18] French torturers were also treated by Fanon. They feared for their sanity, their inability to sleep, and their cruelty to their own families.

Although woefully brief and schematic, these accounts suggest that killers and torturers are likely at times to suffer overwhelming fear from what they have done. It may be tempting to think of Colombian paramilitaries, gangsters, or US police as beyond guilt, but reading Fanon instructs otherwise. However, corpse magic, as I define it, seems quite different, driven not by guilt but by the power of the dead, quite another matter.

Spirit possession is not common in Colombia, certainly not like it is in the Caribbean islands, Venezuela, or Brazil. In general terms, spirit-possession magic pervades popular religion in those societies, while a different set of magical practices, based on the *maleficio*, *sal*, or sorcery bundle (*capacho*), is predominant in the Andean countries of Colombia, Ecuador, Peru, Bolivia, and Chile. In Colombia there was for several years in the 1980s a spirit-possession cult, largely of women mediums possessed by the spirit of the Venezuelan medical doctor José Gregorio Hernández, killed in Caracas by an automobile in the 1920s. (He was beatified by the Vatican in 2021.) But again, spirit possession is uncommon in most of Colombia.

Instances of spirit possession of Colombian paramilitaries are therefore *not* part of a deep tradition of spirit possession. Instead, they emerge from specific circumstances: assassination arouses the spirit of the slain; killing establishes a relationship between slayer and slain. It could also be that the florid beliefs and practices of Venezuela spirit possession, exemplified in the cult of María Lionza at Sorte, have spread west into Colombia and magnified the slayer-slain nexus; this seems to be the case particularly in the eastern plains of Colombia, known as the *llanos*.[19] I wonder if Evangelical religion with its proclivity for possession by the devil does not play a major part here too.

There is another form of spirit possession to consider, and that is the movies, very much including horror movies made in Colombia, in which specters, spirits of the dead, and violence abound. My bodyguard, the ex-elite soldier Andres, often recommended specific movies; one featured soldiers camped in the mist-laden *paramos*, frightened by the dead. When I asked a young woman lawyer born and resident in the Chocó if she was familiar with corpse magic, she at first looked puzzled, then exclaimed, Ah, yes! She had seen it in a movie showing in Medellín!

The story of spirit possession from the plains of eastern Colombia is similar to accounts from other, widely separated parts of the country (Caquetá, Córdoba, and Risaralda). Take the story circulating in 2007 not far from the city of Pereira in the department of Risaralda in central Colombia. It was said that an entire group of paramilitaries was overtaken by the spirits of people they had slain. According to a seventy-year-old peasant witness, the first to succumb was a youngster, who fell to the ground, spuming from the mouth, vomiting, and threatening to shoot everyone.[20] Because the slain from many different hamlets were possessing them, the frightened paramilitaries, known as "the Heroes and Martyrs of Guática," organized a mass exorcism.

In the same region, according to the same source, a comandante by the name of Macaco had to exhume forty corpses (yes, forty!) in 2003 because his fighters were possessed by the spirits of people they had slain. A priest from Pereira by the name of Fabián officiated.[21] It was reported that the exhumed corpses had provoked such fury and anguish among the killers that they lost control, fired off their guns, and spoke incomprehensibly.

THE OTHER SIDE OF THE COIN

Vengeance has also a left-wing progressive side, borrowing from the same spiritual force as corpse magic in which people venerate fallen guerrilla fighters and form a cult around their graves. Elsy Yaneth Castillo Ordóñez described the case of two M-19 combatants whose bodies were buried in the cemetery of Florencia, capital of the province of Caquetá in the foothills where the eastern chain of the Andes descends into the Amazon basin, forming an essential part of the FARC hinterland.[22]

At the time of Elsy Yaneth Castillo's writing in 1989, their tombs were covered with mosaics. Over that of Jairo Capera was an inscription from the book of Matthew (5:10), "How blest are those who have suffered persecution for the cause of right; the kingdom of Heaven is theirs." Capera was an indigenous man who deserted the national government's compulsory military service to join the guerrilla and became famous for his audacity. The national press reported his assassination of two spies working for military intelligence who had infiltrated the guerrilla. According to various testimonies he was seen as a sort of Robin Hood.

The other tomb was that of a woman, Amanda Rincón, born in Florencia and a student in the local university, who participated in the M-19 guerrilla's storming of a party at the Dominican embassy in Bogotá in 1980. Fifteen ambassadors, including the US ambassador, were taken hostage and held for two months. Think of it! Basically, the entire ambassadorial corps, captive for two months—what a movie that would be! Where's our Buñuel?[23] She also participated in the taking of Florencia, the capital of Caquetá, and was killed in action on the slopes of the Andes in Huila.

On Mondays—day of the *ánimas*—and during Easter, at least until 1989 if not to the present day, devotees prayed and brought offerings such as flowers and prayers, asking these dead guerrilla fighters for help. What did they ask for? Work, money, health, and freedom from addiction to cocaine or alcohol.

What are we to make of the fact that in the cases I have cited, paramilitary killers fear the spirits of those they have killed, while the spirits of guerrilla fighters killed by the army can help you? In the one case, the victims wreak vengeance; in the other, miracles.

Preposterous
Equations

Here's the question: What is the more fearsome, corpse
magic or its absence? Which is stranger?
And what of the phone videos of the killing? Are they not
streaming corpse magic?

17 *A Jesuit Seminar in Bogotá*

"But this sore night hath trifled former knowledge."

I first came across what I would later call "corpse magic" in the 1990s, in Lloyd Warner's account of what we might call "the soul" of a dead man entering the body of his slayer. He based this on his 1927 fieldwork among the Murngin (now called Yolngu) in northeast Australia. His description set my mind reeling. Yet it was not in Warner's book, *A Black Civilization*, that I read this but as a quotation in Elias Canetti's *Crowds and Power*. It was an unusually long quotation, three pages, as I recall.

A few years later, in a two-day seminar on violence—organized by CINEP, a Jesuit foundation in Bogotá—I asked a young anthropologist, Elizabeth Reichel, as I recall, to read aloud a Spanish translation of Canetti's Murngin passage.

It resonated terribly with the violence around us, this story of a dead man in his ethereality seeking entry into the killer, expanding him and the animals in the environment, setting the world off-kilter. It was like that old man who, after Macbeth is killed, exclaims that he has seen strange things in his long life "but this sore night hath trifled former knowledge." The horses of the slain king have broken out of their stables, "turned wild in nature." They "would make war with mankind. 'Tis said they eat each other."

Yes, we were in quite a different place and time, but does not a seminar room give license to wander through place and time? A seminar can be a microcosm of things rarely dreamed, such that, yes!, we too could imagine that wildness and feel that "war with mankind."

Our surroundings were suitably fearsome. The CINEP building, a concrete structure, beyond ugly in the best Brutalist manner, sits engulfed by many lanes of traffic, speeding by from the intimation of dawn to late at night. Most everything I hated and feared about Bogotá was in that mindless stampede of automobiles. It was as if the downtown—the Presidential Palace, the Capitol housing Congress, the cathedral, the Palace of Justice—each day swallowed everything, and each day the stampede renewed itself. How many, I wondered, made it back? "'Tis said they eat each other."

What do I mean when I refer to the resonance I felt between what we were listening to in the seminar room and the world pressing in on us? Did we feel the slain entering our bodies? Did we feel we were entering the body of the killer? To say the least, that seems implausible. But who can tell what associations might occur in a tightly bound group, twenty or so people discussing the violence lying thick inside no less than outside ourselves?

The issue was not one of literal identification between the text and us. It was a "conversation" between dissimilars joined by homicide. Yet, that said, is it not the literality that gets under one's skin such that it is more than a conversation? Is it not the image of the victim inhabiting the killer that is devastating and seductive, this in Colombia with a population of forty million, or whatever it was at that time, with countless military-assisted covert assassinations known to the CIA and continual Colombian government cover-ups, not to mention even more killing by gang kids in the poor barrios throughout the land.

Thinking back to the Murngin story or the old man in Macbeth, flex your montage muscles and try to imagine those stories multiplied by millions, not there, not in Murngin-land or Scotland, but in Colombia. Then put the two together, Murngin-land or horses turned cannibal, on the one hand, and Colombia, on the other. Watch the sparks fly. Feel the heat of the conjunction as difference rubs against sameness, my point being not that we are slayers or slain, killers or killed, *but that the contagion emitted by the nationwide killing,* which we in that seminar room had pretty well buffered through habit and fear, burst through at both a physiological and a spiritual level.

Daily life has its predictable rhythms. Your heart settles into them. Then you turn a corner and, out of the blue, the world changes, as if you'd fallen through it. For a moment in the sheltered space that the Jesuits have given over to social research and popular education, we could imagine that dead man, that corpse, that spirit, or whatever we call the active entity at work here, entering into its killer. For a moment we were drawn into the story and into the wilder reaches of our imagining, like Leopold Bloom in his carriage en route to the graveyard.

The baffling entailments of Warner's story—the killer growing in size, being guided to animals to kill—added to the cosmic derangement on the verge of which we were suspended by everyday stories from friends in Bogotá of relatives kidnapped, killings, and befuddling conspiracies. Every taxi ride was ominous, what with stories of the drivers reporting to the army. You were never—but never—to catch a cab on the street. Every glance was suspicious. But you would never admit it. Not even to yourself, despite the surreal gatherings in cafes and living rooms, the downcast eyes and faltering efforts at speech, ticking off the latest kidnappings or assassinations of cousins or friends or friends of friends or colleagues. That was today. Tomorrow or the day after, it would be a different bunch of names and new stories of horses eating each other. This does not even begin to include the kids in gangs across the breadth of the land killing each other for they do not, did not, and never will count in middle-class reckoning.

These spiraling thoughts had a lot to do with the ad hoc theater of the occasion, the group-reading moving slowly, quietly, absorbing us like the soul of the slain being absorbed, detail by detail, surprise by surprise, strangeness into strangeness into the body of the killer and then into the world beyond, transforming all in its passage. Later we would debate how much of this was truly Murngin and how much the anthropologist. But did it matter? And as for "truly Murngin," isn't it likely the anthropologist's informants were stringing him along, just a little, making a good story better, just as—I am sure—the Murngin do with each other?

The slowness was one thing. The immersion into the body, another. And wasn't this just how the *narcorelatos* I recount at the beginning of this book function? It was as if by virtue of our exposure to a radically different culture, through the recitation of this fragment from 1927 fieldwork in northeastern Australia, *we could better take the measure of the violence around us* and begin to imagine, perhaps for the first time, obscure potentials mitigating violence—a sort of hope, really, in the connectedness, physical and metaphysical, binding killer to the killed as recounted in such utter concreteness of spiritual physiology.

The fact that it was read out loud seemed important, as was the fact that we were a group listening together. The sound the words made was as important as their meaning. Not only did they acquire density but they veered off into other registers as if they too—like *narcorelatos*—were *imbued with what they were about.* It was as if we too, all of us, were being connected to the story, to the storyteller, and most of all to the insides of the bodies involved, the body of the dead man walking slowly toward the body of his killer to gain entry via the foot into that enlarging body, and thence to the kangaroo, to the scrub, and to the sky and waterholes beyond. It started off as going inside—like the dark insides in the *narcorelatos* I relate at the beginning of this book—but then things blossomed out to an external, even cosmic, register in which metamorphoses were the order of the day.

That we were in the seminar room of a Jesuit institution trying pretty much on its own at that time to counter the death squads was of great importance. That mission combined with our seminar's focus on the current violence made for a time-out-of-time in which our collective imagination ran riot. The fact that two sociologists, Elsa Alvarado and her husband, Mario Calderón, working for CINEP, had been murdered, together with Elsa's father, by masked men breaking into their apartment in 1997, gives you an idea of the conditions prevailing. Their little son hid in a closet and at the funeral reportedly announced, "I want to live in a closet." Many of the priests, like my friend the anthropologist Gabriel Izquierdo, to whom I dedicate this book, had received death threats and had to leave the country, but they were soon back, unable for reasons of conscience to live outside the struggle.

As for Canetti, I imagine him in the 1950s in that other world, the British Museum reading room, that beautiful Benthamite panopticon once home to the likes of Karl Marx. The long desks radiate out from the center like a cartwheel, at the hub of which were the librarians. When I was reading there in the late 1960s, the ceiling was a light blue dome that to me looked like the sky receding into the empyrean. At the hefty double doors leading into the library stood a man in uniform straight out of Kafka's parable about the Law. And there he is, our Canetti, reading anthropological classics in ways few anthropologists would, their senses dulled by usage. It is refreshing to read him (although Adorno was not a fan).[1] It is as if Canetti, too, is a rare book. He brings new life to these texts in an oracular tone, as if riding a cosmic wave while he tries to relieve his anxieties about obsessive killing by dictators and how that breeds more of the same.

Which calls to mind one of Canetti's most memorable concepts, *the invisible crowd of the dead* ranging through time and space like thunder and lightning, like the starlings of a late afternoon, wheeling over the city and the threshed fields.

Canetti offers no "fixed-explosive" quality à la Breton, no psychologizing, no Marx nor Nietzsche either. He just rattles along, guided by the stories he gleans from an older anthropology, there in the museum under azure skies. Was he on a roll, seduced by secrecy and assassination? Or was he seduced by the fictional possibilities of what he was reading? They were vast, that's for sure.

But how can we "jump" from a society such as Warner studied or from the Nuer or the Arawete to "ours"? Such a jump seems preposterous.

But it happened.

It happened there in that seminar room of the Jesuits in Bogotá.

We all jumped.

It's what we call montage, bringing different images or realities side by side, creating something new and jarring. This parallels, does it not, corpse magic, in which the slain abuts the insomniacal slayer causing madness and death? Montage is the quintessence of corpse magic.

GUILT

You might well ask why I focus on what I call the Nuer-Effect, on the slain entering into the body of the slayer. Why can't I come up with an idea more relevant to our times, such as the torment of guilt?

Yet in a text introduced by Hannah Arendt, the World War II Heideggerian USA soldier-philosopher J. Glenn Gray, who served in Italy and Germany, worries a good deal that such an approach is unsatisfactory. The great majority of soldiers involved in killing and destruction, he writes in 1959, "are able to free themselves of responsibility with ease after the event, frequently while they are performing it."[2]

Our age, Gray claims, seems particularly confused about the meaning of guilt. With the rise of what he calls modern psychology and the predominance of what he calls naturalistic philosophers, guilt has come to be understood exclusively in a moral sense, its older religious and metaphysical dimensions increasingly forgotten.[3] Crucial to this modern view, he might have added, is the displacement of the dead, the new dispensation in which the dead person ceases to exist or else exists "wildly," as Philippe Ariès would have it, in unstable religious and metaphysical frameworks.

As for guilt, I think of my friend accused of sorcery by her neighbor in the sugarcane plantation town. Her neighbor's daughter died in childbirth, and now that neighbor, so my friend suspects, is doing sorcery against her daughter. *Where's the guilt in that?* I ask myself. Is this sort of vengeance connected to the metaphysics Gray has in mind with regard to an older metaphysical system? Is my friend suffering from guilt or is she, by contrast, suffering from the fear of sorcery killing her daughter?

Long out of fashion, the US anthropological distinction of the 1930s and 1940s between guilt and shame cultures comes to mind, an anthropology that hewed to notions of national culture meshed with psychoanalytic insights. As regards my friend, however, while guilt is irrelevant, shame is not nearly as apposite as fear of occult force. And there are plenty of other sorts of fear as well, starting with the gang guys leaning against the wall of the house opposite.

Gray himself worries that the modern concept of guilt is unsatisfactory because it no longer (in the 1950s in the Global North) contains what it used to. What could that be? What did it previously contain? Vengeful spirits, perhaps? What forgotten "older religious and metaphysical dimensions" did our soldier-philosopher have in mind? Why was he dissatisfied? What could he put in their place? Let us leave guilt aside and focus on reciprocity between the living and the dead, in other words, on gift-giving and mimesis. The quintessential text on the gift, by Marcel Mauss, makes no mention of guilt (or of vengeance), though it would seem, at first, easy to read the gift through that lens except for one glaring ethnographic feature, the apparent absence of guilt in the societies he discusses.

What defines the gift is the obligation to give, the obligation to receive, and the obligation to pay back. You could call it the original social contract, what makes us, us. You can think of it as a circle with neither beginning nor end, or a game with more or less clear rules that I guess you could gloss as "laws." Do you feel guilt when you play chess, or soccer? No—unless you cheat like Maradona, in which case you invoke the "hand of God." Social force is what is at work—not guilt, not controls internal to the Great Invention of the Self.

The gift is unstable, as Mauss emphasizes. If you don't follow the rules, it easily pitches into war (which I could gloss as sorcery).[4] Moreover, the things involved in exchange are, Mauss says, likely to be alive with personality, and is this not relevant to corpse magic, with its larger-than-life corpse or specter thereof? Also notable, to my mind, is that vengeance is likely to operate with the same rules as the gift. You cross me and I'll cross you, feud without end.

DOLORES: IMAGE AND GIFT

Some forty years ago, a medical student in Bolivia named Dolores, nearing the completion of her degree, told me how, during one of her afternoon house calls in a small town in the highlands, she comforted a dying man, then moved on to another house to give a tuberculosis injection. TB injections were big then, she emphasized, and the injection had to be given slowly.

As she pressed the plunger millimeter by millimeter, her patient told her a man outside was looking in at the window. "What's he look like?" asked Dolores, humoring him. In reply, he described the dying man she had just left. He was right there. At the window.

As the injection slowly progressed, Dolores's patient explained to her that because she had comforted the dying man, he had returned anxious to reciprocate. He needed to pay her back and she had to ask something of the dead man and receive what he offered.

This exchange seems to me to parallel the impulse under which the slain person visits the slayer each night until he dies of madness and insomnia. How might we call that a sort of gift? "Look at me! Every night! Boring into your heart and soul! Every night until death do us part."

18   *Gun Fetishism*

It is a singular fact that US police often claim when they shoot and kill motorists that the driver has a gun. Rarely does the motorist turn out to have one. But Philando Castile did have one; indeed, he told officer Jeronimo Yanez he had a gun in the car, at which point Yanez, thinking Castile was reaching for it, opened fire and killed him.

Every day, people, white and Black, buy guns to defend themselves from other people who are doing the same. What seems like self-defense becomes an arms race, more like collective suicide. Half of shooting fatalities in the USA are in fact suicide, and half of US suicides are gun-inflicted.

There are some four hundred million guns in the USA, almost twice as many guns as cars. That amounts to a third of the world's guns. The army and police possess a mere seven million. One in three Americans say they have a gun. The average owner has five guns; only 22 percent have only one. Purchases seem to be increasing exponentially, and women account for a growing share. In 2020, Americans bought forty million guns, according to the FBI, of which 42 percent were purchased by women. Guns were responsible for forty-five thousand US deaths that year, 54 percent being suicides. Police officers and army members seem especially prone to suicide, killing themselves with their own weapons, belying the idea that guns are for self-defense.

Gang members killing each other with guns—as in the sugarcane town in Colombia that I discuss—is common in the USA too, notoriously so in Chicago and Baltimore.

Besides the dizzying logic of defending oneself from other self-defenders, the fact that most gun owners own lots of guns suggests a passion if not an addiction, as if amassing weapons is like collecting jewelry, books, or third or fourth houses.

With his own library in mind, Walter Benjamin, in his essay "Unpacking My Library," asks us to consider "true collectors" whose collections, he suggests, may assume divinatory powers and, what's more, come to eventually absorb the collector as part of the collection itself.[1] Transposed to guns, this implies that you, the collector, become a gun, which I assume is the ultimate goal.

Benjamin's essay on book collecting is charming, so much so that Hannah Arendt chose it to open the first collection of his essays in English, which she put together in New York City in 1969 under the title *Illuminations*. In her commentary on the essay, she emphasizes the noncommodity character of the items collected, in Benjamin's case, books, which are so desired for themselves that they become magical.

Is anything collected more than guns in deregulated, Second Amendment America? Four hundred million is quite a lot of guns, bringing to mind Bataille's fascination with profitless expenditure, or *dépense*, forming what he calls a "general economy," which, in the opening pages of his two-volume *Accursed Share*, he equates with possessing jewels or building a church.[2] Now in America we perforce add guns to the list, the gun being both jewel and church.

Thus, amid the panic for self-defense affecting vast swaths of the population there exists something else, and that is the profound attraction to guns in and of themselves such that, as in drug addiction, there can never be enough: big guns, small guns, fat guns, old guns, American guns, Italian guns, Austrian guns, shoulder-holster guns, ladies' purse guns, hunting guns, and war guns posing as hunting guns like the one used to try to kill Donald J. Trump in 2024.

But it's not only quantity that matters. It's the look, the feel, the shine, the glamor. And the name—you can't beat the poetry in the names: the Colt .45, the Smith and Wesson, the Magnum; not to mention what is fondly referred to as "ammo," such as "Dragon's Breath Shells" for shotguns, put out by the Wolf Hill Trading Company. Think about it. *Wolf Hill* pumping out *Dragon's Breath*—a telling instance of the creativity implicit in the adult's imagination of the child's.

When you scroll through images of gun sites online, the motive of self-defense blends with lust for the object itself as supernatural. There is little

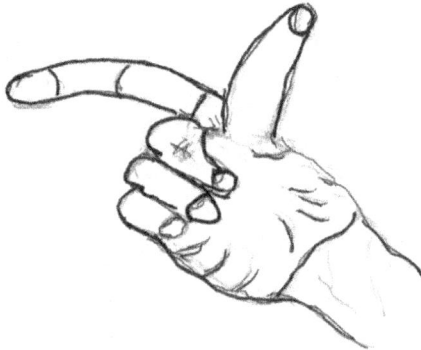

HAND GUN

that can compete for aesthetic impact with color close-ups of guns and cartridges. They seem to embody the industrial revolution and also, in the case of hand guns, emit a spiritual aesthetic that I trace to their death-dealing power combined with their small, stocky, no-nonsense potency, which can be clenched in a fist or secreted snugly in one's nether regions. They are surprisingly cheap too, from five hundred to a thousand dollars for state-of-the-art items.

Gun aestheticism is a defining feature of movies. Guns love movies as much as movies love guns. Guns were made for movies even though they were made centuries before. Guns were made for nicknames like my *gat*, my *rod*, my *piece*, my *heat*, my *chopper*, my *cannon*, and so forth. Guns take on the role of leading man, notably in films made by that US insider/outsider Sergio Leone, whose spaghetti westerns riffed on the ritualized gunfights of Hollywood films. Leone embraces the gun fetish and gives it context—Clint Eastwood's flinty face, his tight-lipped drawl, his Mexican poncho, his white anglo-self set against the black garb of his ugly, over-weight Mexican rival, a truly bad *hombre*.

Hitchcock saw what was coming. His films are scary because they have no guns, just elaborately coiffured ice-cold blonde women whom he pawed off camera. It's a wonder the NRA mounted no campaign against this dis-placement of the gun by such women.

DOES GUN FETISHISM AND HUNTING IN THE USA OUTWEIGH OR CONFIRM THE NUER-EFFECT?

Mass shootings in the USA are overwhelmingly carried out by white men using assault weapons like the AR-15, a gun designed for war. "A lot of people are like, 'Our armed forces use that. That's cool. I want that,'" stated a man who'd overseen marketing for one manufacturer.[3] An editorial in the newspaper *USA Today* quoted an assault weapon owner as saying, "There are very few things that serve such a great form and function, and look cool."[4] This in response to a notably eccentric judge's finding in 2021 that a white seventeen-year-old male hostile to Black Lives Matter had been justified in using an AR-15, as "self-defense," to kill two people taking part in a protest against police killing in Kenosha, Wisconsin.

"That's cool. I want that," says the adman, imagining his imagined buyer's imaginings. Being "cool" raises the question of whether gun fetishism in the USA has attained such mystical intensity as to mitigate the fear that would otherwise arise with Nuer-Effects that kill the killer. For is not the gun as much a charm as a mechanical instrument? Is it not an amulet exercising an apotropaic function?

When my ex-army, ex–French Foreign Legion bodyguard in Colombia anoints his bullets with holy oil and prays each morning to the souls of purgatory, he assumes this logic. He ratifies the fetish of the gun, which in the USA is anointed by the holy oil of the Second Amendment.

In this regard, I think of the humble pea-planting machine that, during the US Civil War, gave birth to the Gatling gun. It was quite an upgrade, from planting peas to firing two hundred bullets a minute, its inventor, a staunch Unionist, being of the opinion that, by displacing swords and bayonets, it would make war less likely and more humane. Peas became bullets and the rest, as they say, is history.

What seems to have most held Nuer-Effects at bay, however, were not only technological advances in the USA but declining belief in the existence of the spirits of the dead from the late nineteenth century onward, a trend these bright-eyed Yankee inventors likely found congenial. But then the dead are still with us, albeit swaddled in layers of ambiguity. Read Despret's *Our Grateful Dead* and look back at the epigraph to this very book.

Even the eminently sensible governor of New York State today talks with her dead mom and finds it best not to deny it.

This leaves the field open to Nuer-Effects or Nuer-Like Effects, but nothing confirms the Nuer-Effect more than rebranding war as hunting, the AR-15 as a hunting rifle.

The murder weapon in the Kenosha case was said by the defense of the murderer to be a *hunting* rifle, not a weapon of war.

This raises a tempting question; why don't we dwell on how "hunting" evokes the tricks and skills of cornering prey so as to maintain law and order in the human world, especially with regard to people of color in automobiles, especially in America where hunting is sacrosanct?

It is the gun as fetish that condenses this skill set of lies, exaggerations, myth, and fear into mystical thrill, as with the BULLET GUY sign outside the trailer gun shop I pass in upstate New York by the side of a peaceful country road. Guns are not drugs. They're legal. So why does it seem so furtive and aggressive, *Bullet Guy*, hermetic as a bank vault and Clint Eastwood's flinty face?

19 *Statistical Legerdemain*

The question I am pursuing throughout this book is whether anything like the Nuer-Effect exists in relation to killings by police in the USA.

Most people seem blissfully unaware that the police kill three people a day in the USA.[1] But some fatal encounters do catch the public imagination, and now and then a name persists in the news: Trayvon Martin in Sanford, Florida, in 2012 (whose killing occasioned the slogan "Black Lives Matter"); Eric Garner in Staten Island; Michael Brown in Ferguson, Missouri; Freddie Gray in Baltimore; Tamir Rice in Cleveland; Walter Scott in North Charleston, South Carolina; Philando Castile in Minneapolis; Sandra Bland in Waller County outside Houston; and more, including, since I first wrote this list, George Floyd, Breonna Taylor, and Ahmaud Arberry. But most names never surface in public consciousness, and most that do are soon forgotten.

In absolute numbers, white fatalities of police violence outnumber those of people of color. But African Americans are killed by police at proportionately higher rates than whites. And the rates for Native Americans are even higher, though all but invisible to the media.

The US government's so-called National Vital Statistics System is a farce. It's been found to underreport police killings by as much as half, as have FBI data. This seems to result from deliberate political decisions. Here we run head-on into the manipulation of data. Since 2015 the most accurate national accounting has been left to two newspapers, one British, *The Guardian*, the other American, *The Washington Post*.[2]

A recent study published in *The Lancet* based on a University of Washington study also shows that US government figures underreported by half the number of police killings for the years 1980 to 2018, the time period coinciding with the War on Drugs and the boom in mass incarceration.[3]

While overall crime figures had dropped since 1990, the *Lancet* article notes, according to a *New York Times* report, that many if not most coroners and medical examiners across the nation lean over backward to accommodate the police and find the causes of police-involved deaths to be accidental, attributable to factors like "preexisting medical conditions"—for example, obesity or emotional turmoil or sickle cell trait, which is racially linked, or drug ingestion, which is what the defense argued unsuccessfully in the George Floyd trial.

A follow-up article in *The New York Times* by Sheila Dewan reported on researchers at the San Diego Medical Center being paid hundreds of thousands of dollars to prove in court that "prone restraint" in police custody does not cause death.[4] Although contested, their conclusions are said to have trickled down into police departments, as justification for such restraint. In many places in the USA, coroners are elected, not chosen based on expertise; they may have no medical training, and may override the findings of pathologists, themselves often cozy with law enforcement, in favor of the police.[5]

No wonder law professor Franklin Zimring asked in 2017 "how a pattern of governmental killing much larger and much more constant than the notorious practice of capital punishment stayed a matter of such low visibility for so long in American public opinion."[6]

Such killings have become, at least intermittently, more visible. In 2012, the first use of the hashtag *BlackLivesMatter* followed the acquittal of George Zimmerman for his killing of Trayvon Martin in Sanford, Florida. In 2017, spectacular protests night after night confronted militarized police in Ferguson following the police killing of Michael Brown. The sustained protests after the video-recorded killing of George Floyd in 2020 had worldwide impact; even so, the headline on a *New York Times* op-ed by Farhad Manjoo read, "Cameras Won't Stop Police from Killing; Body Cams Have Turned Brutality into Spectacle."[7] But while it is true that no police officer seen killing on video had been found guilty in a court of law until the murder of George Floyd, that is not the case in courts of public opinion, national and international. What's more, calling something a "spectacle" by no means confounds its truth and moral impact because that's exactly what these videos of police brutality are—new ways of filming and of look-ing that open the frame to spectacular spectacle, what Nicholas Mirzoeff calls "no one's land."[8]

In the cases of George Floyd and Philando Castile, videos spread at lightning speed to millions of viewers via the haptic eye, the eye that joins vision to touch, collapsing the distance between the seen and the seer. That is the world of the Nuer-Effect mobilized by the phone camera.

20 *Auto-Mobilized Death-Space*

It's time to draw attention to the most common crime scene in America: an automobile pulled over by the police on the side of the road where about a third of US police killings occur.[1] Many, perhaps most, of the instigating events are "pretext stops," a vehicle pulled over, ostensibly because of an illegible registration plate or a cracked taillight, for example. But the deeper reasons seem to be to intimidate the general public and minorities in particular and, second, to get into a sacrosanct private space and fossick around a bit—a strip search on wheels, pulling at this, pulling at that, looking for drugs, looking for bundles of cash, scaring the daylights out of people (see first reason) and, if not planting drugs on them, then at least raising money in fines for a strapped township. (When Michael Brown was assassinated, in Ferguson, Missouri, in 2014, it came to light that most of the locals were Black and heavily in debt because of such fines, with little chance of being able to pay them off as the penalties for late payment mounted. They were trapped on a treadmill.)

I keep asking myself how it feels to be pulled over as the tension mounts in the interior of an auto-mobile? The videos of police shooting give us some idea. Surely for a large chunk of the US population the automobile interior qualifies as one of Foucault's heterotopias, like ships, circuses, colonies, brothels, prisons, and cemeteries or perhaps all bunched together.

The automobile offers the state a golden opportunity for surveillance and control of the population. In a racist society like the USA, the automobile is a state-registered trap, amounting to what I have earlier called "the space of death," a term introduced to me in the Putumayo River drainage of southwest Colombia by my elderly indigenous friend Florencio Mojomboy, describing his voyage into what he called the Space of Death—only in his case he came back to tell the tale.[2]

Unlike Florencio, Philando Castile, stopped by police for a faulty taillight, did not come back.

The angels with their lightning-struck quartz crystals imparting eloquence and justice in Florencio's case, were not present. Yet Castile's passenger, Diamond Reynolds, had something that was, in its own way, as powerful, namely a cell phone video camera streaming into Facebook.

It went "viral," as they say, which I take to be our word for a high-tech version of the Nuer-Effect, the word *viral* feeding into the biospiritual mix of that effect, blending the natural with the supernatural in the void of the automobile.

Diamond Reynolds's video is charged with experience that shatters experience. This video is as close as most of us will ever get to the lived experience of the act of killing *in real time*.

This is what happens with the too-often fatal police-stop, with passengers trapped in the closeted space, suffused with the spiritual intensity of the Nuer-Effect or of something approximating it, namely the biospirituality of state assassination. It may be that the spirit of the slain does not enter into the corpus of the killer in the way I described earlier, drawing on an anthropology of slaying, but does it not enter into the bodies of the video's millions of viewers via the hapticity and spiritual enormity of what is being shown?

To invoke what I call the Nuer-Effect is to evoke sympathetic magic, implying that there is an empathetic bond forged between killer and killed, a bond requiring life-saving rites for the killer, his family, kin, and to some extent the wider social group. Transposed into the USA and indeed the world today, that grouping is what Benedict Anderson, writing on nationalism, termed "the imagined community," a term that I now apply to the almost limitless Nuer-Effected video audience of police killing.

Viewing such videos becomes unmoored soul-stuff in territory known only in insomniacal nightmares like those of the gangsters afflicted with corpse magic I described earlier. Like it or not, we who watch those videos are part of what's happening and not detached viewers.

This is especially so in the USA where, despite the frequency of gun killing, depiction of violence between people is sanitized, as in Hollywood movies with their special effects that used to be the stock in trade of Superman and Captain Marvel comics.

But no matter how much the wagons are circled, death, especially violent death, has a way of escaping. Recall Susan Sontag, in her discussion of Peter Hujar's photographs of people with AIDS: "We no longer study the art of dying, a regular discipline and hygiene in older cultures, but all eyes, at rest, contain that knowledge. The body knows. And the camera shows, inexorably."

This sounds awfully like the mechanism involved in the Nuer-Effect, repurposed for other deaths in other circumstances.

It is this that takes up the slack in a modernity that has abandoned the *ars moriendi*, the art of dying. "All eyes, at rest, contain that knowledge," she writes.[3] Here we might recall Leopold Bloom in his carriage headed for the cemetery, thinking about how the eye of the slain may hold the image of the slayer.

Ruthlessly logical, secular, and perceptive, Sontag here propounds mystical ideas likening the living human body to a camera confronting a body dying from AIDS during the epidemic in which the camera shows what the viewer knows but does not know she knows.

A Los Angeles painter, Henry Taylor, made a painting from the video made by Diamond Reynolds. It freezes the flow of events in a conflation of jarring planes across a flatter than flat surface. We see the oblique angle of the car windows, Castile's body almost horizontal, the white forearm of the cop clenching a black pistol that looks like a toy. There is a patch of blue sky in the yellow window. The image is crude and forceful. It could be a mural honoring victims of violence outside a bodega in Los Angeles or in my Brooklyn neighborhood. It could be one of those colorful facades for the niches of the dead in the cemetery in Buenaventura (see chapter 5). I am reminded of the style adopted by the painter Leon Golub in the 1980s to depict torture and paramilitarism worldwide.

People may differ in their opinion of this painting as art, but what to me is important is that it condenses the video into one image. Taylor's decision, writes Alicia Eler, "to isolate and then combine a few freeze frames from the video into a singular composite image was deliberate—it slows down the moment, making space for contemplation and in-person reflection rather than just reacting online."[4] David Levi Strauss invokes this same effect in his polemic against the melee of "never-ending image streams that ultimately scorch our brains."[5]

"Contemplation and in-person reflection." Is that what predisposes to a Nuer-Effect in the contemporary USA, heart pounding, eyes wide? But "contemplation" and "reflection" seem not quite right, as if the viewer can withstand the pressure of what's depicted. For Taylor's painting extracts from the moving images a stillness that puts everything on hold—as when Benjamin, on the run in France in 1940, invokes a *messianic cessation of happening* as prelude to "a revolutionary chance in the fight for the oppressed past."[6]

"Thinking involves not only the movement of thoughts," he opined, "but their arrest as well. Where thinking suddenly comes to stop in a constellation saturated with tensions, it gives that constellation a shock by which thinking is crystallized as a monad.[7]

Well, what is a *monad*, a strange and even frightening word? Like "Nuer-Effect," it is an *abracadabra* word, referring here to a congealed mystical unity of "oneness," which in the case of Taylor's painting, freighted with incredulity, reminds us that drawing or painting and other forms of witness like the Lascaux cave drawings can complement video. "I swear I saw this," is what his painting says. What did he see? He saw the video and it penetrated him as he entered into it heart and soul. More important he felt the need to enact it, the need to "speak up."

Aby Warburg, who came of age in precinematic times, thought of a painting as a movie frozen in a frame. It is this forced immobilization—*like a traffic stop*—that gives painting its corporeal impact on the viewer, he thought.

In a daring move, Paul Virilio associates war with cinema, an amalgam facilitated, in his eyes, by magic and mysticism.[8] Writing in 1984, by which time photography, film, and video were established tools of warfare and policing, he did not anticipate, however, the reciprocal, that video could become a means of resistance. To my mind, Virilio's *War and Cinema* is outstanding for its focus on the mix of technology *and* magic used in war and civil unrest. Pundits informing us about technology and war are never in short supply. But rarely if ever would they harp on magic.

Virilio draws our attention to the increasing use of visual imaging both in actual warfare and in fictional renditions of war. He understands war as powered by what he calls *sympathetic magic* attuned to "the riveting spectacle of immolation and death agony, the world of ancient religions and tribal gatherings."[9] He could be writing about the horrors of Gaza as I write these lines in February 2024. He goes on to declare, "Terrorism insidiously reminds us that war is a symptom of delirium operating in the half-light of trance, drugs, blood, and union."[10] The "force of arms is not brute force but spiritual force."[11]

It seems that in famously proclaiming that war is politics carried out by other means, Carl von Clausewitz got it only half right. The other half was art and myth, but the "terrorism" Virilio cites seems to me badly misnamed. Think about the two-thousand-pound bombs liberally supplied by the president of the USA and dropped by the Israel Defense Forces on the people of Gaza and ask yourself,

"Who's the terrorist?"

To some extent Virilio's emphasis on image *and* magic is the everyday war-talk we hear now almost forty years later in the wake of October 7, 2023, assertions that the battlefield extends beyond the physical field to the worlds of media and imagination. It seems that the most obtuse general is now aware of that and tries to act accordingly. Surely this elevates the importance of the war artists active since at least World War I. Next will come the cultural anthropologists. It is strange that armies have not leaned into that discipline. Or have they?

The "sympathetic magic" Virilio regards as basic to war is equally present, I think, with policing itself, no less than with video acts of response to policing destined for huge audiences. With cell phones the past twenty years or so, we have entered a new era of warfare *and* counterwarfare.

PULL OVER: THE INTANGIBLE UNTOUCHABLE

What are the police at that moment when the cell phone video captures them in action? They can seem phantasmatic or cartoonish and monstrous (as in Henry Taylor's and Leon Golub's portrayals), not really human, as if all the paranoia and crime of which a society is capable comes to rest not on the species-being of the police but on their species unbeing.

Benjamin thought that police "power is formless, like its nowhere tangible, all-pervasive, ghostly presence in the life of civilized states." This is to be expected, he suggested, because of their "spectral mixture" of law-making and law-preserving violence.[12]

What he was getting at was that, like police traffic stops today, these micro-engagements of police with the citizen are a replay of the violence that gave birth to the state. At once real and mythopoetic, state-creating violence (revolutions, wars of independence, and so forth) is transmuted into law-preserving violence. And the police embody both these events. With every traffic stop, they renew the state, much as the corpse invigorated the Church and the protocorpse figure of Jesus on the Cross still does.

That is what police killing a person in auto-mobilized space means. The police engage a zone tying law to both myth and physical violence. The police exert a ghostly presence due to "formlessness," as Benjamin puts it, referring to the merging of law-founding with law-maintaining violence, which, in the USA, is heavily racialized and, since the 1970s, has been condensed into the War on Drugs, auto-mobilization, and the new Jim Crow of incarceration.

* * *

The First Cop Video. The case of Rodney King in 1991, when up to eight police officers swarmed in on King, is iconic as the first police assault in the USA to be recorded on video. The video evidence seemed clear, but the police were found not guilty.[13] The jury of ten whites, one Hispanic, and one Asian person included no African Americans; the prosecutor was Black, and the trial was held in the whiter-than-white Republican Party stronghold of Simi Valley, where the Ronald Reagan Presidential Library is located. Six days of rioting in Watts and sixty-three deaths followed the verdict. The Marine Corps was called in as well as the National Guard. After suing the city, King was awarded damages of five and half million dollars. He died a few years later from a heart attack in his tiny swimming pool.

The night the police beat him in full view of a video camera, King had been drinking and was speeding on the Foothill Freeway with two friends in a 1987 Honda Excel. A wife-and-husband team in a Highway Patrol car gave chase, and he tried to outrun them.

Imagine the scene. Midnight. Two Black men on the ground. King inside the Excel. White suburb. Cops everywhere. Taser let loose on King. Police jump on him in what is called a "swarm maneuver." A helicopter with searchlights hovers overhead, its rhythmic *whoompf, whoompf, whoompf* raising the hair on the back of your neck. This is theater full of "Virilio effects." And we see only eighty-one grainy seconds in an almost accidental video.

It was by chance that the video was made at all. A plumber by the name of George Holliday, a white man living in the all-white suburb of San Fernando, was awakened by noises and lights. Looking outside, he saw four policemen kicking a man on the ground. Only a month before, he had bought a bulky Sony Handycam and begun filming everything.

Infatuated with his new toy, he reached for his camera, started filming, and two days later submitted the video to a local news station, where it went viral. He had first contacted the police, but they showed no interest. In its eighty-one seconds, the video showed fifty-six attacks with clubs and boots.

A new era was initiated, that of video streaming police violence. Nuer-Effectual red lights flashed, illuminating a body by the side of the highway while a siren screamed like the pig being slaughtered at the fiesta in Clementina Echeverri's video (see chapter 2).

INCARCERATION USA-STYLE AND THE WAR ON DRUGS

I wonder whether mass imprisonment in the USA since the War on Drugs exerts something like the same effect as killing a person?

The body is confined and then, like the souls of the dead, the spirits of the confined are released into the public imagination like homing pigeons on a stupendous scale worthy of all Canetti's strange fulminations concerning the invisible crowd of the dead. The stream of reports from the prison on Rikers Island with its fifty-five hundred prisoners in New York City, not far from where I live, for instance, includes solitary confinement of teenagers younger than seventeen, leading in some cases to their suicide. National Public Radio reports that seven hundred women are claiming sexual assault by Rikers Island prison guards.[14]

Angela Davis, who spent time in prison in California awaiting trial on a murder charge, asks whether prisons are obsolete, whether they serve any useful purpose, and what it would take to think of a society without them?[15] Just as slavery was abolished, she thinks the time is long overdue to abolish the hellholes that form the US prison-industrial complex and seem only to make crime worse. But the legalized sadism she contests is an end in itself, beyond reason.

It seems impossible, no matter how energetic the protest, to shut down Rikers—because of the power of the guards, the way the political system works, and—let's face it—the public's indifference, if not support for in-carceration, all combined with the fact that *prisons, like slaughterhouses and cemeteries*, have been isolated, if not hidden, in this case on an island. In the seven years since a federal monitor was appointed to make Rikers Island safer, city jails have actually gotten more dangerous: A person in custody is seven times more likely to be seriously injured by another de-tainee, and staff are almost twice as likely to be assaulted. The problem, many argue, is that the federal monitor—who lives out of state, flies in for occasional meetings, and makes $400,000 a year—can write reports and make recommendations but can't truly change how Rikers operates.[16]

Is that our choice, to hide the nastiness? Can it really be hidden? Does that not only stir our imagination? In the USA there are currently some 2.2 million people in prison and another 4.7 million on probation or parole, overwhelmingly men of color. Native Americans are even more likely to be imprisoned than African Americans. The figures skyrocketed with the War on Drugs, placing Colombia front and center.

Michelle Alexander saw in the upsurge of incarceration starting in the 1980s the latest manifestation of Jim Crow laws, comparable to the laws enacted in the South after the Civil War to maintain segregation.[17] James Forman Jr., a public defender in Washington, DC, in the 1990s, points as well to the "tough on crime" stance of Black churches and Black conservatives worried about violence and drugs in the inner city.[18]

Not everyone in prison is there for drug felonies, but the War on Drugs initiated by Richard Nixon, boosted by Ronald Reagan, is at the root of today's three fatal shootings by police per day as well as the militarization of the police, including the fifteen-fold jump in SWAT team deployments between 1980 and 2000. The War on Drugs was at heart a War on Blacks—part of Nixon's "southern strategy" to get white southern Democrats to switch allegiance to the Republican Party. It had to look like a war to reassure whites, especially in the South, after the preceding decade's inner-city uprisings and Lyndon Johnson's progressive civil rights legislation. "The Nixon campaign in 1968, and the Nixon White House after that, had two enemies: the antiwar left and Black people," said Nixon aide John Ehrlichman in a recently published interview:

> You understand what I'm saying? We knew we couldn't make it illegal
> to be either against the war or black, but by getting the public to as-
> sociate the hippies with marijuana and blacks with heroin, and then
> criminalizing both heavily, we could disrupt those communities. We
> could arrest their leaders, raid their homes, break up their meetings,
> and vilify them night after night on the evening news. Did we know
> we were lying about the drugs? Of course we did.[19]

The War on Drugs was high-profile theater—drugs assured that—and, as Ehrlichman says, the idea was that it did not seem to be directly aimed at people of color but at drugs. Which is not to say there was no heroin problem or crack-cocaine problem; indeed, those drugs decimated the Black community. At the same time, strengthening the prohibition of such drugs in the USA increased their dollar value while fomenting gang formation and the macabre allure of the drug underworld. It was a war that could expand to include most anything and everything. The police had a free hand. And it was eminently exportable. Witness the War on Drugs and the wars within wars in Colombia and Mexico giving new meaning to magical realism and its relation to US neocolonialism.

PULL OVER: DRUGS, LIFE BLOOD OF EMPIRES

Drugs. A neon word for a neon world. If Marx suggested that religion—the heart of a heartless world—was also the opium of the oppressed, now almost two centuries later, that is no longer metaphor and you needn't depend, like Sherlock Holmes, on British imperialism in Bengal or China for your opium. The Sackler family and Purdue Pharma are right there when you need them for your chronic back pain and mounting despair. In 2020, the CDC reported a national average of 43.3 opioid prescriptions for every 100 Americans.

Getting high and getting wasted has a long history, as old as humankind, I would guess, a panorama of religious ecstasies and lands of Cockaigne, pre-dinner cocktails and all-night boozing, bums in the Bowery, Hogarth's gin palaces in London, the vodka sustaining Russia and the entire Eastern Bloc before, during, and after the USSR. Where, oh where, would humanity be without alcohol and drugs?

Discussing ancient Egypt and Incan Peru in *The Dawn of Everything*, David Graeber and David Wengrow consider "how an intoxicant could gradually become the life-blood of an empire."[20] Alcohol and drugs are not just part of the human condition. They are foundational. It took the contradictory amalgam of neoliberalism and prohibition to make drugs the key ingredient in my "preposterous equations," which in turn make Colombia and the USA come together, click, and multiply.

PULL OVER: FAULTY TAILLIGHT

Is not reality driven by drugs as well as by ideology? Vodka and drugs for the Soviets and their progeny till the liver shrinks; cocaine, heroin, methamphetamines, opioids and their countless derivatives, such as fentanyl, in the USA, where every year life expectancy declines. It is chilling to read Svetlana Alexievich's oral histories concerning *Homo Sovieticus* confronting the crisis at Chernobyl or her accounts of the war against the mujahideen in Afghanistan, with vodka the reward for excellence as well as life support. (And today, in Ukraine?)

With the US War on Drugs, things went crazy. The state found new demons to mobilize against and reality tilted. This we call "culture." Not the culture of drugs but the sustained and profound impact drugs as bio-spirituality have had and continue to have on the sense of reality, justifying out-of-control policing along with out-of-control gangsterism. A new energy was born, hallucinatory and frantic, followed by poor whites in the USA entering MAGA sleepy-time, lotus eaters with opioids to numb the pain as Facebooked algorithms surge through the body politic curdling the soul more than corpse magic ever could.

PULL OVER: SPEEDING

Is not auto-mobilization as big a drug as drugs? Even bigger? Is this why automobiles in the US are every day more obese despite policies to reduce energy consumption? For does not auto-mobilization seduce and coerce as much as drugs? And is not the automobile if driven by a person of color hounded by police almost as ferociously as drugs are? Indeed, the two are entwined. So lovely and loving are auto-mobiles in the ads on TV. Not so lovely when the police, like the elk hunters I described in Siberia, trap their prey. As a timely exercise, it would be rewarding to rework automobile advertisements for an art show in downtown Manhattan or Detroit. Instead of alpine landscapes and desert vistas, base the ads on the mis-en-scène of the police stop as the drama unfolds.

Are they not welded at the hip, automobiles, drugs, and police? You cannot get anywhere in much of the USA except in an automobile. Even in cities, especially the poor parts, which are the most populous, auto-mobilization abounds. Lush advertising for automobiles swamps the nation. Femmes fatales, like figureheads on sailing boats of yore, set the tone. Or else automobiles, true to their fetish character, drive themselves over mountains and deserts, conquering all in their path, appropriating the names of Native Americans and wild animals: Grand Cherokee, Mustang, and Cougar. Inner-city housing may be substandard, but inner-city auto-mobiles include impeccable dream-machines, BMWs, Mercedes, Teslas, Audis, and Cadillacs in mint condition. The staff parking lots at my local police station in Bed-Stuy, Brooklyn, are not short on luxury cars either. (Where do they get the money?)

Auto-mobilization did in fact catch the eye of artists. Nancy Reddin and Ed Kienholz made a number of life-sized installations involving automobiles in the 1960s—a memorable time for civil rights. *Five Car Stud*, started in 1969, displayed five cars in a circle at night with grotesquely masked men bent over a Black man pinned to the ground while the white woman with whom he'd been drinking cowers in a car, vomiting. It was shown first in 1972 at Documenta 5 in Kassel, Germany, curated by the legendary Harald Szeemann. It spent the next forty years unseen (should we say hidden?) in storage in Japan, before being rehabilitated for a show in Los Angeles in 2011.

Back Street Dodge '38, a 1964 installation, featured mannequins making out in the back seat of the automobile, with the door open for viewing. Reddin and Kienholz made two other automobile installations, one with the US Supreme Court, transformed into animals, seated inside a limousine.

When Kienholz died in 1994 at his home in Hope, Idaho, a hole was dug on the mountain where he used to drive up to view the sublime panorama. With Kienholz's corpse in the passenger seat, Reddin, his wife, drove his old Packard into the hole, which was then covered over with

HOPE
IDAHO

dirt, the automobile becoming his coffin set into the mountain in a place called Hope.

PULL OVER: AT THE REST-STOP

"Images fall slow and silent like snow. A beautiful blue substance flows into me." That was William Burroughs in *Naked Lunch*.[21] Altered states of consciousness in the 1960s were a bodily thing as much as an image thing. The music added to the speed-up as well as to the languor. So did the drugs, and so did the passion to protest two colonial wars, one at home and one in Southeast Asia.

PULL OVER: ERRATIC DRIVING

Does not *The War on Drugs* proclaim the obvious; that war is the biggest drug there is?

Toward the end of his 1967 account for *Esquire* magazine of frontline US soldiers in the American war in Vietnam, Michael Herr writes of a birthday party for his photojournalist colleague Tim Page, restricted to a wheelchair after suffering severe brain damage from shrapnel. "He began talking more and more about the war, often coming close to tears when he remembered how happy he and all of us had been there." He had just received an offer from a British publisher to collaborate on a book that would "take the glamour out of war."

Page couldn't get over it.

"Take the glamour out of war! I mean, how the bloody hell can you do that? Go and take the glamour out of a Huey, go take the glamour out of a Sheridan ... war is good for you, you can't take the glamour out of that. It's like trying to take the glamour out of sex, trying to take the glamour out of the Rolling Stones."

"The very idea," he said. "Ohhh, what a laugh! Take the bloody glamour out of bloody war!"[22]

In a chapter entitled "The Enduring Appeals of Battle," J. Glenn Gray writes that the "boundless capacity for self-sacrifice is what is intoxicating and great about war." He cites William James calling war a sacrament, asserting that "society would rot without the mystical blood payment."[23]

"War was and still is the most irresistible—and picturesque—news," wrote Susan Sontag in 2003 in her study of the role of photography in war from the Crimean War onward.[24]

As regards varieties of religious experience among US troops in Vietnam, Herr writes, "Every time there was combat you had a license to go maniac, everyone stepped over the line at least once over there and nobody noticed, they hardly noticed if you forgot to snap back again."[25] He doesn't mention the racial violence within the US Army, notably deadly attacks by white marines on Black marines—a premonition if not the seed for a right-wing armed militia movement within the USA whose growth became impossible to ignore with the Trump-inspired assault on the US Capitol on January 6, 2021, in which militias such as the "Proud Boys" and "Oath Keepers" joined vets and soldiers.[26]

In the USA, the American war in Vietnam was a television staple. Donald Rumsfeld, secretary of defense under George W. Bush, put a stop to that when US troops were sent to the Middle East on his watch. But note Herr: "Night was when it got really interesting in the villages, the TV crews couldn't film at night."[27] Was it this that inspired Virilio, this invisible imagery of war and the prohibition on TV filming ordered by the US secretary of defense? Didn't that indicate the importance of cinema and its magic? But cutting across Rumsfeld was the legion of photographers making still images like Page, and later on the film *Apocalypse Now* (1979), based on the novel *Heart of Darkness* with its "fascination of the abomination."

And not just images but drugs were critical too; drugs on the front line with the soldiers, the reporters, and the photographers; drugs stateside as well.

Drugs and Herr's words are Gilles Deleuze and Félix Guattari's "molecular impulses" moving through bodies, connecting all manner of being and beings. The words hug what the writing is about, then detach, briefly, sometimes go a long way away, then come back into the fray. Like the frontline war experience, I suppose.

Herr writes that men on helicopter crews "would say that once you'd carried a dead person he would always be there riding with you." Of course, it's not the enemy's soul that is riding with you, as in the Nuer-Effect scenario that prompts my inquiry. Or maybe the enemy's soul is incorporated in the body of your fellow soldier as a colonial Nuer-Effect?

Vietnam is a long way from Nuer-land, where two guys battle it out with spears and the "blood" of the slain enters into the slayer. And a long way from Arawete-land, where the soul of the slain sleeps with you and your wife, teaching you songs in your dreams and new dance steps. It's a long way, too, from Murngin-land, where the slayer senses the slain entering his body in an expanding world.

But in this war, is not the helicopter my spirit? And is that what PTSD is, a Nuer-Effect dressed up in an acronym in hock to the mystique of science? Nothing was as magical as the helicopter itself. "Choppers rising straight out of small cleared jungle spaces, wheeling down onto city rooftops, cartons of rations and ammunition thrown off, dead and wounded loaded on."[28]

A whole squad of soldiers dressed in Batman fetishes:

Guys stuck the ace of spades in their helmet bands, they picked relics off of an enemy they'd killed, a little transfer of power; they carried around five-pound Bibles from home; crosses, St. Christophers, mezuzahs, locks of hair, girlfriends' underwear.... One man was carrying an oatmeal cookie through his tour wrapped up in foil and plastic and three pairs of socks. He took a lot of shit about it ("When you go to sleep we're gonna eat your fucking cookie.")

Magical, too, the language, the grunt's Nuer-Effected language and Herr's ear for what mints language afresh—as grounded as *Moby Dick* and as sweeping in terms of the soul and something more, the beyond-words of words and the bottomless political corruption. Yes, that seems to me a Nuer-Effect too, when the soul of the slain and the slayer inhabit not only your body but your prose.

21   *Killing Animals versus Killing Humans*

Retired US Army Lieutenant Colonel Dave Grossman, who invented the discipline of "killology," or at least the term, tours police academies with a presentation about killing. He argues that killing is against human nature, that humans are hard-wired not to kill, and that one kills at psychological cost.

Given his emphasis on this taboo, it would seem that justifying killing to the police, or at least easing the consciences of actual or potential killers, would be a challenge. That could be why, in his post-9/11 lectures that I have seen online, Grossman raises the specter of terrorism, especially with regard to the targeting of US children in schools, overlooking the fact that to date school massacres have been committed by (often young) white US citizens acting in isolation, not by foreign terrorists.

Grossman's efforts imply that police, although morally and politically sustained by an institution, still need extrajudicial justification and cultural psychotherapy for killing. He expresses interest in rituals in what he calls "warrior societies" that are designed to overcome or at least mitigate the sickness and craziness that follows killing another warrior—what I call the Nuer-Effect.

You might wonder, watching Grossman's impressive rants to police academies on YouTube, whether he's not himself stricken by what he intends to heal? He seems to be reenacting his own Nuer-Effected Self as therapy for others. Don't sneer. Anyone, liberal or reactionary, who sets themselves up as an expert on violence, whether anthropologist or violentologist, is likely to be Nuer-Effected sooner or later.

Smart-ass, melodramatic, intelligent, and at times sinister, Grossman's presentations are every inch dramatic performance, bringing to my mind Eduardo Viveros de Castro's descriptions of the spirit of the slain person teaching songs to the killer in the latter's dreams and teaching him new dances. He is possessed and aims at enchanting his audience.

You can also, I believe, see our killologist swelling in size on the stage, like the killer described in Lloyd Warner's 1927 text on the Murngin in northeast Australia. Just as the soul of the victim worms its way into the killer's body in Warner's account, you can sense a throbbing wave of contagion energizing Grossman's rapt audience, spiritually enlarging by the second. In other words—and this is crucial—the Nuer-Effect in the circumstances I describe for the USA, like Warner's description, does not stop with the killer but spreads beyond, way beyond, as befits the size of the US population and its billowing media.

Pacing the stage in full rhetorical flight, Grossman gives voice to the mythology of the policeman's badge as the ultimate sign of warrior status. He informs us that it is called a "shield." He could be in trance with the shield evoking ideas of native warriors and the knights of the Middle Ages. Descending from the stage, he momentarily caresses the shoulder of a seated policewoman, then ascends to the stage once more. It is a poignant moment, this touching, and something more, this gender-sensitized descent and ascent, spreading a halo of Nuer-Effects thanks to the killologist's touching and the corpse magic upon which it implicitly rests of three assassinations per day.

SHIELD BUMP AND WAR FEVER

In Craig Atkinson's 2016 documentary film *Do Not Resist*, concerning the militarization of US police, there is a shot of two police officers one night in August 2014 leaving the battlefield of protests against the police killing of an unarmed Black teenager, Michael Brown, in Ferguson, Missouri. Like football players exultant after scoring a goal, they perform a ritual known as "the shield bump" in which they hold up their plastic body shields and then bring them together—*bump*.

When mellow-voiced Leonard Lopate, the NPR interviewer, asks Atkinson about this scene, he also asks about Dave Grossman affirming that, after street battles, police "have the best sex ever."

It is a tense moment. Lopate and Atkinson seem embarrassed and tread warily. Grossman repeatedly returns to the theme of sex. Indeed, it would be no exaggeration to say that sex forms the backbone to his inquiry into

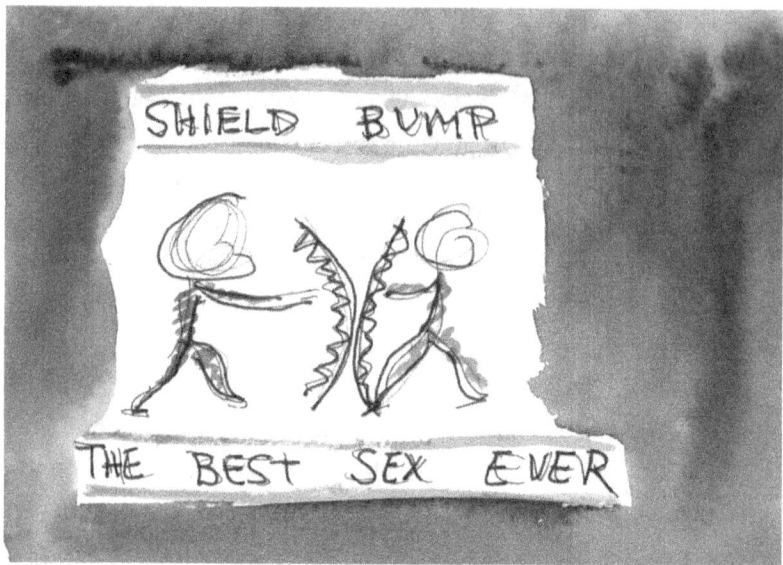

SHIELD BUMP

THE BEST SEX EVER

killing, it being his argument that while in the West the study and discourse of sex has been liberated (*pace* Foucault), killing as a subject for analysis remains swaddled in taboos and denial. (He has a point.) "Every society has a blind spot, an area into which it has great difficulty looking. Today that blind spot is killing. A century ago it was sex."[1]

Yet surely killing is one thing, killing on behalf of the state another?

Grossman presents anecdotal evidence as to the sexuality of killing done with state authorization. A soldier links the massacre at My Lai with the pleasure and guilt of masturbation. A British paratrooper confides that an attack in the Falklands was the most exciting thing since "he got his leg across." I myself recall a *New York Times* report of a female pilot in the first Gulf War writing her parents in the same vein, words to the effect that "flying into combat was the most exciting thing since my first date." (She was shot down.) An Israeli military psychologist predictably recalls an Israeli machine gunner in orgasmic ecstasy squeezing the trigger, his weapon hammering, and the flight of his tracers "rushing out into the dark shore."[2] A Vietnam vet compares having a weapon to "having a permanent hard-on. It was a pure sexual trip every time you got to pull the trigger."[3]

As antidote and proof, Thomas Pynchon had the key character in *Gravity's Rainbow* get a hard-on whenever a German V-2 rocket was approaching

England. Scientists were intrigued. The War Office wanted to adopt the phenomenon into their defense system. Paranormal psychologists and spiritualists were called in.

"Anyone entering military service for the first time," writes J. Glenn Gray, "can only be astonished by soldiers' concentration upon the subject of women and, more especially, upon the sexual act." The most common word is *fuck* as adjective, adverb, verb, and noun in practically every sentence spoken. We "spent more time in the service of Eros during our military careers than ever before or after." He continues. "For their part, millions of women find a strong sexual attraction in the military uniform, particularly in time of war."[4]

This opens things up. It seems there is a fever to war affecting women as much as men, a fever that affects society as a whole. Mauss and Hubert might have called this *mana*. War unleashes mana. With World War II in mind, Gray noted that in wartime marriages multiply and the birth rate increases. He recalls the Greek myth of the love affair between Aphrodite, goddess of love, and Ares, god of war. Two children were born from their union, the ever-youthful Eros and the beautiful Harmonie. We might recall William James on war as sacrifice and as blood debt—crazy stuff indeed, eyeball-rolling scary, that in my opinion seems pretty accurate. The path here is steep and perilous, as full of mystery as it is of tenderness and cruelty, bound as it is with the widespread practice of torture, rape, and defilement of women.

Is not the capture by men of the enemy's women and the protection of "their own" women an underlying trope of war, beginning with *The Iliad*?

To Grossman's conviction that humans are hard-wired not to kill, contrast the deluge of stories attesting to an innate or almost innate love—yes love!—of destruction. Gray tries masterfully to wind a path through these contraries, but cannot.

Resisting dialectics, Bataille emphasizes the not fitting together of oppositions and the propulsive dynamism thereby unleashed, come what may, in which all societies indulge in their different ways at different times. Mass shootings in the USA is one such way, gun fetishism another. Bataille's examples are banquets, potlatch, religious ecstasies, sumptuous expenditure—and *war*. In fact, he regards twentieth-century wars as more massive acts of *dépense* than all acts of *dépense* prior to 1949 when his book was published.

LIKE BATAILLE, THE COLONEL WONDERS

Lieutenant Colonel Grossman draws attention to the rarity in the US today of direct experience of the killing of animals. Back in the day, he says, kids on farms witnessed such killing at close proximity, including some involving animals regarded as family pets. They may well have assisted in the castration of bulls and pigs.

In 2016, when I was researching Colombian landlords' use of death squads to make way for oil palm, I stayed with a family in a village surrounded by an encroaching oil palm plantation. Their teenage daughter had a pig that roamed through the area where we took our meals. With lightning speed it would steal our plastic plates even if they bore no more than a trace of food. We watched this ever-nimble pig while in the back of our minds savoring the meal he would one day become. The teenager's father, I might add, was an adept castrator, and next door a monkey on a rope spent the day somersaulting. In other words, we lived in the thick of human-animal relationships in which killing, castrating, and eating one's companions was commonplace.

At the end of this tiny settlement about once a week a cow was slaughtered on the street by my new friend Ariel and his sons. The village nurse had a flock of sheep. Her mother was one of the two midwives that delivered babies in the village. And surrounding the village were the killer paramilitaries hired by the oil palm plantation.

In other words, animal slaughter and human birth were integral parts of everyday reality, as were death squads. There was no concealment of killing. None at all. The pig ate our scraps, and we ate the pig, while my colleague Juan Felipe García and many of the villagers not only litigated in courts of law but physically resisted the death squads.[5]

In *Pig Earth*, a collection of stories published in 1979 concerning peasant life in a French alpine village, John Berger describes the killing of a cow in the village abattoir. The cow's owner knows its habits as well as he knows his fellow villagers. He has followed her life since birth. He has taken her into the mountains in summer and back down in winter. It is an ecology of persons, animals, and mountains that ends in killing for money. Shrewd calculations of profits are based on the rhythms of birth and death. If she is not killed now and calves, the cow can no longer be milked, will lose weight, and will be worth less. Flashes of bitterness occur between the old man and his younger wife who together work the abattoir. The son shoots the bolt into the masked cow's brain. It is a family affair, interspecies at that.

In a quite different way this awareness of killing cattle and pigs also exists in the western Colombian town of fifty thousand people where I first came across corpse magic. I recall with stark clarity a queue of people huddled in the cold at sunrise some thirty years ago, outside the slaughterhouse in the center of town. They were waiting to drink the fresh blood, said to be a tonic. You can't get much closer to animals than drinking the warm blood flowing from their just-killed bodies.

Other associations come to mind, such as cattle rustling, the close ties between butchers and regional mafias, the reserving of choice cuts such as *loma biche* for fancy restaurants in Cali, the butchers, jocular and hoary, male and white, selling muscle meat while a hundred meters away Black women, spattered in blood and grease, sell intestines and internal organs. *Triperas*, they were called, after tripe, famous for their flashing knives. "Don't mess with me," they seemed to say, while smiling.

Here killing and the selling of meat for consumption formed a close bond at many levels of awareness and sociology. There was the fresh blood drunk at sunrise, the association with criminality, the sharp gender distinction—*triperas* peddling organ meats versus red meat and hoary masculinity. You could say everyone in town was "in the know," that killing and eating were closely connected activities, until the cocaine-moneyed businessmen set up money-laundering supermarkets with freezers. That was in the 1980s, just as the drug war took off in Colombia along with the birth of local gangs and killing by the army, by paramilitaries, and by the FARC and other guerrilla groups.

Nowadays, however, children and young adults in the rural Colombia that I know are repulsed at the thought of killing even a chicken, though some seem to have no compunction about killing a person. Few young adults know how to cook a meal. They buy fast food, especially chicken produced in terrible conditions. By at least 2015, everybody was eating chicken without any idea of how the animals lived and died. Fast food had arrived, deathlessly, magically contrived, but there was one killing people still recognized and knew well, and that was not of animals.

In *Every Twelve Seconds*, Timothy Pachirat's remarkable account published in 2011 of his undercover fieldwork in a Nebraska slaughterhouse, we read in unforgettable Nuer-Effecting detail what has long been rendered invisible because of gag rules enacted by state legislatures at the behest of meat industries. It appears that these industries are scared if not sacred. They are scared of something like three hundred million human carnivores in the USA getting turned off by killing (of animals, not humans) and by the negative effects of meat on human longevity. The brilliant young US congresswoman known as AOC was derided by Republicans early on in her tenure: If the Green New Deal becomes a reality, they bellowed, "she'll take away your hamburger."

In April 2020, a month into the COVID-19 pandemic, President Trump declared that the animal slaughtering industry (called "meatpacking"), along with gun shops, were "essential," and that slaughterhouse workers had to return to their killing even though their work conditions significantly increased the chance of they themselves being killed by the virus.

Unlike the rest of us, slaughterhouse workers are certainly aware of the killing of livestock (a curious word, *live-stock*; compare Diego Rivera's "frozen assets," chapter 9). A safety supervisor tells the author of *Every Twelve Seconds* to stay away from "knocking," meaning the actual killing. "Man, that will mess you up. Knockers have to see a psychologist or psychiatrist or whatever they're called every three months."

"And why's that?"

"Because man that's killing. That shit will fuck you up for real."

The author, who briefly tried his hand at knocking before going back to hanging livers in the cooler, goes on to note that the effect of "knocking" makes possible the construction of killing as something "other," even on the "kill floor."[6]

What does he mean? What is involved in construing killing as "other"? He means that the persons doing the actual killing, the knockers, as well as those working in other sections of the kill floor, manage to kill by mythologizing killing, investing it with "almost supernatural evil powers." Pity he does not explain more. Are the knockers victims of the Nuer-Effect, crazed by what they do?

It is worth pointing out that Nuer-Effects can come from reading about killing as much as from killing itself. Reading *Every Twelve Seconds*, for instance, you are likely to become haunted by the images it engenders—just as it's difficult to shake off *narcorelatos*. This effect seems stronger and more likely to occur when it is animals being killed, as compared with humans—and therein lies a mystery.

J. Glenn Gray comes to mind here, with his sense that our language of guilt, implicating modern psychology, impedes understanding of killing. But colloquial language here does an end-run around that psychology: "That shit will fuck you up for real."

Gray refers us to the killing not of animals but of soldiers by other soldiers. This raises the question of whether it is possible that Nuer-Effects in industrialized societies are more likely to be generated by the killing of animals than of humans, bringing to mind a remark by cartoonist Chuck Jones, of Bugs Bunny fame, that it is more difficult to humanize humans than animals.[7]

The spiritual link between animals and humans is in my opinion one reason why abattoirs are concealed from view and also why a freaky antiseptic aura shrouds the styrofoam-embedded steak in the supermarket cooler. Red meat appears as if by magic. *Voilà!* No long knives flashing here. No grease or blood either, a mystery without mysteriousness, like the way your everyday taillight problem can enter into the sacred of an everyday police stop.

22 *The Taboo on Portraying Killing*

Killing is hedged in by fierce taboos. Because of that, it has been a famous subject for religiously inspired Christian image making.

Numerous painters and sculptors have interpreted biblical stories such as Judith beheading Holofernes in the Old Testament, and John the Baptist's severed head presented to Salome in the New Testament. Caravaggio painted versions of both, and in *David with the Head of Goliath* depicted his own head, bloody and misshapen, as that of Goliath. This would not go over well today. But Caravaggio? What can you say?

You can't get away from the fact that killing is a major theme in religious representation, at least in Judeo-Christian tradition, notably with the Crucifixion, which became important from the fifth century after the death of Christ onward.

I find it strange that many Christians and Jews seem never to tire of saying how violent and militant is Islam. Yet the Hebrew Bible mixes the harshness of God's rule with awful tales of killing, while Christianity manifests a profound attraction to suffering, of Self as much as of Other, manifest in the abject humility of Christ and the saints, many of whom go so far as to inflict upon themselves torture and death. This does not seem altogether healthy.

Let us contemplate one of the many versions of Judith beheading Holofernes, paintings that date from the Middle Ages through to the twentieth century.[1] In Caravaggio's version, the sweep of light and shadow resonates with a pervasive sense of shock. Holofernes's eyes and mouth are wide open in disbelief: "Is this really happening? Is this happening to me?" It is a portrait of death in life, of the very moment of the kill, neither dead nor alive but in some fathomless in-between state. It is also a wholly remarkable feminist image, erupting from biblical times no less than Caravaggio's.

As with Artemesia Gentileschi's and Lucas Cranach the Elder's paintings of Judith in action, what we see is decapitation porn, shocking and titillating. It is not only the wonderfully skilled painting involved but the transgression of the taboo that makes the images leap out. In our own time, such images of bodily violation would be censored by law or taste—much more so in Euro-America than in Colombia, where I used to see pages of the afternoon newspapers like *El Caleño* laid out on the footpath on the side of the plaza opposite the church of the town in which I lived. Photos of near-naked young women were juxtaposed with photos of mutilated, naked or semi-naked corpses on the facing page. While the Mass proceeded in the church, there was this other ritual on the other side of the plaza.

COMEDY

If in our time the corpse offers boundless opportunity for comedy, especially in film, is it any surprise therefore that Judith cutting off Holofernes's head can do so?

Well, yes, to me it was a surprise, rather delightful, at that, when in 2018 I read Brianna Rennix and Lyta Gold's sillier-than-silly smart-ass commentary on some twenty paintings of this bloody event.[2] Their exchange is funny, partly because they are so sharp, partly because through humor they shatter the pomposity of Art History, bringing to light fundamental aspects of the paintings you might otherwise not see, and partly because in their lightheartedness they themselves transgress the transgression of the taboo. They are more Bataille than Bataille.

Bataille struggles manfully to convince us that laughter, eros, and death are intrinsically connected. Yet his efforts fail for want of examples and, even more, for want of the attitude toward art, and indeed life, that these young women exude.

One thing Rennix and Gold bring out is what fun it is to imagine what Judith is thinking as she decapitates. Look at her face? What is she saying to her servant? What are the two of them saying to us? What do their postures communicate? At the same time, we surely enjoy the reckless anachronisms they offer, connecting things of our time—clothing styles, handbags, and so forth—with details in centuries-old paintings imagining an event that occurred more than a millennium before the paintings themselves. This montage of now and then fertilizes the disturbing mix of taboo and transgression that these paintings evoke in response to the violence of patriarchy.

INTERFACIALITY

If the face is the window to the soul, yet also a mask, what happens when two or more faces face each other and one of the faces, like that of Holofernes, is, in his eye-bulging spasm, passing from life to death?

There is another face to contend with, apart from those of Judith, Holofernes, and the servant, and that is our own face, the face of the viewer. We do not actually see our face looking, but do we not feel it's transcription in our soul? We are mimetically bound to the scene we gaze at. We become part of it according to Emmanuel Levinas's insistence that (1) I exist in the face of the other and (2) the face is the evidence that makes evidence possible.

In which case, what is the painter of this scene to do? The stakes are daunting as one of the faces in which I exist is halfway to amputation, which imperils mine too.

THE STILLED IMAGE

Midway between life and death, seized by shock, Caravaggio's Holofernes offers us a momentary glimpse of the Nuer-Effect in its making.

You might assume that brutality ineffably defies representation as Judith's knife slices through Holofernes's throat, his eyes staring in disbelief. But, far from it, the brutality enhances the beauty and congealed repose that is the upsurge of life as it disappears.

Yet can a painting compete with the reality of the slaughterhouse kill floor or the guillotining of the king and queen that led to their Louvre palace becoming—of all things!—a public art museum without the enormity of its origin receiving much, if anything, by way of recognition? Whom among the millions of visitors staring at the Mona Lisa each year knows this or cares?

The bourgeois individual (as Bataille would have it) like myself looks at paintings of decapitation and feels disturbed. But how does that compare with a video of beheadings carried out by ISIS in Iraq, or the video streamed by the perpetrator himself of the massacre of worshippers in the mosque in Christchurch, New Zealand?

I don't know. At first it seems that the moving picture hits with more force, yet does not a painting take advantage of stillness? Does not stillness amplify the "fixed-explosive" quality André Breton points to in *Mad Love*?

Moreover, the still image for Warburg is not so much a still image as a *stilled* one. Goethe, writing about the sculpture of Laocoön and his sons, excavated in Rome in 1506, had made a similar distinction. Of course, being a sculpture it is still. But more than that it is *stilled*. A pertinent image here is another of Caravaggio's severed heads, that of the Medusa. The story was if you locked eyes with her when she was alive, or even with her decapitated head, you would be *petrified*—turned to stone, hence stilled, and hence the power of using her severed head to still others if, like Perseus, you managed to cut her head off without looking directly into her face.

Bearing such a charm you can "still" the Other; that is, use this charm to petrify the person who harmed you, as in Rogerio Velásquez's description I have cited of the Chocó corpse magic that does its work by dazzling the murdered person's shadow (see chapters 1 and 5). Does this provide a clue to Warburg's obsession with the image as fixed movement? How can a still image evoke movement? How can a still image freeze movement so it is both decidedly still *and* motile? *Is not this paradox the realm of the living-dead*, of the corpse both alive and dead activated by corpse magic, as in horror stories like Bram Stoker's *Dracula* and my stories from western Colombia?

Haunted by the notion of images as stilled movement, as "treading water," so to speak, Warburg wrote himself a note: "To attribute motion to a figure that is not moving, it is necessary to reawaken in oneself a series of experienced images following one from the other—not a single image; a loss of calm contemplation." And, following Goethe, he described the

Laocoön Group, with its writhing serpent enclosing three human figures, as like a flash of lightning or a wave petrified as it approaches shore.[3]

Warburg suggested, as had Goethe, that you should blink in front of such a depiction, close and open your eyes so as to "catch" the movement, in effect using your eyelids as the shutter in a movie projector.

Is this "blink-effect" the same as the victim's nightly visits to the assassin as part of the corpse magic I describe in western Colombia? With drawn-out slow-motion vengeance as its goal, the stilled image moves into action. What the corpse sorcerers or stories about them have figured out is how to perfect Warburg's and Goethe's scheme. Lightning flashes. The wave trembles just before breaking as it approaches the shore. Surfboard riders are experts at gauging this stilled movement.

There seems little need with the Laocoön to blink to sense its movement. But then, it is more than movement. It is also its cessation, the Surrealist "fixed explosive."

In a pathbreaking essay on what he called "the third meaning" in film imagery, Roland Barthes singled out the "freeze-frame," a single frame extracted from a movie or comic strip. But nowhere, I dare say, is this "freeze" more obvious than in depictions of a drop-dead gorgeous woman cutting off the head of a tyrant.

Barthes's point about the "third meaning" was its "pointlessness," its open-endedness and anarchy with regard to "meaning." It not so much resists symbolic and semiotic connections as consumes them where interpretation exhausts itself. Such, I believe, is the biospirituality of the Nuer-Effect and, even more so, of the visual representations influenced by it. Two extremes meet, movement and stasis: severing the head of Holofernes, all movement; the face of Judith, stock-still, more than serious, concentrated and calm—a study in frozen movement. Meanwhile, the onlooking servant, whom I take to be a stand-in for the viewer of the painting, expresses the enormity of the erotic mix of assassination and liberation. It's up to you, the viewer, to experience time's collapse in the image.

In Caravaggio's Holofernes and in his Goliath, the eyes and mouth of the head are wide open in astonishment, rage, pain, and disbelief. The latter is Caravaggio's own head, while it has been surmised that the young

David is his assistant, who was probably his lover at the time. Caravaggio did not need to blink. His being-killed face is the evidence that makes evidence of Nuer-Effectuality possible. It is not Judith who embodies the Nuer-Effect but us, the viewers.

DESUBLIMATION

These paintings of decapitation position the viewer in the *corporeal* space of embodiment I am claiming for the Nuer-Effect and the *narcorelato*.

If ever there was embodiment it is found in the *narcorelato*. For these tales exercise *desublimation*, meaning that they reverse the movement of sublimation that Freud postulated, transforming sexual instincts into art by means of repression.[4]

Consider the Catholic Mass in which the body of Christ is eaten, an astounding event if taken literally but rendered "as if" thanks to sublimation, thus transposed into the higher realms of symbolism.

Narcorelatos circumvent this. They dwell in the Rabelaisian "lower realms," where is found, in Mikhail Bakhtin's interpretation, a ferment generative of life, enthusiastically dismissive of good taste and social hierarchies (read, Stalinism and its heirs). Taboos are broken joyfully left and right in an ecstatic if not erotic redemption passing through the melee of desublimation. It is an old story, claims Bakhtin, older than Christ, and one that defines his being, his message, and his holiness.[5]

The same Rabelaisian move was made surrealistically by Bataille when in 1929–1930, as editor of *Documents*, he wrote essays such as "The Big Toe," "The Language of Flowers," and "The Solar Anus."[6] In these essays, the ludic pull of the sublimatory is entertained with élan, playing with the Hegelian dialectic—the head in relation to the big toe, for example. Such play amounts to a perpetual-motion machine in which the toe, proximal to earth's earthiness, trumps the idealization of the head, thought, and the airy heavens because these cannot exist without the feet or the body's materiality. What's more (Surrealist Bataille here pulls our leg), the big toe can come across, especially with age, as an absurd-looking, indeed surreal, piece of anatomy (as shown by the larger-than-life photos provided

THE BIG TOE

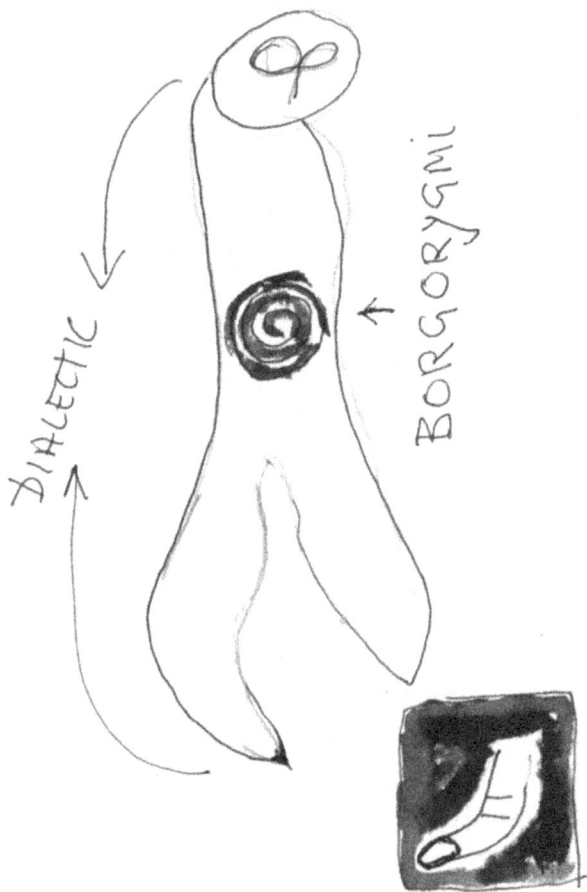

DIALECTIC

BORGORYGMI

by J. A. Boffard). Even more, as the big toe exceeds the dialectical head–foot back-and-forth, it inhabits what Bataille elsewhere calls "base materialism," a realm immune to meaning. It just is.

In Bataille's essay, the big toe jumps out of dialectic. An unstable ricochet, back and forth between the sublimatory and the desublimatory, ends—but is there an end?—with his highlighting the circular movement of the contents of the human intestines and the echoing sound of the bowels in a sort of chthonic laughter known as borborygmi or the growling of the stomach. *Borborygmi!* You have to love the sound of this word, in a nonsublimatory and loving sort of way, of course—the sound of a dialectic without end.[7] Like the awkward corporeality of the big toe, the sound of the bowels is basely material and desublimatory.

What the *narcorelato* achieves, in my opinion, is a "big toe effect," a picture, a story, a reaction with Rabelaisian flare hovering over horror mixed with the grotesque. Think of Vladimir's story as he passes ever so quietly by the riverbed where the corpses hang, one dead, the other still alive, screaming, both en route to becoming corpse-containers for cocaine.

This Rabelaisian flare not only generates Nuer-Effects but *is* those effects, their spread and diffusion beyond the actual event depicted. At bottom, what is the Nuer-Effect, after all, if not the epitome of enfleshment as the spirit of the slain enters your body in desublimating waves even when encountered secondhand for us listening to Vladimir's *narcorelato*? What do I recall now? The motorbike of *alto cilindraje* (I hear it purring) as the mist rises off the stream by the hung corpses being stuffed with a coca derivative, a man screaming, and Vladimir's cunning as our launch passes over the river of floating flowers.

23 *Nuer-Effect:*
   Present or Absent or Both?

In previous pages I have drawn attention to corpse-spirit excitation stemming from assassination as with the spiritual effluvium streaming from the Crucifixion, ancient Greece corpses, and the magical healing properties attributed to state-assassinated corpses in eighteenth- and nineteenth-century Britain (Hardy, Boswell, Laqueur) and fifteenth- to eighteenth-century Germany (Augsburg, Kathy Stuart); and considered the emotional if not spiritual satisfaction of corpse mutilation as enacted between Protestants and Catholics in early modern France (Natalie Zemon Davis), in 1930s Spain (Bruce Lincoln), and during the Colombian Violencia. I've circled, in particular, around a number of corpse exhumations in western Colombia, beginning with a break-in on New Year's Eve 2014 into a cemetery in a sugar plantation town, a break-in motivated, so I was told, by the intruders' fear that a fresh corpse had been magically arranged to kill its killer or killers.

This has led me to claim that, alongside the endless return of the Crucifixion since the early Middle Ages, we can surely add what I call Nuer-Effects as spiritual entailments of assassination. These striking stories from anthropology and ancient Greece and so forth, in which the slain person in some form enters into the body of the slayer and in which cosmic perturbation may occur, seem to me relevant when we consider cell phone videos of killing by US police.

PHOTOGRAPHY OF THE UNTOWARD DEAD: AFTERLIVES

In considering photography with regard to what I call Nuer-Effects, I am drawn to Aby Warburg's idea of the "afterlives" of images, what he called *nachleben*, analyzed recently with great panache by Georges Didi-Huberman.[1] Afterlives are survivals, which is why Didi-Huberman focused on the early Oxford anthropologist E. B. Tylor's *Primitive Culture* published in 1871 in which the idea of cultural survival of customs and beliefs was fundamental. By the 1920s this idea had been abandoned by British anthropologists in favor of *functionalism*. But for us, faced with cell phone videos of police killing in the USA, the notion of afterlives is obviously relevant, adding weight to those images as moving force with immense corporeal impact.

The notion of the body uppermost in Didi-Huberman's approach to Warburg owes much to Nietzsche's view of history, involving a physiology of history that can almost be measured and displayed like the twitching of a muscle plotted as a myogram or an earthquake recorded on a seismogram. Indeed, the idea of an earthquake is not far from what both Nietzsche and later Warburg had in mind for the seismogram that is, in their estimation, the ideal historian of culture, sensitive to power and aesthetics. In this, they seem to me to share the sensitivity to spirits of the dead possessed by prevocal infants and some elderly people in the gold mining village I describe at the beginning of this book.

Warburg's three years in a mental asylum for schizophrenia or manic depression, and Nietzsche' legendary mental breakdown in Turin—scene of his famous attempt to rescue a horse being beaten—indicate the cost likely to be incurred by such seismically sensate minds-in-body. This vulnerability seems to me to belong to the same family of sensitivities as the Nuer-Effect in which the murdered person enters the body of the killer.

Nietzsche begins *The Use and Abuse of History* quoting Goethe: "I hate everything that merely instructs me without increasing or directly quickening my activity."[2] That quickening is to be understood quite literally and forms the backdrop to a view of the body, sustained by Nietzsche's sympathetic reading of ancient Greek texts that runs through his work starting with *The Birth of Tragedy*, figured by the character of Dionysus in myth and theater.

Dionysus suggests a quicksilver capacity for mimesis to the degree that—as Nietzsche writes—such a creature cannot *not* become Other.[3]

There is likely, then, to be a confluence between viewer and viewed in which the viewed enters into the body of the viewer, and vice versa, something that Benjamin (a fan of Warburg) claimed in the 1930s happens when we watch a movie or kids enter into the colors of illustrations in childrens' books.

In *The Hour of Our Death*, Philippe Ariès contrasts the pre-Enlightenment "taming" of death to its "wildness" thereafter. When, in European history, a taboo sensibility determined the handling of the corpse, then death was tamed. But when the taboo sensibility is expunged—when taboo itself is tabooed—then death becomes "wild." Moreover, as regards the modern corpse, such wildness comes not so much from the denial of death as from the contortions undertaken in pursuit of such denial. Consider, for example, at the start of the COVID-19 pandemic in March and April 2020, how the public caught only an indirect (albeit highly dramatic) glimpse of open graves being dug on Hart Island off the Bronx in Long Island Sound. The rows upon rows of neat and deep empty spaces in the red soil one after the other said it all. Something very bad was on the way. We also saw body bags being loaded onto refrigerator trucks in Manhattan, photos that had considerable impact. But the day after that, the curtain was closed and no more such photos were published. What we got instead were daily statistics and unintelligible multicolored mini-graphs with tiny arrows shooting off in all directions. No wonder many people denied the existence of COVID and still do or are indifferent.

But for other people, those early images stuck, as forbidden images usually do. As far as the eye could see, empty graves one after the other, and at the same time, as if in response to those voids, illicit videos taken with shaking hands showing heavy shapes in body bags being loaded onto tractor-trailers in New York City. When I say "illicit videos," I mean in some sense wrong, in some sense taboo where law and lore conflate.

We never saw a body.

But those trembling videos of shiny black bags seemed more shocking than images of actual corpses could be. The concealment suggested more than the naked body could show and the taboo grew before our eyes as a contorted version of the public secret—that which we all knew but preferred or dared not put into speech or image.

As I was writing these lines at the end of August 2020, two months before the diselection of Donald Trump, a man said to belong to the right-wing "Patriot Prayer" militia was shot dead in Portland, Oregon. An aerial photograph posted by CNN is emblematic. It is nighttime. An ambulance, a police car, and police officers form a circle. In its center, in a pool of light, are crouched several people, one wearing a black-ribbed riot-gear jacket. At the center of the center is a white rectangle. It is a sheet covering a body. That's it, as close as CNN and the ever-obliging circumstances allow you to get. But the white rectangle seems more powerful than the corpse.

Next day, August 31, a photograph in *The New York Times* credited to Mason Tringa showed the same God's-eye aerial view but with a change. The spectral pool of light surrounds the now-visible corpse, which lies supine, white, and naked from the waist up. It is the body of a young man whose face and head are obscured by the body of a medic. Around the perimeter of the halo of light stand ten police and medics, bulky in their bulletproof gear as if an invasion is imminent. They seem mesmerized, like guardians focusing the energy of the body as the president of the republic furiously tweets that he'll order a military invasion of Portland.

Such photos are rare. It is a mystery to me that they could be taken and more to the point circulated in mainstream media.

Then five days later, US marshals and local police in Portland, no doubt emboldened by the president's tweets, assassinated—there is no other word—an Antifa activist named Michael Reinoehl, who had claimed in a video to have killed the Patriot Prayer militiaman in self-defense.

It was a Hollywood Classic. Reinoehl was mowed down "resisting arrest." As soon as he got into his automobile, unmarked SUVS traveling at high speed penned him in and, according to over twenty witnesses interviewed by the press, the police opened fire without warning. They sprayed some forty bullets in the general direction of the lone man seated at the wheel. Some shots bounced off fences, others entered homes. The police claim that Reinoehl fired at them. What did he fire? Well, under questioning the police claimed he fired one shot. But witnesses disputed even that, and it turns out that the six-round magazine of his pistol was full. As so often happens his auto-mobile became his tomb, in this case riddled with bullets.

But as far as I know there was no photo.

Pretty much the same with 9/11. A famous photograph taken for the Associated Press by veteran photojournalist Richard Drew, showing a single body falling from the World Trade Center on September 11, 2001, was published once and once only in the US morning papers. A very few other photos of falling bodies were also printed in the first two to three days. Then they stopped altogether. It was asserted that such images exploited the deaths of the people shown, stripping them of their dignity, invading their privacy, turning tragedy into pornography. A bystander using a video camera was chased by a fireman: "Don't you have any human decency?" On YouTube in January 2022, I found textual references to bodies falling from the World Trade Center but not one image.

There are, however, exceptions. Tom Junod has referred to the "internet underbelly," one part of which is the site "Best Gore." Here you can see images elsewhere deemed taboo, such as the decapitation of Daniel Pearl in Pakistan and autopsy photos of Nicole Brown Simpson in Los Angeles.[4]

In language reminiscent of my tongue-twisting figure-eight formulation of the taboo of the taboo, Junod concludes that perhaps hundreds of people jumped from the Twin Towers (note the uncertainty as to the number), but we "deem their deaths unworthy of witness—because we have somehow deemed the act of witness, in this one regard, unworthy of us."[5] The story of their jumping was image enough.

But months later in the plantation town on which I focus in western Colombia, the falling bodies were still being shown endlessly, as I recall, in places providing easy public viewing, such as stores around the plaza.

Upstate New York barely a month after the attack, the artist Carolee Schneemann produced a series of images showing the shadowy outlines of nine falling bodies. She did this by scanning and making enlarged prints of the few newspaper photos that had appeared.

On October 12, 2011, this work, called *Terminal Velocity*, was shown in the back room of a Manhattan gallery where, according to the artist, "it received hostile, aggrieved reactions," even though, in her view, the images, far from demeaning the dead, consecrated them.[6]

So, making some thing or some event sacred is bound to its reciprocal, as with the fireman screaming, "Don't you have any human decency?" The sacred and the indecent go hand in hand. Can you say the same with regard to cell phone videos of police killing in the USA? Can you say they *consecrate* as much as they profane such that the sacred shines through?

What then of photos of lynching or of Emmett Till, a fourteen-year-old Black teenager from Chicago who was tortured, killed, and mutilated by white men in Mississippi in 1955? Against the advice of close associates, his mother insisted that his disfigured face and body be photographed and the image circulated. This had a huge impact. Here the mother takes control and breaks the taboo on showing death, killing, and mutilation, just as the Black teenage girl who took the cell phone video of George Floyd's murder took control seventy years later, by which time photo technology could live-stream assassination in real time.

IMAGES OF GLOBAL SOUTH CORPSES, INCLUDING CHRIST

As the US invasion of Iraq presided over by the Bush-Cheney team progressed, photos of soldiers' coffins were not permitted because too many US dead would be politically costly. The rule seems to be that if US papers or television news run a photograph or footage of a corpse, the product of violence, it is far more likely to be of a body from the Global South: three-year-old Alan Kurdi from Kobani, dead on a Turkish beach in 2015; a saint such as Che Guevara; or the phantom-like figures glimpsed falling off a plane carrying refugees out of Kabul in August 2021.

In October 1967, Guevara's emaciated corpse was shown worldwide, suspended over a washtub in the laundry room of a small hospital in a Bolivian town. He was captured alive, then killed on the orders of the Bolivian president, although the CIA had wanted him alive. Once killed, his hands were amputated, ostensibly for fingerprints. Thirty years later, in 1997, his body was returned to Cuba.

In Brian Moser's photograph, taken the first day, the corpse has been arranged by the army like a hunting trophy.[7] It is still wild, alive in death, eyes wide open, with Bolivian officers staring at it. A man said to be CIA lurks in the background. The good guys may have brought down a formidable opponent, but he was more mythic than real anyway, and in death capable of arousing the world.

The most famous photograph was taken the second day by Freddy Alborta. It shows the cleaned-up corpse beatified like a Christian martyr. John Berger pointed out its remarkable resemblance to Andrea Mantegna's 1480 painting *Lamentation over the Dead Christ*, with Christ placed not vertically on the Cross as is customary but laid out, as was Che, on a horizontal surface with his feet facing the viewer. But while Mantegna's Christ lies on a marble slab, Che lies on a washtub in a poor country town. Like the photos of Che's dead body, Mantegna's image is disturbing. If ever there was corpse magic in a literal sense, this is it, aura radiating out in waves, the head at farthest remove, eyes closed but dominating the picture.

It is disorienting, what you could call a "worm's-eye view," with your eye at slab level, likely to be immersed in what it views as the posture curtails the distance been subject and object. With the head in the distance and the toes in your face, does not this image magnify Bataille's comic treatment of Hegel and Marx, heads and toes, destabilizing perception? The fact that it teeters on the edge of utter blasphemy yet also utter sanctity is what makes this image of the god miraculous.

Unlike the familiar vertical Christ, crucified, arms outstretched, Mantegna's Christ bears the weight of itself in itself. This is not a corpse that is about to fly skyward to join the Father in Holy Patriarchy. It looks like it will stay put. Likewise Che—the revolutionary—was already a saint, indeed, a Marxist Christ, cigar clenched in his teeth, scattering the moneylenders.

Mantegna makes you realize how strange are the standard representations of Christ, his near-naked body dying or just dead. Stilled. Not still. Images of corpses may be taboo. Newspaper editors may tie themselves and their "standards guys" in knots deciding what to show or not to show when it comes to death and murder. But then there's Christ: naked, dead, and everywhere—and nowadays if not Him, then a simple gold cross bereft of transgression as a pendant suspended from a woman's neck, hovering between faith, art, and breasts.

As an experiment, try to imagine Mantegna Christs replacing the usual version of the Crucifixion. Imagine sculptures, horizontal, *jutting out feet*

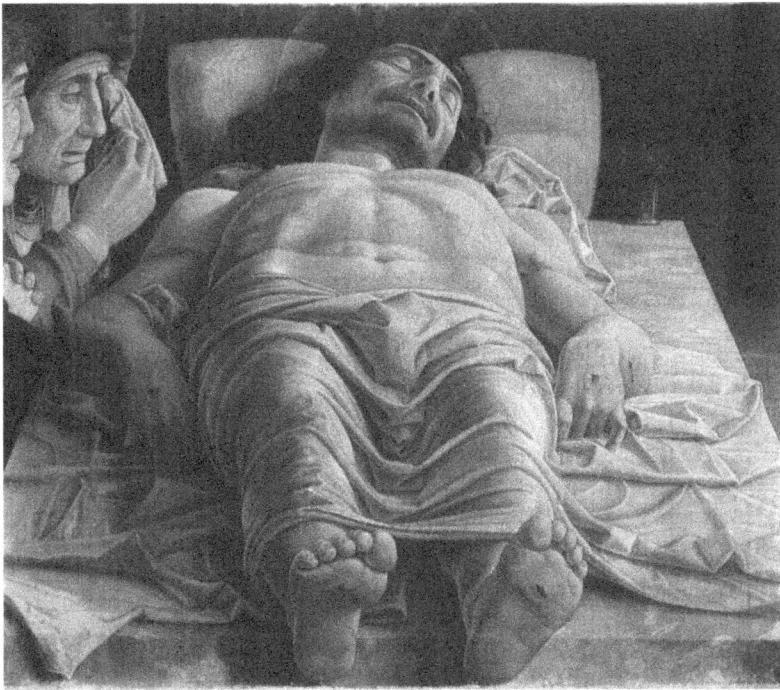

first from walls with such force that you are impelled to join the majesty of feet, legs, generous hints of genitalia, and Bataille's big toes with the head, remote in the Hegelian distance contemplating the turgid dreams of corpse magic.

A century later, around 1520, Hans Holbein tried something similar with a painting he made in Basel depicting a horizontal dead Christ squeezed in a coffin. This radically unfamiliar orientation, the compression of the body with barely an inch of free space, the fact that the image is life-size and hung at the viewer's eye-level, all contribute to the dramatic display of what seems to be a real corpse. Indeed, it is so real as to seem more like an anatomical drawing to be used for medical instruction than a religious painting.

Given such pointed realism, what is unexpected is that something magical steps out of the frame. How can that be? Such is the wont of the Nuer-Effect, and such is what held Dostoevsky spellbound in his visit to Basel, described in his novel *The Idiot*. For Dostoevsky, Christianity is to be continuously tested against the reality of human existence, here represented by the realer-than-real corpse that does away with traditional piety in favor of a greater one. Within Christian doctrine are we not all responsible for Christ's recurring murder, and does that not reinstitute the Nuer-Effect for us who stand by this coffin in the disturbing quietude of burgher Basel? It is said that Dostoevsky's wife had to drag him away from the painting for fear he would suffer an epileptic attack.

There is a story that Holbein fished the corpse that served as his model out of the Rhine, which flows through the city. As I stand in Basel staring at Holbein's Christ, I think of the corpses floating downstream in Colombian rivers today. Are these corpses *my* models, other Christs, you could say?

As for the adamant exposure of the corpse in its nakedness and torment, is that what makes churches sacred, that *nakedness and torment of the corpse*? If death is fenced in by fierce taboos, and nakedness too, what of their combination when the covering sheet is withdrawn or the body bag unzipped? It very much seems that what makes things sacred is the breaking of taboos, as with nakedness and not just death but murder and not just murder but state-sanctioned murder. The true miracle here is that this has become so dull.

In that regard, Leo Steinberg's book *The Sexuality of Christ in the Renaissance and in Modern Oblivion* provides a startling alienation effect with its eye-popping visual testimony to the flouting of taboo north and south of the Alps in paintings of Christ on the cross.[8]

We are likely to be amazed at these images, but does not their camp genital display reveal the larger truth: that Crucifixion imagery is always already transgressive in terms of sex and death torment?

The mystery of the mystery of Christ lies not only in the ritualized state murder but in the fact that the story of a victim of colonial and local priestly rule was chosen to break the mold and give rise to a world-dominating religion. Let us not forget that in their separate ways both Che and Christ were regarded as saints because they were portents or prophets of revolution. Like Che, Christ the Jew was of the Global South. It was the Christians who converted his assassination into the exemplary instance of corpse magic that Nietzsche called *ressentiment*, the cunning of the weak.

CELL PHONE VIDEOS AS LASCAUX CAVE IMAGES

You went to the city to march against police violence. I never imagined I would see a murder on a TV news broadcast. Recently I've seen several.

This fragment from an email I received in 2020 from the writer Joe Broderick living in Bogotá expresses his amazement at the new normal of showing killing. That was the year of Black Lives Matter marches and growing public awareness about police killing. No stranger to stories of assassination in Colombia, Joe was struck by this video from the USA as something he never thought possible; the public visualization of murder, specifically murder done by police.

Let me backtrack a little to consider storytelling in relation to such videos. In 1936 Walter Benjamin famously argued that the denial of death together with the decay of craft production spelled the end of the oral storyteller. But what if, in much of the world outside the Global North, death is not denied, and what if one craft has not disappeared but instead grown increasingly visible, namely, the craft of killing people enabled by the War on Drugs?

And what if other crafts have arisen in concert with and reaction against that craft, such as the abundance of phone videos of abuse by US police? Has not the storyteller and craft production proven more resilient than Benjamin assumed? Artisans may have been eclipsed by the factory system, but now, in less than two decades, everyone in the Global South and North has become an artisan of phone photography and video storytelling.

THE LASCAUX CAVE PAINTINGS UPDATED TO THE INTERIOR OF AUTO-MOBILES

With the innovation of cell phone photography and video the past fifteen years, it has become possible to show killing as it is happening in real time for a mass audience.[9] To the degree that Bataille's intuition has merit—that the Lascaux cave paintings can be considered as reactions to the breaking of taboos on killing and that by such means homage is paid to the creatures slain—might we develop my conceit that the interior of the automobile is our modern Lascaux, only now the hunted, not the hunter, makes the image?

Some Lascaux experts suggest that the cave paintings were made by seers and shamans. Be that as it may, do not the videos of police killing attain those same powers? Plato took us out of the cave where he thought we mistook images for reality. Today, back in the cave that is the automobile, we engage with images that portray realities long suppressed by Plato's Republic and its police. But now, thanks to phone videos, the interior of the cave shows the truth no matter how much the auto-mobile is the dream-house of illusions in other ways.

Sometimes the images take a long time coming or are incomplete, as happened in the case of twenty-nine-year-old Sandra Bland, who ended up dead, hanging herself, so police alleged, in a Texas jailhouse. "I will light you up," said Officer Encinia, the man who arrested her, brandishing his taser.

"Light you up." Hunter that he was, Encinia had tailgated Bland in a way that confused her such that she misused a turn signal, which gave him the absurd excuse to pull her over. She refused to exit her automobile, her cave, her safe place, her trap. It took four years before her cell phone video was released by the police. Four years. As for the police camera footage, the police altered it. So much for police videos.

Killing has existed in Western literature as far back as *The Iliad*. But that's been manifestly second-order representation using language and the art of storytelling. Now, however, with phone videos and surveillance cameras, the meaning of actual killing is there, in your face, shared instantly by millions of people in what I take to be a storm of Nuer-Effects, meaning spirit contagion attendant on killing. What does "in your face" imply, after all? A slap, an affront, an ontological assault? The images are in your face in that they defy the taboos on showing actual violence and actual state murder. They do so in a Space of Death wherein new channels of communication expose what for so long and in so many places and situations has been concealed.

Like hunting, cell phone photography such as this is dependent on being in the right place at the right time—as when a girl on her way to the store in Minneapolis is confronted by an automobile with its door open, a large policeman kneeling on the neck of his prey. She pulls out her phone and starts filming. Immediacy is what matters. And raw presencing, meaning not so much an image of something as an image *which is itself part of that something.*

Think of the police killing Philando Castile as recorded by his companion in the passenger seat, *live-streaming* to her video audience with her four-year-old daughter crying in the back seat. The viewer of this life-stream turned death-stream becomes part of the action, a body amid bodies, a participant observer dragged in by the enormity of what is being streamed there in the confines of the automobile with its supposedly broken taillight.

It is like spying, too, both on the part of the person making the video and on our part, we who come later looking at the display of what you are not meant to see behind the police wall. Thanks to this video you now become intimate with the secret in the closeness of the cave. Perhaps spying is the wrong word. It's more like initiation, a process involving revelation of a secret as prelude to the Nuer-Effect's diffusion through the bodies of observers, like you, me, and this text in between.

Bataille suggests that the Lascaux paintings can be thought of as a response to killing where "he who gives death also enters into death."[10] Is this what is happening with police murder? But what does that mean, "enters into death"? Does it mean that the police-person, now an elemental part of the slayer-slain nexus, is in for the ride and becomes spiritualized, meaning contaminated? Does it mean us?

And if for Bataille such cave paintings are the "birth of art," intimate with killing, what of phone videos of assassination by police practicing the ancient art of hunting?

Consider the police as hunters roaming the highway in search of prey.

Consider the sudden stoppage, lights flashing, as a messianic moment when past and present touch each other with nothing in between but the gun in the automobile window.

Consider the hunted making paintings of the hunters.

Consider Plato's contention that the slain person's "soul joins forces with the very memory of the murderer to bring all possible distraction upon him and all his works."

I call this corpse magic.

It has been my distraction as well.

FIN

ACKNOWLEDGMENTS

Many people helped me along the way. I want especially to thank the following: William Amú, Lucy Biafera, Jesse Bransford, Joe Broderick, Alhena Caicedo, Daniel Campo, Jon Carter, Alberto Castrillon, Maria Del Rosario Ferro, Juan Felipe Gárcia, Nancy Goldring, Merien Grueso, Nina Lang, Luís Carlos Mina, Olivia Mostacilla, Rachel Moore, Todd Ramón Ochoa, Jasmine Pisapia, Valentina Restrepo, Axel Rojas, Carolina Saquel, Brigitte Weingart, and Lilia Zuniga.

NOTES

METHOD IN THE MADNESS . . .

1. These figures come from several sources, chiefly *The Washington Post*, *The Guardian*, *The New York Times*, and the Gun Violence Archive. A recent study published in *The Lancet* shows that US government figures underreported by half the number of police killings for 1980–2018, the period of the War on Drugs and mass incarceration; see Tim Arango and Sheila Dewan, *New York Times*, October 1, 2021 (dated September 30, 2021), and Sheila Dewan, "Studies on Use of Police Holds Are Challenged," *New York Times*, October 4, 2021.

CHAPTER 1

1. The murder rate in 2021 was around 80 killings per 100,000 inhabitants. Some 80 percent of this was due to gangsters killing each other. Compare this with 25/100,000 for Colombia as a whole in 2021, and 18/100,000 for Chicago in 2019.

2. Rogerio Velásquez, "Ritos de la muerte en el alto y bajo Chocó," *Revista colombiana de folclor* 2 (1961): 164–65.

3. The Spanish is "revestida de extraños resplandores" (Velásquez, 139). Velásquez received his formal anthropological training, be it noted, because French anthropologists associated with the Musée de l'Homme under the direction of Paul Rivet, having fled the Nazis, set up or enlarged schools of anthropology in Barranquilla and in Popayan, where Velásquez studied. Did they teach Hertz's essay on the dead? As far as I know, this was the only time there were Black students of anthropology in Colombia until the end of the twentieth century.

4. "Memorias de un 'para' (el diario de 'Don Mario')," *La Semana*, March 16, 2007. Also see "El dossier paramilitary," *La Semana*, May 11, 1989.

5. Johanna Pérez Gómez, "Supernatural Bulletproof Men: An Ethnography of Sorcery and Paramilitary Powers in Colombia's Eastern Plains," PhD diss., Department of Anthropology, University College London, 2022, 107–11.

6. To me this sounds "Venezuelan," such spirit possession being the basis of the popular cult of María Lionza. See Michael Taussig, *The Magic of the State* (London: Routledge, 1997). As far as I know, Colombia's eastern plains can be coextensive with Venezuelan culture of the dead.

7. Drinking the ashes of a written spell is a procedure for learning English among the Kuna of the San Blas Islands off the Caribbean coast, as described by Baron Nordenskiöld and Rubén Pérez in *An Historical and Ethnographic Study of the Cuna Indians* (Gothenburg: Ethnografiska Museum, 1938). Written words can of course be magical in themselves, and when swallowed, more so—not only here or with the Kuna.

8. Pérez Gómez, 56.

9. Pérez Gómez, 191.

10. See Taussig, *Shamanism, Colonialism, and the Wild Man* (Chicago: University of Chicago Press, 1987), for a discussion of this composite human-animal. Compare the October 9, 2023, statement of the Israeli minister of defense, Yoav Gallant, that "we are fighting human animals and shall act accordingly." With regard to my analysis of the infrahuman combined with the superhuman, note both the characterization "human animals" and the assertion of reciprocity: we "shall act accordingly."

11. Elizabeth Gallón Droste, *Útica* (pub. by author, Bogotá, 2022), and personal communication.

12. Gallón Droste, *Útica* and personal communication.

13. E. Louis Backman, *Religious Dances in the Christian Church and in Popular Medicine*, trans. E. Class (1945; London: Allen & Unwin, 1952), 133.

14. Gerardo Reichel-Dolmatoff and Alicia Dussán de Reichel-Dolmatoff, *The People of Aritama* (London: Routledge, 1961). The book gives no date for the fifteen months of fieldwork, but I assume it was in the 1940s. A negative review of the book was published by Orlando Fals-Borda (who was born close to the village studied) in *Hispanic American Historical Review* 43, no. 2 (1963). The later Spanish-language edition has a laudatory blurb by Claude Lévi-Strauss. The book is a mine of intelligently presented information but strangely does not unpack what could be the most interesting material, namely the mixing and, presumably, tensions that enter as dynamic force in the interaction of indigenous and *mestizo* cultures.

15. Anakana Schofield, *New York Times*, op-ed, March 7, 2021.

16. James Joyce, *Ulysses* (1922; London: Penguin, 1968), 137.

17. Todd Ramon Ochoa, *Society of the Dead: Quita Manaquita and Palo Praise in Cuba* (Berkeley: University of California Press, 2010).

18. Friedrich Nietzsche, *Twilight of the Idols*, trans. R. J. Hollingdale (London: Penguin, 1980), 84.

19. Walter Benjamin, *The Arcades Project*, trans. Howard Eiland and Kevin Mc-Laughlin (Cambridge, MA: Harvard University Press, 1999), 476.

20. Benjamin, "On the Concept of History" (usually known as "Theses on the Philosophy of History"), in *Selected Writings*, vol. 4, *1938–1940*, ed. Howard Eiland and Michael W. Jennings (Cambridge, MA: Harvard University Press, 2003), 396.

21. James Forman Jr., *Locking Up Our Own: Crime and Punishment in Black America* (New York: Farrar, Straus and Giroux, 2017).

22. Benjamin, *Arcades Project*, 470.

CHAPTER 2

1. See, for example, Grupo de Memoria Histórica, *La masacre de El Salado* (Bogotá, Taurus: 2009) and *¡Basta ya! Colombia: Memorias de guerra y dignidad*, (Bogotá: Imprenta Nacional, 2013).

2. Mikhail Bakhtin, *Problems of Dostoevsky's Poetics* (Minneapolis: University of Minnesota Press, 1984), chap. 4.

3. Notably, German Guzmán, Orlando Fals Borda, and Eduardo Umana Lina, *La Violencia en Colombia: Estudio de un proceso social*, 2 vols., Monografías Sociológicas, 12, Facultad de Sociología, Universidad Nacional (Bogotá: Tercer Mundo, 1962). This is, I think, the major text, published but six years after the leaders of the two parties forged a power-sharing agreement. The three authors were a sociologist, a lawyer, and a priest, and it represented the birth of Colombian sociology as a discipline.

4. Michael Taussig (pseud. Mateo Mina), *Esclavitud y libertad en el valle del río Cauca* (with one chapter by Anna Rubbo) (1975; Bogotá: Editorial Universidad de Los Andes, 2011), 140–42.

5. For example, Karl Marx, "The Fetishism of Commodities and the Secret Thereof," in vol. 1 of the first English-language edition of *Capital*, trans. Samuel Moore and Edward Aveling (Moscow: International Publishers, 1967).

6. Fyodor Dostoevsky, "Bobok—From Somebody's Diary," in *Bobok* (1873; London: Read and Co. Classics, 2018), 11.

7. James Joyce, *Ulysses* (1922; London: Penguin, 1968), 138.

8. "Tom and Jerry," Wikipedia, accessed May 24, 2024.

9. James J. Parsons, *Antioqueño Colonization in Western Colombia*, rev. ed. (1968; Berkeley: University of California Press, 2021).

10. Johanna Pérez Gómez, "Supernatural Bulletproof Men: An Ethnography of Sorcery and Paramilitary Powers in Colombia's Eastern Plains," PhD diss., Department of Anthropology, University College London, 2022.

11. Eric Levenson and Josh Campbell, CNN, June 10, 2021.

12. See Sharon E. Hutchinson, *Nuer Dilemmas* (Los Angeles: University of California Press, 1966).

13. Compare with Georges Didi-Huberman, *The Surviving Image: Phantoms of Time and Time of Phantoms: Aby Warburg's History of Art*, trans. Harvey Mendelsohn (2002; University Park: Pennsylvania University State Press, 2017), and Philippe-Alain Michaud, *Aby Warburg and the Image in Motion*, trans. Sophie Hawkes (2007; New York: Zone, 2013).

14. Sigmund Freud, *Jokes and Their Relation to the Unconscious*, in *The Standard Edition of the Complete Psychological Works of Sigmund Freud*, ed. James Strachey (London: Hogarth, 1953–1974), 8:192. See also Taussig, *Mimesis and Alterity: A Particular History of the Senses* (London: Routledge, 1993), 46.

15. Sergei Eisenstein, *Eisenstein on Disney*, ed. Jay Leyda (London: Methuen/ Calcutta: Seagull Books, 1988), 24–35.

16. Hutchinson, 106.

17. Walter Benjamin, *One-Way Street*, in *Reflections: Essays, Aphorisms, Autobiographical Writings*, ed. Peter Demetz (New York: Schocken, 1978), 68.

18. Sarah Iles Johnston, *The Restless Dead: Encounters Between the Living and the Dead in Ancient Greece* (Los Angeles: University of California Press, 1999).

CHAPTER 3

1. Georges Bataille, *The Tears of Eros*, trans. Peter Connor (1961; San Francisco: City Lights, 1989), 36–37.

2. Leo Frobenius, "Dessins rupestres du sud de la Rhodésie," *Documents*, no. 4 (1930): 185–89.

3. Éveline Lot-Falk, *Les rites de chasse chez les peuples sibériens* (Paris: Gallimard, 1953); Bataille, *The Cradle of Humanity: Prehistoric Art and Culture* (New York: Zone, 2005), 163.

4. Rane Willerslev, *Soul Hunters: Hunting, Animism, and Personhood Among the Siberian Yukaghirs* (Berkeley: University of California Press, 2007).

5. Walter Benjamin, "On the Mimetic Faculty," in *Reflections: Essays, Aphorisms, Autobiographical Writings*, ed. Peter Demetz (New York: Schocken, 1978).

6. Fragment 35, "Elk Dreamers" (anonymous informant), in *Lakota Belief and Ritual*, collected by James R. Walker at Pine Ridge, Dakota, between 1896 and 1914, ed. Raymond DeMallie and Elaine A. Jahner (Lincoln: University of Nebraska Press, 2014), 135.

7. See Nietzsche on police as criminals in *The Genealogy of Morals*, trans. Walter Kaufmann and R. J. Hollingdale (New York: Vintage, 1989), 82.

8. Joseph Ypes Brown, "The Unlikely Associates: A Study in Oglala Sioux Magic and Metaphysic" (1970), *Studies in World Religion* 15, nos. 1–2 (Winter–Spring 1983).

9. Frank G. Speck, *Naskapi* (Norman: University of Oklahoma Press, 1935), 210–12.

10. See Marshall Sahlins, *The New Science of the Enchanted Universe* (Princeton, NJ: Princeton University Press, 2022); and Bataille, *Theory of Religion* (1948), and *The Accursed Share* (1949), both trans. Robert Hurley (New York: Zone, 1992, 1988).

11. Speck, 74.

12. Speck, 110, 113.

13. Bataille, *Accused Share*.

14. E. E. Evans-Pritchard, *Nuer Religion* (New York: Oxford University Press, 1956), 248–86.

15. Jacques Derrida, *The Gift of Death*, trans. David Willis (Chicago: University of Chicago Press, 1995).

16. See David Graeber and David Wengrow, *The Dawn of Everything: A New History of Humanity* (Farrar, Straus and Giroux, 2021), and the copious literature and films on New Guinea ritual warfare such as the acclaimed *Dead Birds* (1963), directed by Robert Gardner.

17. Henri Junod, *The Life of a South African Tribe*, 2 vols. (1912–1913; Hyde Park, NY: University Books, 1962); see 2:478–81.

18. Junod, *Life of a South African Tribe*, 2:478.

19. Junod, *Life of a South African Tribe*, 2:476.

20. Sharon E. Hutchinson, *Nuer Dilemmas* (Los Angeles: University of California Press, 1966), 106.

21. Marcel Mauss (and Henri Hubert), *A General Theory of Magic* (1902; London: Routledge, 1972), 171.

22. W. Lloyd Warner, *A Black Civilization: A Study of an Australian Tribe*, rev. ed. (1937; New York: Harper & Row, 1958), 152 ff. Murngin is a name used by early anthropologists. The more common name today is Yolngu.

23. Warner, 144.

24. Peter Sutton, *The Politics of Suffering: Indigenous Australia and the End of the Liberal Consensus* (Melbourne: Melbourne University Press, 2011).

25. William Shakespeare, *Macbeth*, act 4, scene 3.

26. Eduardo Viveiros de Castro, *From the Enemy's Point of View: Humanity and Divinity in an Amazonian Society* (Chicago: University of Chicago Press, 1992).

27. Viveiros de Castro, 239.

28. Viveiros de Castro, 239, 246.

29. The idea of an "anachronistic knot" appears in Georges Didi-Huberman, *The Surviving Image: Phantoms of Time and Time of Phantoms: Aby Warburg's History of Art*, trans. Harvey Mendelsohn (2002; State Park: Pennsylvania State University Press, 2017), 33.

30. Sarah Iles Johnston, *The Restless Dead: Encounters Between the Living and the Dead in Ancient Greece* (Los Angeles: University of California Press, 1999), 140–50.

31. Johnston, 87.

32. Johnston, 27–28.

33. Johnston, 28.

34. Johnston, 86.

35. Johnston, 129.

36. Hutchinson, 106.

37. Timothy Bella, Ben Brasch, and Dan Rosenzweig-Ziff, "Alex Murdaugh Sentenced to Life in Prison in Murder of Wife, Son," *Washington Post*, updated March 3, 2023.

CHAPTER 4

1. See Yezid Campos Zornosa, *El baile rojo: Relatos no contados del genocidio de la UP* (Bogotá: Icono, 2003).

2. See Comisión de estudios sobre la violencia, "La violencia urbana en Colombia en el decenio del ochenta," in *Colombia: Violencia y democracia: informe presentado al Ministro de Gobierno* (Bogotá: Universidad Nacional de Colombia, 1987), 56–81.

3. See Michael Taussig, *Law in a Lawless Land: Diary of a Limpieza in Colombia* (Chicago: University of Chicago Press, 2005).

4. See Taussig, *Law in a Lawless Land*, 99.

5. Carlos Mario Perea Restrepo, *Con el diablo adentro: Pandillas, tiempo paralelo y poder* (México, DF: Siglo XXI, 2007), 167–69.

6. The famous robbery in 1980 by the M-19 guerrilla of the Colombian army's weapons depot in the north of Bogotá also occurred on New Year's Eve. The guerrilleros left a note: "Feliz Año Nuevo y Feliz Armas Nuevas" ("Happy New Year and happy new arms"). Friends of mine were arrested and tortured for this. It opened up a new phase in state violence.

7. William Shakespeare, *Macbeth*, act 2, scene 2.

8. Carolina Bohórquez, "Rituales de brujería acechan a las cementerios del Pacífico" [Sorcery rites stalk the cemeteries of the Pacific], *El Tiempo*, February 11, 2015.

CHAPTER 5

1. Johanna Pérez Gómez also notes priests as experts on sorcery in "Supernatural Bulletproof Men: An Ethnography of Sorcery and Paramilitary Powers in Colombia's Eastern Plains," PhD diss., Department of Anthropology, University College London, 2022, 81–83. How expert is debatable.

2. *The Odyssey*, book XI.

3. Carolyn Walker Bynum, *Fragmentation and Redemption: Essays on Gender and the Human Body in Medieval Religion* (New York: Zone, 1991), 107.

4. Rogerio Velásquez, "Ritos de la muerte en el alto y bajo Chocó," *Revista colombiana de folclor* 2 (1961): 138–39.

5. Velásquez, 139.

6. *The Guardian*, October 12, 2014.

CHAPTER 6

1. Michel Taussig, *Shamanism, Colonialism, and the Wild Man: A Study in Terror and Healing* (Chicago: University of Chicago Press, 1987).

2. Michael Taussig, *The Devil and Commodity Fetishism* (Chapel Hill: University of North Carolina Press, 1980).

3. Norman O. Brown, "Dionysus 1990," in *Apocalypse and/or Metamorphoses* (Berkeley: University of California Press, 1992).

4. Hendrix, Nidia Gongora, Alex Play, and Junior John, *Quién los mató* (video, 2024).

CHAPTER 7

1. See Michael Taussig (pseud. Mateo Mina and Anna Rubbo), *Esclavitud y libertad en el valle del río Cauca* (1975; Bogotá: Editorial Universidad de Los Andes, 2011).

2. See Wolfgang Schivelbusch, *Three New Deals: Reflections on Roosevelt's America, Mussolini's Italy, and Hitler's Germany, 1933–1939* (New York: Picador, 2007).

3. On Carabobo, see Taussig, *The Magic of the State* (London: Routledge, 1997). On Saddam Hussein's arch, see K. Makiya, *The Monument* (Berkeley: University of California Press, 1991).

4. Gerardo Reichel-Dolmatoff and Alicia Dussán de Reichel-Dolmatoff, *The People of Aritama* (London: Routledge, 1961), 355.

5. Reichel-Dolmatoff and Dussán, 355.

6. Reichel-Dolmatoff and Dussán, 356–60.

7. Michel Foucault, "Heterotopias," *Diacritics* 16, no. 1 (Spring 1966): 22–27.

CHAPTER 8

1. Walter Benjamin, *The Arcades Project*, trans. Howard Eiland and Kevin McLaughlin (Cambridge, MA: Harvard University Press, 1999), 84 [C1a2].

2. Carlos María Perea Restrepo, *Con el diablo adentro: Pandillas, tiempo paralelo y poder* (México, DF: Siglo XXI, 2007), 11–12.

3. E. A. Wallis Budge, *Amulets and Superstitions* (1930; London: Dover, 1978), 336–49.

CHAPTER 10

1. Gerardo Reichel-Dolmatoff and Alicia Dussán de Reichel-Dolmatoff, *The People of Aritama* (London: Routledge, 1961), 354.

2. Fustel de Coulanges, *The Ancient City* (1864; New York: Doubleday, 1956), 21–25.

3. *The Odyssey of Homer*, trans. Samuel Butler (Roslyn, NY: Walter J. Black, 1944), book XI, 132.

4. Nadezhda Mandelstam, *Hope Against Hope* (New York: Modern Library, 1999), 231.

5. The literature and filmography on the return of the dead is immense. See the French film series, *Les Revenants*. Also N. C. Y. Mandeville Cacioloa, *Afterlives: The Return of the Dead in the Middle Ages* (Ithaca, NY: Cornell University Press, 2015).

6. William of Newburgh, *Historia Rerum Anglicarum*, book 5, chap. 24 (4–7), accessed online.

7. Barbara Newman, "A Thousand Slayn," *London Review of Books* 42, no. 21 (November 5, 2020).

8. Vinciane Despret, *Our Grateful Dead*, trans. Stephen Muecke (Minneapolis: University of Minnesota Press, 2021), 49–50.

9. Philippe Ariès, *The Hour of Our Death* (New York: Knopf, 1981), 38.

10. John Berger, "Drawn to That Moment,"in Jim Savage, *Berger on Drawing* (Occasional Press, 2007).

11. Michael Taussig, *The Nervous System* (New York: Routledge, 1991), 20, 47, 49.

12. The phrase is Bataille's.

13. Thanks to Brigitte Weingart of Berlin for alerting me to this film.

CHAPTER 11

1. Mary Shelley, *Frankenstein* (1818; London: Penguin, 2006).

2. Michel Foucault, *The History of Sexuality*, vol. 1 (New York: Vintage, 1980), 35.

3. Michael Taussig, "Viscerality, Faith, and Skepticism: Another Theory of Magic," *Hau, Journal of Ethnogrphic Theory* 6, no. 3 (2016). See also Taussig, *Defacement: Public Secrecy and the Labor of the Negative* (Palo Alto, CA: Stanford University Press, 1999).

4. Nietzsche on truth in *The Gay Science* (Cambridge: Cambridge University Press, 2001), 200–201 (sect. 344, "Why Not Deceive?").

5. Marx, *Capital: A Critique of Political Economy*, vol 1., trans. Samuel Moore and Edward Aveling (Moscow: International Publishers, 1967), 71–83.

6. Online I found this Magritte painting dated 1936 with the title *Le travail caché*, *caché* being French for "hidden" or "stored." This captures what I am getting at, like capital, hidden or stored.

7. E. Louis Backman, *Religious Dances in the Christian Church and in Popular Medicine* (1945; London: George Allen & Unwin, 1952).

8. Blaise Cendrars, *Sky: Memoirs* (1949; New York: Da Capo, 1996).

9. Backman, 9–43.

10. Backman, 140–46.

11. James George Frazer, *The Golden Bough*, part III, *The Dying God*, 3rd ed. (London: Macmillan, 1911), 92.

12. Natalie Zemon Davis, "The Rites of Violence," in *Society and Culture in Early Modern France* (Stanford, CA: Stanford University Press, 1975), 179–81.

13. Thomas W. Laqueur, *The Work of the Dead: A Cultural History of Mortal Remains* (Princeton, NJ: Princeton University Press, 2015), 105–6.

14. Bruce Lincoln, "Revolutionary Exhumations in Spain, July 1936," *Comparative Studies in Society and History*, April 1985, 241–60.

CHAPTER 12

1. Max Horkheimer and Theodor Adorno, *Dialectic of Enlightenment*, trans. John Cumming (1944; New York: Herder and Herder, 1972).

2. Friedrich Nietzsche on error, for example in *The Gay Science* (Cambridge: Cambridge University Press, 2001), 200–201, sect. 344.

3. Thomas W. Laqueur, *The Work of the Dead: A Cultural History of Mortal Remains* (Princeton, NJ: Princeton University Press, 2015), 200–220.

4. Bataille, "Abattoir," in "Chronique Dictionaire," *Documents* 6 (1929): 329–31.

5. Philippe Ariès, *The Hour of Our Death* (New York: Knopf, 1981), 23.

6. Alan Klima, *The Funeral Casino: Meditation, Massacre, and Exchange with the Dead in Thailand* (Princeton, NJ: Princeton University Press, 2002).

7. Denis Hollier, *Against Architecture: The Writings of Georges Bataille* (Cambridge, MA: MIT Press, 1992), xiii.

8. Susan Sontag, introduction to Peter Hujar's *Portraits in Life and Death* (New York: Da Capo, 1976).

9. Walter Benjamin, "Critique of Violence" (1920–1921), in *Reflections*, ed. Peter Demetz (New York: Harcourt Brace Jovanovitch, 1978), 277–300.

CHAPTER 13

1. E. Louis Backman, *Religious Dances in the Christian Church and in Popular Medicine*, trans. E. Class (1945; London: Allen & Unwin, 1952), 1–44.

2. James Joyce, *Ulysses* (1922; London: Penguin, 1968), 108.

3. Joyce, 136.

4. Joyce, 135.

5. Joyce, 137.

6. Joyce, 125.

7. Walter Benjamin, "The Storyteller."

CHAPTER 14

1. Gabriel García Márquez, *Relato de un náufrago* (Barcelona: Tusquets, 1970).

2. García Márquez, *Relato*, 106, 109.

3. Rogelio Velásquez, "Ritos de la muerte en el alto y bajo Chocó," *Revista colombiana de folclor* 2 (1961): 158.

4. Ida Harris in *Yes! The Death Issue*, Fall 2019.

5. As described in the mid-twentieth-century biography of San Pedro Claver by Gabriel Porros Traconis; see Velásquez, 147.

6. Velásquez, 145, citing the church journal *La Aurora*, 1959 and 1960.

CHAPTER 15

1. Thomas Hardy, "The Withered Arm." I thank Chris Lamping for this reference.

2. Thomas Laqueur, "Crowds, Carnival, and the State in English Executions, 1604–1868," in *The First Modern Society: Essays in English History in Honour of Lawrence Stone*, ed. A. L. Beier et al. (Cambridge: Cambridge University Press, 1989), 72. See also Peter Linebaugh, "The Tyburn Riot Against the Surgeons," in *Albion's Fatal Tree*, ed. Douglas Hay et al. (New York: Pantheon, 1975), 110.

3. See Kathy Stuart, *Defiled Trades, and Social Outcasts: Honor and Ritual Pollution in Early Modern Germany* (Cambridge: Cambridge University Press, 2001).

4. Roger Caillois, "The Sociology of the Executioner: Tuesday, February 21, 1939," in *The College of Sociology*, ed. Denis Hollier (1979; Minneapolis: University of Minnesota Press, 1998), 233–47.

5. Caillois, "Sociology of the Executioner"

6. Michael Taussig, "The Language of Flowers," in *Walter Benjamin's Grave* (Chicago: University of Chicago Press, 2006), 189–218.

CHAPTER 16

1. Thomas W. Laqueur, *The Work of the Dead: A Cultural History of Mortal Remains* (Princeton, NJ: Princeton University Press, 2015), 105–6.

2. Michael Taussig, *Shamanism, Colonialism, and the Wild Man* (Chicago: University of Chicago Press, 1987).

3. *New York Times*, September 18, 2021.

4. *New York Times*, November 19, 2023.

5. I am not counting people killed by political violence such as that involving the army, paramilitaries, FARC *disidentes*, or the ELN guerrilla.

6. Gabriel García Márquez, *One Hundred Years of Solitude*, trans. Gregory Rabassa (1967; New York: Harper, 2006).

7. García Márquez, *One Hundred Years*, 22–23.

8. Walter B. Cannon, "Voodoo Death," in *American Anthropologist*, no. 44 (1942): 169–81.

9. Mélina Gautrand, French doctoral student in anthropology, personal communication.

10. Mélina Gautrand, personal communication.

11. See Johanna Pérez Gómez, "Supernatural Bulletproof Men: An Ethnography of Sorcery and Paramilitary Powers in Colombia's Eastern Plains," PhD diss., Department of Anthropology, University College London, 2022. I explore the magical power attributed by the "civilized" to indigenous people in considerable detail in *Shamanism, Colonialism, and the Wild Man.*

12. Claudia Steiner, "Almas en Pena," in *A la sombra de la Guerra. Ilegalidad y nuevos órdenes regionales en Colombia*, ed. Álvaro Camacho et al. (Bogotá: Universidad de los Andes, 2009). The students whose theses provided the invaluable fieldwork descriptions were Liz Carolina Lozano, Natalia Castellanos, and Matthew Arose Magak. See also Luz María Sierra, "Fantasmas de víctimas descuartizadas levan locura a varios 'paras' en Meta y Casanare," *El Tiempo*, November 24, 2007.

13. Luz María Sierra.

14. Frantz Fanon, *The Wretched of the Earth*, trans. Richard Philcox (New York: Grove, 2021), 183; quoted in Schatz, *The Rebel's Clinic* (New York: Farrar Straus and Giroux, 2024), 248 (Kindle).

15. Schatz, 387 (Kindle).

16. Fanon, 219.

17. Molano was the classic novelist manqué. Alienated from academic sociology, which he studied under Alain Touraine in Paris (sociology itself being a novelty in Colombia in the 1950s), he picked up a tape recorder and began to record small-town and rural people's accounts of their experience during the 1940–1960 Violencia and later. His originality lay in the way he edited the transcripts, even to the point at times of combining different speakers to form one speaker. For the middle class, the inimitable language of this discourse, its introspection and storytelling, was new and breathtakingly unfamiliar except perhaps their exchanges with their servants.

18. Shatz, 250 (Kindle).

19. See Taussig, *The Magic of the State* (London: Routledge, 1997); Pérez Gómez.

20. Iván Noguera, "Paramilitares acudieron a un exorcismo para romper supuesto maleficio de sus víctimas," *El Tiempo*, November 24, 2007.

21. Noguera.

22. Elsy Yaneth Castillo Ordóñez, "Religiosidad popular en el Caquetá: El culto de los muertos," paper delivered to the October 1989 Congress of the Colombian Anthropological Association in Villa de Leyva, Boyacá.

23. I am thinking of the film *The Discreet Charm of the Bourgeoisie* (1972), directed by Luis Buñuel.

CHAPTER 17

1. "Elias Canetti: Discussion with Theodor W. Adorno," *Thesis Eleven*, no. 45 (May 1996).

2. J. Glenn Gray, *The Warriors: Reflections on Men in Battle* (New York: Harcourt Brace, 1959), 172.

3. Gray, 174.

4. Marcel Mauss, *The Gift* (1925; Glencoe, IL: Free Press, 1954).

CHAPTER 18

1. Walter Benjamin, "Unpacking my Library," in *Illuminations*, ed. Hannah Arendt (New York: Schocken, 1968), 59–68.

2. Georges Bataille, *The Accursed Share*, trans. Robert Hurley (1949; New York: Zone, 1988).

3. *Washington Post*, July 26, 2022.

4. *USA Today*, editorial board statement, November 19, 2021.

CHAPTER 19

1. These figures are available thanks to *The Washington Post* and *The Guardian*, though only since 2015.

2. See Franklin E. Zimring, *When Police Kill* (Cambridge, MA: Harvard University Press, 2017).

3. See Tim Arango and Sheila Dewan, *New York Times*, October 1, 2021 (dated September 30, 2021).

4. Sheila Dewan, "Studies on Use of Police Holds Are Challenged," *New York Times*, October 4, 2021.

5. Michael LaForgia and Jennifer Valentino-DeVries, "How a Generic Trait in Black People Can Give the Police Cover," *New York Times*, May 15, 2021; Jennifer Valentino-DeVries, Mike McIntire, Rebecca R. Ruiz, Julie Tate, and Michael H. Keller, "How Paid Experts Help Exonerate Police After Deaths in Custody," *New York Times*, December 26, 2021.

6. Zimring, 5.

7. Farhad Manjoo, "Cameras Won't Stop Police from Killing; Body Cams Have Turned Brutality into Spectacle," *New York Times*, June 3, 2020; also see Tom Jackman, "How Police Body Cams Failed Us," *New York Times*, December 13, 2023, a long insightful article on how police departments stall, often for years, release of body-cam footage.

8. Nicholas Mirzoeff, *The Appearance of Black Lives Matter* (Miami: [NAME] Publications, 2017), ebook.

CHAPTER 20

1. Compare with the forty thousand people who die each year from traffic accidents, the commonest cause of death of people under fifty.

2. Michael Taussig, *Shamanism, Colonialism, and the Wild Man* (Chicago: University of Chicago Press, 1987), p. 7, chaps. 25–27. See also Howard Rolin Patch, *The Other World, According to Descriptions in Medieval Literature* (Cambridge, MA: Harvard University Press, 1950), and R. (Tom) Zuidema and U. Quispe M., "A Visit to God: The Account and Interpretation of a Religious Experience in the Peruvian Community of Choque-Huarcaya," in *Bijdragen tot de Taal-, Land-en Volkerunde* 124, no. 1 (1968): Leider 22–39.

3. Susan Sontag, introduction to Hujar's *Portraits in Life and Death* (New York: Da Capo, 1976).

4. Alicia Eler in *Star Tribune*, June 23, 2017.

5. David Levi Strauss, in *The Critique of the Image in the Defense of the Imagination* (Brooklyn: Autonomedia, 2020).

6. Walter Benjamin, "On the Concept of History," in *Selected Writings*, vol. 4, *1938–1940* (Cambridge, MA: Harvard University Press, 2003), 396.

7. Benjamin, "On the Concept of History."

8. Paul Virilio, *War and Cinema: The Logistics of Perception* (1984; London: Verso, 1989).

9. Virilio, 7.

10. Virilio, 7.

11. Virilio, 8.

12. Benjamin, "Critique of Violence," in *Reflections: Essays, Aphorisms, Autobiographical Writings*, ed. Peter Demetz (New York: Schocken, 287. See also Jacques Derrida, "Force of Law: The 'Mystical Foundation of Authority,'" in *Deconstruction and the Possibility of Justice*, ed. Drucilla Cornell, Michel Rosenfeld, and David Gray Carlson (New York: Routledge, 1992).

13. A later trial found one police officer guilty.

14. NPR online, reported by Christopher Werth, August 10, 2024.

15. Angela Y. Davis, *Are Prisons Obsolete?* (Seven Stories Press, 2003).

16. NPR online, November 17, 2022.

17. Michelle Alexander, *The New Jim Crow: Mass Incarceration in the Age of Colorblindness* (New York: New Press, 2010).

18. James Forman Jr., *Locking Up Our Own: Crime and Punishment in Black America* (New York: Farrar, Straus and Giroux, 2017).

19. Dan Baum, "Legalize It All," *Harpers Magazine*, February 2024. See also Charles Blow, *New York Times* op-ed, January 31, 2024.

20. David Graeber and David Wengrow, *The Dawn of Everything: A New History of Humanity* (Farrar, Straus and Giroux, 2021), 406 (Kindle).

21. William Burroughs, *Naked Lunch*, ed. James Graerholz and Barry Miles (1959; New York: Grove, 2001), 91.

22. Michael Herr, *Dispatches* (1968; New York: Random House, 1991), 248–49.

23. J. Glenn Gray, *The Warriors: Reflections on Men in Battle* (New York: Harcourt Brace, 1959), 47.

24. Susan Sontag, *Regarding the Pain of Others* (New York: Farrar, Straus and Giroux, 2003).

25. Herr, 58.

26. Kathleen Belew, *Bring the War Home: The White Power Movement and Paramilitary America* (Cambridge, MA: Harvard University Press, 2019).

27. Herr, 41.

28. Herr, 9.

CHAPTER 21

1. Dave Grossman, *On Killing: The Psychological Cost of Learning to Kill in War and Society*, 270 (Kindle).

2. Grossman, 2350 (Kindle).

3. Grossman, 2355 (Kindle).

4. J. Glenn Gray, *The Warriors: Reflections on Men in Battle* (New York: Harcourt Brace, 1959), 61–62.

5. Juan Felipe García, *El Exterminio de la isla de Papayal* (Bogotá: Editorial Pontificia Universidad Javeriana, 2019); Michael Taussig, *Palma Africana* (Chicago: University of Chicago Press, 2018).

6. Timothy Pachirat, *Every Twelve Seconds: Industrialized Slaughter and the Politics of Sight* (New Haven, CT: Yale University Press, 2013), 159.

7. Chuck Jones, interviewed in 1989 by Terry Gross on *Fresh Air*; replayed on NPR, February 25, 2002.

CHAPTER 22

1. I am thinking of Caravaggio, Lucas Cranach the Elder, Artemisia Gentileschi, and Sandro Botticelli. The paintings of Salome with John the Baptist's head on a platter are legion.

2. *Current Affairs*, online, September 17 and 27, 2018.

3. Philippe-Alain Michaud, *Aby Warburg and the Image in Motion* (2007; New York: Zone, 2013), 83, 85.

4. On desublimation, see Norman O. Brown on Jonathan Swift in *Life Against Death* (Middletown, CT: Wesleyan University Press, 1959); also Gilles Deleuze, "From *Ressentiment* to Bad Conscience," chap. 4 in *Nietzsche and Philosophy* (1962; New York: Columbia University Press, 1983), 211–12n8.

5. Katerina Clark and Michael Holquist, *Mikhail Bakhtin* (Cambridge, MA: Harvard University Press, 1984), 249–51.

6. In Georges Bataille, *Visions of Excess: Selected Essays, 1927–39*, ed. Allan Stoekl (Minneapolis: University of Minnesota Press, 1991).

7. Jacques Derrida, "From Restricted to General Economy: A Hegelianism without Reserve," in *Writing and Difference*, trans. Alan Bass (Chicago: University of Chicago Press, 1978), 251–77.

CHAPTER 23

1. Georges Did-Huberman, *The Surviving Image: Phantoms of Time and Time of Phantoms: Aby Warburg's History of Art*, trans. Harvey Mendelsohn (2002; University Park: Pennsylvania University State Press, 2017).

2. Friedrich Nietzsche, *The Use and Abuse of History*, trans. Adrian Collins (1874; New York: Macmillan, 1957), 5.

3. Nietzsche, *Twilight of the Idols*, trans. R. J. Hollingdale (London: Penguin, 1980).

4. Tom Junod, "The Falling Man," in *Picturing Atrocity*, ed. Gregory Batchen et al. (London: Reaktion, 2014), 171.

5. Junod, "Falling Man."

6. Personal communication via email from Rachel Churner, director of the Carolee Schneemann Foundation, January 2022.

7. A detailed description is provided by Richard Gott, "The Ribs of Rosinante," *London Review of Books* 19, no. 16 (1997). Together with the British photographer Brian Moser, Gott was the first journalist on the scene and identified the body. Moser's photographs, taken the day before the press arrived, show a far less theatricalized version of the body than photos taken subsequently.

8. Leo Steinberg, *The Sexuality of Christ in Renaissance Art and in Modern Oblivion*, 2nd ed. (Chicago: University of Chicago Press, 1996).

9. Compare with the film *The Act of Killing* (2012) by Joshua Oppenheimer, in which killers in Indonesia's 1965–1966 state-backed mass murder of alleged communists reenact their actions for the camera.

10. Georges Bataille, *Cradle of Humanity: Prehistoric Art and Culture* (New York: Zone, 2005), 171.

INDEX

aborigines, 56

Accursed Share, The (Bataille), 145, 208

Act of Killing, The (film), 273n9

Adorno, Theodor, 147

Africa, 52–54, 61, 170, 182

African Americans, 212; Black space, 17; blackness of funerals, 170; "tough on crime" stance, 222–23

Agrippa, 132–33

AIDS, 217; "art of dying," 154

AIZ (magazine), 115

Akhmatova, 120

Alborta, Freddy, 252

alchemy, 90, 132–33; double pelican system, 144

alcohol, 195; as foundational to humanity, 224

Alexander, Michelle, 223

Alcxievich, Svetlana, 224

Algeria, 190–92

Algerian Liberation Front (FLN), 190

All Souls' Day, 17, 19

Alvarado, Elsa, 202

Amazonia, 58–61, 77

American Way of Death, The (Mitford), 160; embalming chapter, 32–33

Anderson, Benedict, 216; imagined community, 216

animals, 22, 90, 136, 151, 169, 199, 225–26, 235, 260n10; cave paintings as equivalent to Christian iconography, 48; cruelty to, as entertainment, 37; drawing of, 46–48; fast food, 236; as humans in another or hybrid form, 47, 52, 59; killing of, 51–52, 56, 126, 150, 152, 201, 234, 236–37; as sacred Other, 51; sacrifice, 52; "skinners," 175; as superhuman, 46, 52

ánimas, 15, 19, 195. *See also* souls of the dead

Anthropologie, 151

anthropology, 45, 189, 204, 219, 246; of slaying, 216

Antigone (Sophocles), 127

Apetitos de Familia (video), 38–39

Apocalypse Now (film), 228

apotropaica, 153; apotrapaism, 153, 174, 192

Aragon, Louis, 106

Arango, Ariel, 85

Arawete, 60, 153, 190, 203, 229; as Tupi-Guaraní people, 57

Arberry, Ahmaud, 212

Arcades Project, The (Benjamin), 24, 26, 106

Arendt, Hannah, 203–4, 208

Ariès, Philippe, 23, 141, 149, 171, 182, 204; soullessness of modern death, 169; "tamed" vs. "wild" death, 125, 127, 132, 248

arreglados, 69

Arroyave, Miguel, 11–12

ars moriendi (art of dying), 125, 154, 217

Asia, 53, 227

Atkinson, Craig, 231

Augsburg (Germany), 175, 178, 246

Australia, 44, 55–56, 61, 201–2, 231

automobiles, 27, 36, 50, 111, 193, 200, 211, 216, 227, 249, 257; as adult toys, 105; advertising, 106, 225; auto-mobilization, 225–26; brand names, 225; as coffin, 106; as crime scene, 215; as genius loci, 105–6; as heterotopia, 215; installations involving, 226; interiors as modern Lascaux, 256; as moving landscape and sacred site, 26; as shrine, 102; strangeness of, 103; state assassination, 112; as state-registered site of surveillance and trap, 215; as tomb or river, 112

Azande people, 182

decapitation, 241, 250; decapitation porn, 239; paintings of, 243, 272n1

decenteredness, spiritual geography of, 107

Deibler, Anatole, 176

Deleuze, Gilles, 59, 228

Democratic Party, 223

Democratic Socialism, 135

Deneuve, Catherine, 31, 34, 135

denial of denial, 126–27

dépense, 23–24, 92–93, 145, 160, 208

Derrida, Jacques, "gift of death," 52

desacralization, 178

Despret, Vinciane, 123, 210–11; ontological tact, 129

Detroit (Michigan), murder rate, 68

Dewan, Sheila, 213

Dialectic of Enlightenment (Horkheimer and Adorno), 147

Didi-Huberman, Georges, 246–47; anachronistic knot, 263n29

Dinka people, 54

Dionysis, capacity for mimesis, 247

Discreet Charm of the Bourgeoisie, The (film), 269n23

disenchantment, 135; with nature, 132; reechantment as means of, 133–34, 153–54

Divina Commedia (Dante), 34, 52

Do Not Resist (documentary), 231

Documenta 5, 226

Documents (magazine), 48, 149, 243; dictionary entries, 150–51

Dostoevsky, Fyodor, 34, 144, 150, 253–54

Dowd, Maureen, 183

Dracula, 135

Dracula (Stoker), 121, 241

Drew, Richard, 250

Droste, Elizabeth Gallón, 14

drug trafficking, 8, 67, 89, 94, 180

drugs, 27, 70, 77, 94, 110, 211, 215, 219, 221–22, 224, 227; as biospirituality, 225; effect on Black community, 223; "molecular impulses," 228

Dumont, René, 151

Durkheim, Émile, 73, 172; sacred, as force of attraction and repulsion, 139

Dying God, The (Frazer), 140

Eastwood, Clint, 209, 211

Echeverri, Clemencia, 38–39, 221

Eco, Umberto, 73

Ecuador, 16, 109, 193

Egypt, 138–39, 224

Ehrlichman, John, 223

Eisenstein, Sergei, 43, 115

Elias, Norbert, caviling, 169

El Sur de Bolívar, 8–9

Eler, Alicia, 217, 218

embalming, 32–33

England, 42, 141, 178. *See also* Britain

Enlightenment, 105, 112, 126, 130–31, 133, 135, 143, 147, 155, 161; disenchantment with nature, 132; taboo of taboo, 152

entables (mafia gold mining), 17

Escobar, Pablo, 37, 72

espanto (spooked out), 19–20

Europe, 111, 125, 135, 171, 178; corpse defilement, 141; dancing over graves, 138–39, 141

evangelicals, 166; and gangsters, 156

Evans-Pritchard, E. E., 52

Every Twelve Seconds (Pachirat), 236–37

"everyday common," 8

executioners, 175, 178; as alter ego to kings, 176

extractavismo académico (academic extraction), 79

Facebook, 216

Fals-Borda, Orlando, 260n14

Fanon, Frantz, 190, 192; lived experience, 191

Federal Bureau of Investigation (FBI), 212

Feingold, Ken, 36

Ferguson (Missouri), 215, 231

Finnegans Wake (Joyce), 35

Fitzcarraldo (film), 114

Five Star Stud (Reddin and Kienholz), 226

Floyd, George, 22, 27, 43, 212–14, 251

folk-law, 188

folklore, 188

Forman, James, Jr., 27, 222–23

Foucault, Michel, 133, 231–32; biopolitics, 148; heterotopias, 103–4, 215

frailejón, 8

France, 32, 46, 115, 141, 176, 191, 218, 246

opioid prescriptions, 224

Oppenheimer, Joshua, 273n9

Other, 45, 49, 121, 238, 241, 247; animal as sacred Other, 51; magic and violence as reciprocal, 90; slain, 61

Our Grateful Dead (Despret), 129, 210–11

Pachirat, Timothy, 236

Page, Tim, 227–28

Palestine, 179, 183, 191–92

Palo (religious practice), 25, 74

Panama, 187

paramilitaries, 3, 12, 16, 30, 38, 67–68, 70, 88–89, 94, 190, 192; corpse defilement, 142; killing with machetes, 42; mystical visions of, 119; possessed by spirits of victims, 189–90, 193–95; sorcery, effort to ban, 187–88; as superstitious, 14–17

Paris (France): catacombs, 148–49; La Villette as "Blood City," 152; Père Lachaise, 150; slaughterhouses, 150

Parscale, Brad, 183

patriarchy, violence of, 240

Pearlman, Daniel, 250

People of Aritama (G. Reichel-Dolmatoff and A. Reichel-Dolmatoff), 119, 121

Perea, Carlos Mario, 71, 109

Pérez Gómez, Johanna, 11, 14, 41, 264n1

Peril (Woodward and Costa), 183

Peron, Eva, 175

Peru, 193, 224

Petro, Gustavo, 181

Phenomenology of Spirit, The (Hegel), 173

photography, 246–47; in war, 228

Pig Earth (Berger), 234

Plath, Sylvia, 123

Plato, 60–62, 74, 138–39, 157, 256, 258

police killings and violence, 21–22, 27, 74, 128, 153, 157–58, 192, 207, 210, 212, 259n1; assassination, 1–2, 55; in automobiles, 215, 220; ghostly formlessness, 220; haptic eye, 214; imagined community, 216; militarization, 223, 231; Nuer-Effect, 214, 221; phone videos, 40, 43, 48, 55, 197, 213–16, 219–21, 246–47, 251, 255–57; pretext stops, 215; shield bump, 231; swarm maneuver, 221; traffic stops, 220; viral feeding, 216

political capital, 110

polygony, 56

Portland (Oregon), 249

posttraumatic stress disorder (PTSD), as Nuer-Effect, 229

Primitive Culture (Tylor), 247

prison-industrial complex, 222

profanation, 73

Proud Boys, 228

Proust, Marcel, *mémoire involontaire*, 44

psychogeography, 161

Purdue Pharma, 224

Pynchon, Thomas, 232–33

¿Quién Los Mato? (Who Killed Them?) (video), 93–98

Rabelais, François, 28–29, 243, 245

racism, 180, 215, 220

Rag & Bone, 151

Reagan, Ronald, 223

Rebel Without a Cause (film), 106

reciprocity, 260n10; between living and dead, 204–5

Reddin, Nancy, 226–27

reenchanted space, 110

Reichel, Elizabeth, 199

Reichel-Dolmatoff, Alicia Dussán de, 102–3

Reichel-Dolmatoff, Gerardo, 102–3

Reinoehl, Michael, 249

Renaissance, 132–33

Rennix, Brianna, 239

Republican Party, 220, 223

revenge, 180–81; citizens' surrender of, 184; defund the police, 183; envy, 182; pleasure of, 183

Reyes, Raúl, 16

Reynolds, Diamond, 26–27, 216

Ricardo, David, 33

Rice, Tamir, 212

Richard the Lionheart, 144–45

Richardson, Tony, 32

Rincón, Amanda, 194

Rivera, Diego, 136–37; frozen assets, 236

Rivet, Paul, 259n3

Rome, 119, 141, 148

Ronald Reagan Presidential Library, 220

Rule of Law, 1, 62, 182–83

Tate, Sharon, 42
Taylor, Breonna, 212
Taylor, Henry, 27, 217–20
Tears of Eros, The (Bataille), 47
Tennessee Valley Authority (TVA), 98
Terminal Velocity (Schneemann), 250
terrorism, 219, 230
Texas Chainsaw Massacre, The (film), 42–43
Thailand, 149
"Theses on the Philosophy of History" (Benjamin), 55, 98, 156
Third Reich, 147, 159
Thonga people, 53
threshold people, 20
Thury, Héricart de, 148
Till, Emmett, 251
Tolstoy, Leo, 125, 154
Tom and Jerry (cartoon), 35–37
Tomei, Marisa, 105
Tosquelles, François, 192
Touraine, Alain, 269n17
Tringa, Mason, 249
Trouble with Harry, The (film), 31
Trump, Donald, 160, 208, 228, 236, 249; grievance politics, 183
Tunis (Tunisia), 190, 192
Tylor, E. B., 247

Ukraine, 224
Ulysses (Joyce), 23, 35, 104, 127, 152, 163–65; funeral march, 161–62, 201, 217
Un chien andalou (film), 36
Un chien délicieux (video), 36
Unidad Popular Party, 17, 67
United Fruit Company, 187, 189
United States, 3, 51, 77, 105, 106, 112, 124, 135, 180, 191, 213, 219, 224, 228; automobiles, 225; auto-mobilization, 225; cremation, 169; culture of death, 169; defund the police, 183; evangelicals' voting power, 156; gang members, 207, 223; gun fetishism, 210, 233; guns in, 207–8; hunting as sacrosanct, 211; MAGA, 225; mass imprisonment, 221; mass shootings, 210, 233; meat consumption, 150; murder rate, 68; neocolonialism, 223; Nuer-Effect, 62, 218, 231; police assassination, 55; police killings, 22, 26, 40, 45, 50, 58,

157–58, 192, 212, 216, 247, 251, 255; racialized, 220; shootings, 207; slasher films, 42–43; slavery, 170; War on Drugs, 224. *See also* police killings and violence
"Unpacking My Library" (Benjamin), 207–8
untouchables, 175–76
Uranus, 60
Uribe, Álvaro, 89
US Capitol, assault on, 228
Use and Abuse of History, The (Nietzsche), 247

Velasco, Luis Alejandro, 168
Velásquez, Rogerio, 7, 88–89, 137–38, 154, 169, 171, 241, 259n3
Venezuela, 193, 259n6
vengeance, 24–26, 44, 57, 156–57, 179, 195, 205; corpse magic, 184–86, 194, 242; curse tablets, 61; envy, 182; as heart of power, 181; justice as euphemism for, 183; passive-aggressive, 188–89; self-pity, 188–89; vengeance economy, 180
vengeance magic, 73–76, 80, 85, 89; black cross, 83–84. *See also* corpse magic
Vertov, Dziga, 115
vicio, 94
Vietnam, 191–92, 229
Vietnam War, 227; antiwar movement, 180; religious experience among US troops, 228; as television staple, 228
Violencia (Zapata), 29–30
Virilio, Paul, 228; sympathetic war, 219; "Virilio effects," 221; war and cinema, 218
Viveiros de Castro, Eduardo, 57–59, 153, 230
von Clausewitz, Carl, 219
voodoo, 24, 74

War and Cinema (Virilio), 218–19
war games, 53
War on Drugs, 2, 27, 142, 180, 212, 220–22, 224, 227, 255, 259n1; as exportable, 223; as theater, 223; as War on Blacks, 223
Warburg, Aby, 2, 157, 248; afterlives of images, 246–47; blink effect, 242; images as stilled movement, 241–42; *nachleben*, 246–47; painting, like traffic stops, 218
warfare, 227; cell phones and counterwarfare, 219; *dépense*, 233–34; photography in, 228; as sacrament, 228; as sacrifice

and blood debt, 233; torture, rape, and defilement of women, 233

Warhol, Andy, 175

Warner, W. Lloyd, 55–56, 199, 201, 203, 231

Washington, DC, murder rate, 68

Waugh, Evelyn, 32–34, 126–27, 140, 169

Weekend (film), 103

Wengrow, David, 224

What's the Matter with Kansas? (Frank), 183

whiteness, 170

Whitney Biennale (2017), 27

Whitney Museum, 151–52

Willerslev, Rane, "becoming Other," 49

William of Newburgh, 121–22

Wire, The (TV series), 155

"Withered Arm, The" (Hardy), 172–73; hangman's rope, 176, 178

witnessing, 39

Wittgenstein, Ludwig, 147

Wolf Hill Trading Company, 208

Woodward, Bob, 183

World Bank, 68

World Trade Center, falling bodies, 250

World War I, 219

World War II, 233

Wretched of the Earth, The (Fanon), 190

Xenophon, 61

Yanez, Jeronimo, 207

Yolngu, 199. *See also* Murngin people

Yukaghir people, 49

Zambrano, Marco Polo, 30

Zapata, Tomás, 29–30

Zimbabwe, 48

Zimmerman, George, 213

Zimring, Franklin, 213

zombies, 24